W9-BWS-475

World Book
Discovery Science Encyclopedia

Matter and Energy

a Scott Fetzer company
Chicago
www.worldbook.com

For information about other World Book publications, visit our
website at www.worldbook.com or call
1-800-WORLDBK (967-5325).

For information about sales to schools and libraries, call
1-800-975-3250 (United States); **1-800-837-5365** (Canada).

World Book, Inc.
233 N. Michigan Ave.
Chicago, IL 60601
U.S.A.

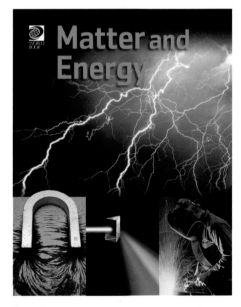

Library of Congress Cataloging-in-Publication Data

Encyclopedia of matter and energy.
    pages cm. -- (World Book discovery science encyclopedia)
  Includes index.
  Summary: "An encyclopedia of topics concerning matter and energy, covering
their properties and interactions in the physical world. The book includes such basic
concepts as heat and work, as well as more advanced concepts of physics, such as
superconductors and the Higgs boson. Features include drawings, diagrams,
photographs, and activities"-- Provided by publisher.
  ISBN 978-0-7166-7521-1
  1. Physics--Encyclopedias, Juvenile. 2. Matter--Encyclopedias, Juvenile. 3. Force
and energy--Encyclopedias, Juvenile. I. World Book, Inc.
QC25.E53 2013
530.03--dc23
                              2012050648

Printed in China by Shenzhen Donnelley
Printing Co., Ltd., Guangdong Province
1st printing July 2013

Front Cover:
© A.T. Willett, Alamy Images; © Art Directors &
TRIP/Alamy Images; © ACE Stock Ltd/Alamy
Images; © Michael Ventura/Alamy Images

Back Cover:
© Shutterstock; © Shutterstock; © Shutterstock

Staff

Executive Committee

President
Donald D. Keller

**Vice President and Editor
in Chief**
Paul A. Kobasa

**Vice President, Sales and
Marketing**
Sean Lockwood

Vice President, International
Richard Flower

Controller
Anthony Doyle

Director, Human Resources
Bev Ecker

Editorial

**Associate Director,
Annuals and Topical Reference**
Scott Thomas

**Managing Editor,
Annuals and Topical Reference**
Barbara A. Mayes

**Manager, Sciences,
World Book Encyclopedia**
Jeff De La Rosa

**Senior Editor,
Annuals and Topical Reference**
Christine Sullivan

Staff Editors
Michael DuRoss
Daniel Kenis
Nick Kilzer

Senior Researcher
Mike Barr

**Manager, Contracts
& Compliance
(Rights & Permissions)**
Loranne K. Shields

Manager, Indexing Services
David Pofelski

Administrative Assistant
Ethel Matthews

Editorial Administration

Director, Systems and Projects
Tony Tills

**Senior Manager, Publishing
Operations**
Timothy Falk

**Associate Manager, Publishing
Operations**
Audrey Casey

Graphics and Design

Senior Manager
Tom Evans

**Coordinator, Design Development
and Production**
Brenda B. Tropinski

Senior Designers
Matt Carrington
Don Di Sante
Isaiah Sheppard

Contributing Designer
Lucy Lesiak

Media Researcher
Jeff Heimsath

Contributing Photographs Editor
Carol Parden

Manager, Cartography
Wayne K. Pichler

Senior Cartographer
John M. Rejba

Production

**Director, Manufacturing
and Pre-Press**
Carma Fazio

Manufacturing Manager
Barbara Podczerwinski

Production/Technology Manager
Anne Fritzinger

Senior Production Manager
Jan Rossing

Production Specialist
Curley Hunter

Proofreader
Emilie Schrage

How to use World Book Discovery Science Encyclopedia

http://bit.ly/13kOpzd

- Hundreds of illustrations
- Guide words
- Phonetic spellings
- Related article lists
- Experiments and activities
- QR codes

World Book Discovery Science Encyclopedia is filled with information about basic science concepts, tools, and discoveries as well as the world around us. Entries on people who have made important contributions to science are included, too. All entries are written in a way that makes them easy to understand.

Finding entries is easy, too. They are arranged in alphabetical order. There is also an index in each volume. The index lists all the entries, as well as topics that are covered in the volume but that are not themselves entries.

Science experiments and activities are also included in this volume. These and the many other features of *World Book Discovery Science Encyclopedia* make it an encyclopedia that you can use for research as well as reading just for fun.

Easy alphabetical access
Each letter of the alphabet is highlighted to help you locate entries alphabetically.

Nn

Natural gas liquids

Natural gas liquids are certain chemical compounds that can be obtained in liquid form from natural gas. These compounds rank among the world's most valuable energy resources. Natural gas liquids, also called *NGL's*, are widely used as fuel. They are also used in manufacturing industrial chemicals and other products.

There are several important NGL compounds. From lightest to heaviest, they include ethane, propane, butane, pentane, hexane, and heptane. Chemical manufacturers use ethane in making *ethylene*, an important industrial chemical. Butane and propane, and mixtures of the two, are classified as *LPG* (liquefied petroleum gas). LPG is used chiefly as a heating fuel in industry and homes. Pentane, hexane, and heptane are called *natural gasoline* or *condensate*. These substances are blended with other kinds of gasoline used for transportation.

Other articles to read include: **Ethylene; Fuel.**

Neon

Neon is used to make colorful signs.

10	Ne
Neon	20.1797

Neon atomic symbol

Neon is a colorless, *odorless* (scent-free) gas. It is one of the gases that make up the protective layer of air around Earth called the *atmosphere.*

Neon is also a *chemical element.* A chemical element is a material that is made of only one kind of atom. Neon was discovered in 1898 by the British chemists Sir William Ramsay and Morris W. Travers. They named the gas for the Greek word that means *new.*

Neon is mainly used in certain kinds of lamps and in tubes to make colorful signs. Neon light can be seen even in fog. That is why neon lamps are used as beacons to guide airplanes at many airports.

Neon signs are made by filling glass tubes with neon gas. Electric current makes the tubes glow. The tubes can be made of colored glass or coated with different colors of powder to make signs of various colors.

Other articles to read include: **Element, Chemical; Gas.**

Neutralization

Neutralization *(NOO truh luh ZAY shuhn)* is when an *acid* and a *base* combine to form a salt. An acid is a chemical that has a sour taste and can burn the skin if it is strong enough. A base feels slippery and tastes bitter. Strong bases can also harm the skin. Baking soda is one type of base.

In water, acids and bases break down, forming positive and negative particles. These particles come together in a different combination to form a salt. The salt usually appears as crystals once the water has dried up. If the neutralization reaction is complete, the final salt is usually *neutral.* Being neutral means that it is neither an acid nor a base. Neutralization is important in many branches of industry. It is also important in the human body.

Other articles to read include: **Acid; Base; pH.**

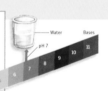

To test the strength of an acid or base, scientists may use an indicator called pH paper. The *pH* (potential of hydrogen) *number* shows the concentration of hydrogen ions in a solution. When the paper is dipped into a solution, the color changes. The color can then be checked against a color chart to determine the pH of the solution. Neutral substances, such as water, have a pH of 7.

Neutron

A neutron *(NOO tron)* is a part of an *atom.* Atoms are tiny bits of matter. Neutrons, along with particles called *protons,* form the *nucleus* (center) of nearly all of the various kinds of atoms. A neutron has no electric charge. Protons have a positive charge.

Only the atoms of hydrogen, the most common *chemical element,* contain no neutrons. A chemical element is a material with only one kind of atom. Neutrons and protons make up almost all of an atom's *mass* (amount of matter). A cloud of negatively charged particles called *electrons,* which orbit the nucleus, makes up the rest.

A neutron is about one-millionth of a *nanometer (NAN oh MEE tuhr)* wide. A nanometer is approximately ⅟₁₀₀,₀₀₀ the width of a human hair. Neutrons are made up of even tinier particles called *quarks.* Scientists use neutrons to make chemical elements *radioactive.* Scientists shower an element with neutrons. After the elements absorb the neutrons, they give off *radiation* (energy or tiny particles of matter).

Other articles to read include: **Atom; Electron; Proton; Radiation.**

Neutrons and protons form the *nucleus* (center) of atoms and make up almost all of an atom's *mass* (amount of matter). They are held together by an extremely powerful force.

Illustrations
Each volume of *Discovery Science Encyclopedia* contains hundreds of photographs, drawings, maps, and other illustrations. Each illustration is labeled or explained in a caption.

Pronunciations
The phonetic spelling for unusual or unfamiliar words is given. A key to the pronunciation is in the front of each volume.

Related references
The references listed at the bottom of many articles tell you which other articles to read to find out more or related information.

Guide words
Guide words at the top of a page help you quickly find the entry you are seeking.

Experiments
Many experiments are found in *Discovery Science Encyclopedia*. These experiments extend or enrich the subject of the article they accompany and are suitable for use at home or in the classroom.

Activities
Many activities are found in *Discovery Science Encyclopedia*. These simple activities, which can be done at home or in the classroom, extend or enrich the subject of the article they accompany.

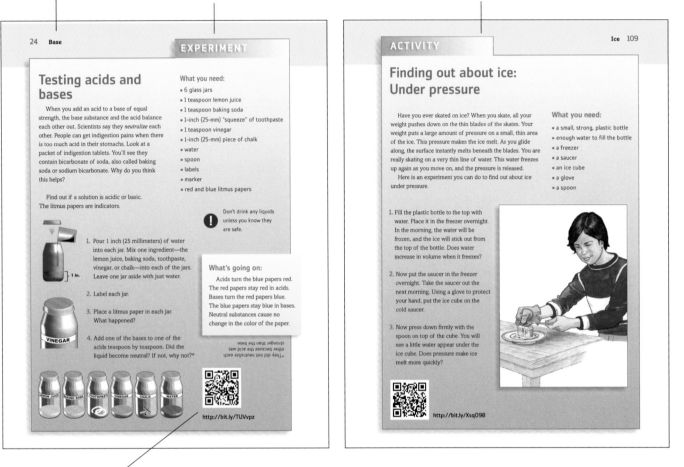

24 Base

EXPERIMENT

Testing acids and bases

When you add an acid to a base of equal strength, the base substance and the acid balance each other out. Scientists say they *neutralize* each other. People can get indigestion pains when there is too much acid in their stomachs. Look at a packet of indigestion tablets. You'll see they contain bicarbonate of soda, also called baking soda or sodium bicarbonate. Why do you think this helps?

Find out if a solution is acidic or basic. The litmus papers are indicators.

What you need:
- 6 glass jars
- 1 teaspoon lemon juice
- 1 teaspoon baking soda
- 1-inch (25-mm) "squeeze" of toothpaste
- 1 teaspoon vinegar
- 1-inch (25-mm) piece of chalk
- water
- spoon
- labels
- marker
- red and blue litmus papers

Don't drink any liquids unless you know they are safe.

1. Pour 1 inch (25 millimeters) of water into each jar. Mix one ingredient—the lemon juice, baking soda, toothpaste, vinegar, or chalk—into each of the jars. Leave one jar aside with just water.

2. Label each jar.

3. Place a litmus paper in each jar. What happened?

4. Add one of the bases to one of the acids teaspoon by teaspoon. Did the liquid become neutral? If not, why not?*

What's going on:
Acids turn the blue papers red. The red papers stay red in acids. Bases turn the red papers blue. The blue papers stay blue in bases. Neutral substances cause no change in the color of the paper.

*They did not neutralize each other because the acid was stronger than the base.

http://bit.ly/TUVvpz

Ice 109

ACTIVITY

Finding out about ice: Under pressure

Have you ever skated on ice? When you skate, all your weight pushes down on the thin blades of the skates. Your weight puts a large amount of pressure on a small, thin area of the ice. This pressure makes the ice melt. As you glide along, the surface instantly melts beneath the blades. You are really skating on a very thin line of water. This water freezes up again as you move on, and the pressure is released.

Here is an experiment you can do to find out about ice under pressure.

What you need:
- a small, strong, plastic bottle
- enough water to fill the bottle
- a freezer
- a saucer
- an ice cube
- a glove
- a spoon

1. Fill the plastic bottle to the top with water. Place it in the freezer overnight. In the morning, the water will be frozen, and the ice will stick out from the top of the bottle. Does water increase in volume when it freezes?

2. Now put the saucer in the freezer overnight. Take the saucer out the next morning. Using a glove to protect your hand, put the ice cube on the cold saucer.

3. Now press down firmly with the spoon on top of the cube. You will see a little water appear under the ice cube. Does pressure make ice melt more quickly?

http://bit.ly/Xsq098

QR codes
This symbol is a QR code. You can find QR codes on all the pages with experiments and activities in the *World Book Discovery Science Encyclopedia*. Simply scan a code with your smartphone or tablet to see a video about the experiment or activity or related information about the subject of the project. (You will need to download a QR code reader to your device if you have not already done so.) If you do not have a mobile device, you can still access the videos linked to experiments and activities by keying in the URL beneath each QR code into a browser on your computer.

You can also find a QR code on the opposite page. This code links to a video explaining how to use the *World Book Discovery Science Encyclopedia*.

A library of all the videos and related information included in the *World Book Discovery Science Encyclopedia* can be found at
http://www.worldbook.com/all/item/1876.

Key to pronunciation

World Book Discovery Science Encyclopedia provides the pronunciations for many unusual or unfamiliar words. In the pronunciation, the words are divided into syllables and respelled according to the way each syllable sounds. The syllables appear in *italic letters*. For example, here are an article title and the respelled pronunciation for it:

Absorption *(ab SAWRP shuhn)*

The syllable or syllables that get the greatest emphasis when the word is spoken are in capital letters *(SAWRP)*.

Aa

Absolute zero

Absolute zero is the lowest temperature possible. It is equal to −273.15 °C, or −459.67 °F. Scientists think that nothing can be colder than absolute zero. A widely accepted scientific law says that nothing can even reach absolute zero. Scientists have cooled special substances to within a few billionths of a degree above absolute zero. Scientists have discovered that many materials have unusual properties at temperatures near absolute zero. For example. some materials develop the ability to conduct electric current without resistance.

Some temperature scales are based on absolute zero. One of these is the Kelvin scale. On this scale, absolute zero equals zero kelvin (0 K). The word *degree* and the degree symbol (°) are not used with the Kelvin scale.

The Kelvin scale is related to the Celsius scale. The temperature in kelvins equals the Celsius temperature plus 273.15. For example, 20 °C equals 293.15 K. The Kelvin scale is named for Lord Kelvin (William Thomson), the British scientist who invented the scale in the 1800's.

Other articles to read include: **Celsius scale; Temperature.**

Absorption

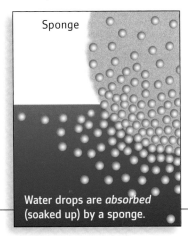

Sponge

Water drops are *absorbed* (soaked up) by a sponge.

Absorption and adsorption

Absorption *(ab SAWRP shuhn)* occurs when a material takes in matter or energy or both. A sponge *absorbs* (soaks up) water, which is matter. The water spreads through the sponge.

Water in a lake absorbs *oxygen*, one of the main gases in air. Oxygen from the air spreads through the lake water. Fish use this oxygen in much the same way people use oxygen from the air they breathe.

Energy can also be absorbed. Sound is a type of energy. Heavy drapes can absorb sound in a room. The sound energy spreads through the fabric of the drapes, rather than reflecting as an echo.

Adsorption *(ad SAWRP shuhn)* takes place when one material collects on another. Charcoal water filters use adsorption. The charcoal pulls tiny unwanted particles out of the water. The charcoal does not soak up the particles. The particles just stick to the surface of the charcoal pieces.

Other articles to read include: **Capillary action**

Adsorption

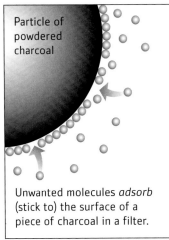

Particle of powdered charcoal

Unwanted molecules *adsorb* (stick to) the surface of a piece of charcoal in a filter.

Acceleration

A car accelerates when the driver steps on the gas pedal. Slowing down is also a kind of acceleration, sometimes known as deceleration.

Acceleration *(ak SHEL uh RAY shuhn)* is any change in the speed or direction of an object's movement. An object's speed and direction are called its *velocity (vuh LOS uh tee)*. Acceleration is how much the velocity changes over a certain time.

Think of a car going down a straight highway. The car's speedometer says the car is going 40 miles (64.3 kilometers) per hour. Stepping on the gas pedal makes the car go faster. After 20 seconds, the car is going 60 miles (96.5 kilometers) per hour. The car has accelerated 20 miles (32.1 kilometers) per hour in 20 seconds. We could say the car's velocity increased by an average of 1 mile (1.6 kilometers) per hour for every second it was accelerating. After one second of acceleration, the car would be going 41 miles (66 kilometers) per hour. After two seconds, it would be going 42 miles (67.6 kilometers) per hour.

The car can slow down, too. In physics, slowing down is also considered a kind of acceleration. It is sometimes called deceleration *(dee SHEL uh RAY shuhn)*.

A change in direction is another kind of acceleration. For example, the moon orbits Earth at a fairly constant speed. But it is continuously accelerating, changing direction to maintain its nearly circular path.

Other articles to read include: **Motion; Velocity.**

Acid

An acid is a type of chemical. All acids are alike in some ways. They have a sour taste. They make people's skin prickle or burn. A special paper called blue litmus *(LIHT muhs)* paper turns red if it is dipped in acid. Acids can melt many substances. Some are strong enough to melt certain metals.

Continued on the next page

Many acids are found in nature. For example, a person's stomach contains an acid that helps digest food. Other acids are found in citrus fruits, vitamin C, and aspirin. The proteins in living things are made up of *amino (uh MEE noh)* acids.

Many acids are poisonous, and some acids cause bad burns. Strong acids are used in industry for making paints, plastic, and other products.

Chemicals called *bases* can *neutralize* acids. That is, adding a base to an acid will weaken the acid until the two are balanced.

Other articles to read include: **Acid; Base; Litmus; pH.**

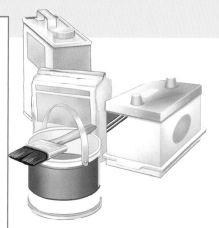

Acids are used to make many items, including paper, paint, fertilizer, and car batteries.

Acoustics

Acoustics *(uh KOOS tihks)* is the study of sound. It includes how sounds are created, sent, and received. Acoustics can also mean the quality of sound in a place.

People use acoustics in the design of rooms and buildings. They can use it to make a room quiet. They can also design rooms that provide improved conditions for listening to speech and music. Acoustics is important in the design of auditoriums, churches, halls, libraries, and music rooms.

Several things affect the acoustics of a room. The room's size and shape affect the quality of sound. So does the ability of the ceiling, walls, and floor to absorb or block unwanted sound. The surfaces in a room can also reflect sound. These reflections are called reverberation. Over long distances, reverberation can sometimes be heard in the form of echoes.

Acoustics is also used in the control of *noise pollution* (unwanted sound). Major sources of noise pollution include airplanes, construction equipment, factories, and motor vehicles.

People control noise pollution in many ways. They may lower the level of noise something makes. In addition, they might block the passage of noise from one place to another. Finally, they might use devices to absorb noise. For example, mufflers quiet the noise of automobile engines. Heavy walls can block noise. Furnishings of special material can absorb noise.

Intense noise can damage a person's hearing. People who work in noisy places may wear earplugs or earmuffs for protection.

Other articles to read include: **Echo; Sound.**

Acoustical tiles in a school auditorium improve students' ability to hear by dampening background noise and *reverberations* (sound reflections).

A set of 5 apples

A set of 3 apples

Putting the two sets together creates a new set of 8 apples.

You add when you put together two or more sets to find out how many there are altogether.

Basic addition facts can be arranged in an easy-to-use table. To find the answer to the problem 1 + 3, for example, first find the row that starts with 1. Then find the column that starts with 3. At the point where the row and column meet, you will find the answer.

Addition

Addition *(uh DIHSH uhn)* is a way of putting together two or more things (sets) to find out how many there are altogether. To find out how many things you have added to make a new set, you can count them together. Only things that are alike can be added.

Basic statements in addition are called *addition facts*. There are 100 basic addition facts. You can learn them all easily if you look for patterns in addition. When you learn the addition facts, you will be able to add things quickly.

You can write an addition statement like this:

5 + 3 = 8
We say "Five plus three equals eight."

Addition is one of the four basic operations in arithmetic. The others are division, multiplication, and subtraction.

Other articles to read include: **Division; Multiplication; Number; Subtraction.**

+	0	1	2	3	4	5	6	7	8	9
0	0	1	2	3	4	5	6	7	8	9
1	1	2	3	4	5	6	7	8	9	10
2	2	3	4	5	6	7	8	9	10	11
3	3	4	5	6	7	8	9	10	11	12
4	4	5	6	7	8	9	10	11	12	13
5	5	6	7	8	9	10	11	12	13	14
6	6	7	8	9	10	11	12	13	14	15
7	7	8	9	10	11	12	13	14	15	16
8	8	9	10	11	12	13	14	15	16	17
9	9	10	11	12	13	14	15	16	17	18

Aerodynamics

Aerodynamics (*air oh dy NAM ihks)* is the study of forces that push and pull on an object as it moves through the air or another gas. Scientists use aerodynamics to study the flight of airplanes. They also use it to study air-related forces that act on cars and other objects moving along the ground. A similar study is used for ships and submarines moving through water. It is called *hydrodynamics.*

Scientists study two main forces in aerodynamics: *lift* and *drag.* Lift is the force that raises an airplane off the ground. It is caused by the way air moves across the airplane's wings. The air under the wings pushes upward on them.

Drag is the force that slows down a moving object. It is caused by air rubbing against the object. Much work in aerodynamics has to do with making the amount of drag smaller. Lowering drag makes it easier for an object to move through the air.

Other articles to read include: **Force; Motion.**

Aerodynamic forces act on skiers as they speed down a mountain. A wind tunnel can be used to test how these forces affect their position and equipment.

Aerosol

Aerosol *(AIR uh sahl)* is a mixture of tiny particles in a gas. The particles may be drops of liquid. Or they may be solid bits. The particles are *suspended* (spread) throughout the gas.

Smoke is a kind of aerosol. It is made up of tiny particles in the air. Clouds and fog are aerosols of water.

The atmosphere is full of tiny aerosols. Some of them come from nature. These include pollen, volcanic ash, and dust. Human activities also release small particles into the air. These aerosols can contribute to air pollution.

Some products are sold in containers called *aerosol cans.* The product is dissolved in a *propellant* in the can. The contents of the can are sealed under pressure. Opening a valve releases a burst of propellant gas. The product is released with the gas as an aerosol.

Devices called *inhalers* convert medicine into aerosols. The medicine can then be breathed into the lungs. Such aerosols are used to treat asthma and other breathing problems.

Other articles to read include: **Chlorofluorocarbon.**

Aerosol cans release particles of a liquid or solid along with a propellant gas.

Alchemy

Alchemy *(AL kuh mee)* is an ancient way of studying and experimenting with matter. Alchemy combines principles of chemistry, magic, and philosophy in the study of truth and knowledge. People who practice alchemy are called alchemists. Much of alchemy involves efforts to change natural materials into useful or valuable substances. For example, alchemists once tried to change cheap metals into silver or gold. Today, the few people who practice alchemy mainly seek spiritual changes in themselves.

Most alchemists thought that matter consisted of four *elements* (basic parts): (1) water, (2) earth, (3) air, and (4) fire. They also thought that all metals could be changed into one another.

Ancient societies in Egypt, India, and China practiced alchemy. Alchemy became very popular in Europe in the 1600's. But in the 1700's, many scholars began to criticize alchemy. They pointed out that it was not scientific.

Alchemists developed some of the methods used in modern chemistry. For example, they carried out experiments in laboratories and carefully measured the substances they worked with.

Other articles to read include: **Matter.**

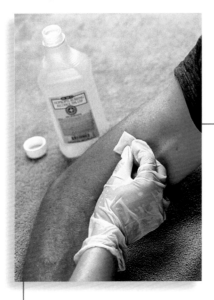

Rubbing alcohol is used to destroy germs on skin before an injection.

Alcohol

Alcohol *(AL kuh hawl* or *AL kuh hol)* is a type of chemical. There are many kinds of alcohol. But all of them contain the *chemical elements* carbon, oxygen, and hydrogen. A chemical element is a material that contains only one type of atom.

People use alcohol in many ways. It is an important part of such drinks as beer and wine. People use a kind of alcohol called *rubbing alcohol* on sore or itchy places on their skin. Alcohol is used as a *disinfectant* and as an *antiseptic*. A disinfectant destroys germs on nonliving objects. An antiseptic destroys—or stops the growth of—*germs* on living tissue. Alcohol is also added to many kinds of soap because it breaks up dirt and grease.

Car owners use a liquid called *antifreeze* to keep their engines from freezing in winter. Antifreeze contains an extremely poisonous form of alcohol. Workers in factories use alcohol to help make such products as paint, plastic, and varnish.

Other articles to read include: **Antifreeze; Disinfectant.**

Algorithm

An algorithm *(AL guh rihth uhm)* is a way of solving a math problem using steps. Each step has precise instructions. Many algorithms involve performing the same operation over and over until a certain result is achieved. People often use computers to carry out algorithms.

One of the most famous algorithms is called Euclid's algorithm It is used to find the *greatest common divisor* of any two whole numbers. The greatest common divisor is the largest number by which two numbers can be evenly divided.

We will call the larger number *a* and the smaller number *b.* Here are the steps for Euclid's algorithm:

First, divide the larger number, *a*, by the smaller one, *b (a ÷ b)*. We will call the remainder *r.*

If the remainder r is 0, then b is the greatest common divisor of a and b. But if r is not 0, then divide b by r (b ÷ r).

If the new remainder is 0, then *r* is the greatest common divisor of *a* and *b.* If the new remainder is not 0, then repeat the previous step, this time replacing *r* with the new remainder.

For example, you can use the algorithm to find the greatest common divisor of 15 and 10. First, divide 15 by 10. The answer is 1 with a remainder of 5. Now divide 10 by the remainder, 5. The answer is 2, with no remainder. This result means that 5 is the greatest common divisor of 15 and 10.

Other articles to read include: **Euclid; Mathematics.**

Alloy

An alloy *(AL oy* or *uh LOY)* is a mixture of a metal with one or more other materials. The main metal in an alloy is called the *base* metal. The materials added to an alloy may or may not be metals.

An alloy behaves differently than its base metal. A good alloy makes the base metal harder or stronger. For example, steel is an alloy of iron with a small amount of carbon mixed in. Steel is much stronger than iron. Stainless steel is an alloy of iron combined with a metal called *chromium (KROH mee uhm)*. Things made of stainless steel do not rust.

People have made alloys for several thousands of years. The first alloy was *bronze,* a mixture of copper and tin. People first made bronze about 5,500 years ago.

Other articles to read include: **Chromium; Metal.**

United States coins used for everyday business are made of alloys. Pennies are zinc coated with copper. Nickels contain copper and nickel. Dimes, quarters, and half dollars are pure copper coated with an alloy of copper and nickel.

Aluminum

13 **Al** 2 8 3
Aluminum
26.981538

Aluminum
atomic symbol

Aluminum (*uh LOO muh nuhm*) is a silver-colored metal that weighs less than most other metals. Aluminum does not rust and does not wear out easily. It resists damage from weather and chemicals. People use aluminum more than any other metal except iron and steel. Aluminum can be formed into almost any shape. It can be rolled into thick plates to make armored tanks. It can be rolled thin enough to make chewing-gum wrappers or wire or cans.

By itself, aluminum is soft and not very strong. So it is almost always mixed with small amounts of other elements. Adding copper, magnesium, or zinc helps to make aluminum strong. It also gives aluminum other features that make it one of the most useful metals.

Aluminum makes up about 8 percent of Earth's crust. But aluminum, by itself, is never found in nature. Aluminum is combined with other elements in soil or rocks, called *aluminum ore*. Heat and chemicals are used to get pure aluminum from the ore.

Other articles to read include: **Element, Chemical; Corrosion; Metal.**

Aluminum mixed with other metals that add strength is widely used in the construction of airplanes.

Alvarez, Luis Walter

Luis Walter Alvarez *(AL vuh rehz)* (1911–1988) was an American scientist. He worked with *atoms*. Atoms are tiny bits of matter. Alvarez built machines called *bubble chambers*. The bubble chambers helped him look for the even smaller parts that make up atoms. In 1968, he won the Nobel Prize, a top award for scientists, for his work.

A few years later, Alvarez and his son, Walter, found evidence of a huge meteorite crash on Earth. Many meteorites contain the metal iridium. But Earth's surface has little of the metal. The Alvarezes found lots of iridium in soil from 65 million years ago. They proposed that the extra iridium came from a large meteorite crash on Earth's surface. They also linked this crash to the disappearance of the dinosaurs. Many scientists now agree with that idea.

Other articles to read include: **Atom.**

Luis Walter Alvarez (right) and his son Walter proposed that an asteroid that crashed into Earth 65 million years ago played a role in the extinction of the dinosaurs.

Ammonia

Ammonia *(uh MOHN yuh)* or *(uh MOH nee uh)* is a colorless gas. It has a strong smell that stings the nose. Breathing pure ammonia can be dangerous and may even cause death. Ammonia is safe if mixed with a large amount of air.

The ammonia sold in bottles is really ammonia water. It is made by mixing ammonia gas into water.

Ammonia is a *chemical compound*. Chemical compounds are made from two or more chemical elements. A chemical element is a material that contains only one kind of atom. Ammonia is made from two gases, *nitrogen* and *hydrogen.*

People use ammonia for many things. Ammonia water is good for cleaning glass and other things around the house. Ammonia is also used in making fertilizers, drugs, chemicals, and plastics.

Other articles to read include: **Gas; Hydrogen; Nitrogen.**

Ampere

The *ampere (AM pihr or am PIHR)* is a unit used to measure an *electric current* (the movement of many electrons). Ampere is often written *amp* for short. The ampere measures an electric current's rate of flow.

A 100-watt light bulb uses about 1 ampere of current at 100 volts. Calculators and computers use currents so tiny they are measured in *milliamperes* (thousandths of amperes) or *microamperes* (millionths of amperes). Large industrial equipment uses currents measured in *kiloamperes* (thousands of amperes).

The ampere was named for the French physicist André-Marie Ampère, who discovered the laws of *electromagnetism* in the 1820's. Electromagnetism is the branch of physics that studies the relationship between electricity and magnetism.

Other articles to read include: **Ampère, André-Marie; Electricity.**

A device called a multimeter can be used to measure electric current in amperes in a circuit. Multimeters also measure such other electrical quantities as *voltage* (force) and resistance.

André-Marie Ampère

Ampère, André-Marie

André-Marie Ampère *(ahn DRAY mah REE ahn PAIR)* or *(AM peer)* (1775–1836) was a French mathematician and *physicist (FIHZ uh sihst).* A physicist is a scientist who studies matter and energy. Ampère discovered the laws of *electromagnetism* in the 1820's. Electromagnetism is the branch of physics that studies the relationship between electricity and magnetism. The *ampere,* or *amp,* the basic unit of electric current, is named for Ampère.

Ampère said that electric currents produce magnetism. He showed that two wires with electric currents running through them in the same direction attract each other like magnets. They repel force away from each other if the currents run in opposite directions.

He also found that an electric current flowing through a coiled wire attracts certain metals like a magnet. A magnet created by an electric current is called an *electromagnet.* This discovery led to the invention of the *galvanometer (GAL vuh NOM uh tuhr),* an instrument for detecting and measuring electric currents.

Other articles to read include: **Ampere; Electricity.**

Angle

An angle is made by two *rays* that start at the same point. A ray is a part of a line. The point where the two sides of an angle meet is called the *vertex.*

The size of an angle is measured in units called *degrees* (°). When the two sides make a square corner, the angle is called a *right angle.* A right angle measures 90°. An angle of 180° is called a *straight angle.* Its sides make a straight line. People use a tool called a protractor to measure and draw angles.

Other articles to read include: **Geometry; Triangle.**

Acute

Right

Obtuse

Straight

Antifreeze

Antifreeze is a material that lowers the *freezing point* of a liquid. The freezing point is the temperature at which a liquid turns into a solid. The freezing point of water is 32 °F (0 °C). Antifreeze contains an extremely poisonous form of alcohol.

Antifreeze keeps water from freezing in cold weather. For this reason, it is used in the cooling systems of automobiles and other vehicles. A car's cooling system uses water to keep the engine from getting too hot.

Antifreeze also raises the *boiling point* of water, which is 212 °F (100 °C). As a result, antifreeze keeps the water in a car's cooling system from boiling under extreme heat.

Other articles to read include: **Alcohol; Freezing point.**

Antifreeze added to the water in a car's cooling system keeps the water from freezing in extreme cold.

Antimatter

Antimatter is much like ordinary matter but with certain properties, such as electric charge, reversed. Both matter and antimatter consist of *elementary particles*. The parts of an atom—protons, neutrons, and electrons—are the most familiar elementary particles. In 1931, the British physicist Paul Dirac predicted that antimatter existed. In 1932, the American physicist Carl D. Anderson discovered evidence of *antiparticles* (particles of antimatter). In 2009, scientists discovered that lightning produces antimatter.

The elementary particles of antimatter have the same *mass* (amount of matter) as their counterparts in ordinary matter. For example, the *positron* is the antimatter counterpart to the electron. It has the same mass as an electron but has a positive charge, rather than a negative one.

Antimatter particles can bind together just like ordinary particles. For example, a positron and *antiproton* (the antimatter counterpart of a proton) can combine to form an antihydrogen atom. When matter and antimatter particles come into contact, they are destroyed. For this reason, antimatter on Earth is usually destroyed instantly, through contact with ordinary matter.

Other articles to read include: **Mass; Matter.**

Archimedes

Archimedes *(AHR kuh MEE deez)* (287?–212 B.C.) was an important ancient Greek scientist and inventor. He made many discoveries in mathematics and science. He also invented many machines. Archimedes lived on the island of Sicily in the Mediterranean Sea.

Archimedes explained how levers and pulleys work. Levers and pulleys are machines that can move heavy objects with little effort. Archimedes also explained why some things float in water.

Archimedes invented weapons to defend his city, Syracuse, against attacks by the Roman Empire. One weapon was a more effective catapult. The catapult is a machine that throws heavy rocks. Archimedes also invented a machine that could lift Roman ships out of the water, shake them, and drop them. Eventually, the Romans captured Syracuse. According to one story, Archimedes was killed by a soldier while working on a geometry problem.

Other articles to read include: **Mathematics.**

Archimedes

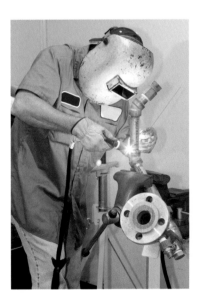

Argon, which does not react easily with other chemicals, is used in one type of arc welding to shield the area to be joined from outside substances in the air.

18	Ar	2 8 8
	Argon	
	39.948	

Argon atomic symbol

Argon

Argon *(AHR gon)* is a *chemical element* that forms less than 1 percent of Earth's atmosphere. A chemical element is a material that contains only one type of atom. Argon is a colorless, odorless, tasteless gas. Some light bulbs are filled with argon and a little nitrogen. Argon is also used in one type of *arc welding*, a process that uses heat to join metals. The argon protects the metal from oxygen in the air, which can damage it.

Argon is always being released into the atmosphere. It comes from the *decay* (breakdown) of radioactive potassium in Earth's crust. When the potassium decays, it changes into argon.

Argon is called a *noble gas*. Noble gases do not react easily with other chemicals. Argon and the other noble gases were discovered in 1894 by British scientists Lord Rayleigh and Sir William Ramsay.

Other articles to read include: **Element, Chemical; Gas; Noble gas; Potassium.**

Arsenic

Arsenic *(AHR suh nihk or AHRS nihk)* is a poisonous *chemical element* . A chemical element is a material that contains only one type of atom. Arsenic can cause cancer. It is used to make poisons for animal pests, insects, and weeds. It is also added to some metals to make them harder.

In the past, people used arsenic as a medicine. They thought it could cure some diseases. Arsenic is not used as a medicine today.

There are three forms of arsenic, called *gray, yellow,* and *black* arsenic. When gray arsenic is heated, it changes directly from a solid to a gas.

Arsenic is usually found in rocks called *ores* that also contain sulfur or oxygen or metals. The ore is heated to separate the arsenic from the other materials in the ore.

Other articles to read include: **Element, Chemical.**

| 33 | **As** | 2 8 18 5 |
| Arsenic 74.92160 | | |

Arsenic atomic symbol

Arsenic is a poisonous chemical element. It should be handled with protective equipment.

Ash

Ash is the powdery material left over after something has been burned in a fire. Ash can be found in a fireplace after a wood fire. Ash is also left over from burning cardboard, cloth, coal, paper, and many other materials.

Ash hold clues to the material that was burned. That is because chemicals from the burned material remain in the ash. For example, a chemical called *calcium* can be found in the ash of burned milk. This is because milk contains calcium. Likewise, ash from burned seaweed contain a chemical called *iodine* .

Most ash gets thrown away, but some ash can be useful. Wood ash, for example, can be added to soil as a fertilizer to help some kinds of trees and plants grow.

Other articles to read include: **Combustion; Fire.**

Ash contains chemicals that offer clues to the kind of material that was burned.

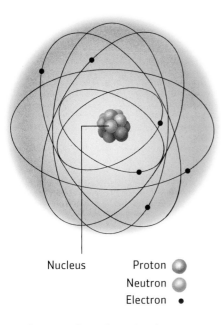

Nucleus   Proton
                 Neutron
                 Electron

An atom has three basic types of particles: protons, neutrons, and electrons. The protons and neutrons are in the *nucleus* (the center of the atom). The electrons whirl at fantastic speeds through the empty space around the nucleus.

Atom

The atom is one of the building blocks of matter. The matter around us is made up of atoms. Atoms are very tiny. A human hair is more than 1 million times as wide as an atom. The smallest speck of matter that can be seen with an ordinary microscope contains more than 10 billion atoms.

An atom is made up of smaller bits, called subatomic *(SUHB uh TOM ihk)* particles. The main subatomic particles are *protons (PROH tonz), neutrons (NOO tronz),* and *electrons (ih LEHK tronz).*

Protons and neutrons make up the nucleus *(NOO klee uhs),* the center of an atom. The electrons orbit the nucleus. An atomic nucleus is very small. If an atom could be made 4 miles (6.4 kilometers) wide, the nucleus would only be about the size of a tennis ball. The area containing the electrons is mostly empty space. The nucleus of an atom is held together by a very powerful force. This force helps contain a tremendous amount of energy. Scientists can split the nucleus to release some of this energy, called *atomic energy.* Nuclear energy is used in power plants to make electric current.

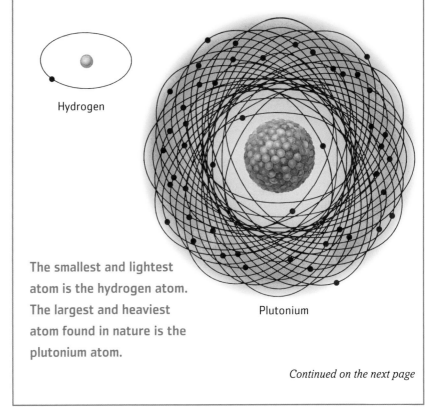

Hydrogen

Plutonium

The smallest and lightest atom is the hydrogen atom. The largest and heaviest atom found in nature is the plutonium atom.

Continued on the next page

Electrons are always moving at high speed. In just a millionth of a second, an electron makes billions of trips around the nucleus.

The most basic materials in nature are called *chemical elements*. A chemical element is made of only one kind of atom. The gases hydrogen and oxygen and the metals iron and lead are chemical elements.

All atoms of a particular chemical element have the same number of protons in their nucleus. A hydrogen atom, for example, has only 1 proton. A uranium atom has 92 protons.

Atoms can link together to form units called molecules *(MAHL uh kyoolz)*. Most chemicals are molecules made up of different kinds of atoms. For example, two hydrogen atoms join with one oxygen atom to form a molecule of water.

Other articles to read include: **Electrons; Matter; Neutron; Nucleus; Proton.**

Avogadro, Amedeo

Amedeo Avogadro *(AH mah DEE oh AH vuh GAH droh)* (1776-1856) was an Italian scientist. In 1811, he proposed an idea about gas that became famous. Avogadro's law had to do with *volumes* of gas. *Volume* is the amount of space something fills. Avogadro's law says that equal volumes of gas at the same temperature and pressure have the same number of chemical units. These units are the tiny *atoms* or *molecules* that make up the gas.

Using his law, Avogadro was able to figure out the *mass* (amount of matter) of atoms and molecules. At first, Avogadro's ideas were not accepted by most other scientists. His ideas did not catch on until 1858. Then, an Italian scientist named Stanislao Cannizzaro took up Avogadro's ideas and added to them.

Avogadro was born in Turin, Italy, on Aug. 9, 1776. He died on July 9, 1856.

Other articles to read include: **Gas; Volume.**

Amedeo Avogadro

Bb

Bacon, Francis

Francis Bacon (1561-1626) was an English *philosopher,* writer, law expert, and politician. A philosopher is a person who studies truth and knowledge. Bacon was one of the earliest and most important people to support science experiments and to study them.

Bacon helped develop the *scientific method* of solving problems. The scientific method is an orderly way of doing scientific research. The general steps include identifying a problem, gathering *data* (information), developing a *hypothesis (hy POTH uh sihs)* (possible explanation), performing experiments, figuring out the results, and drawing a conclusion.

Bacon believed that the mind jumps to conclusions, which keeps it from learning truths. But he believed that the mind could discover important truths if used properly. These truths would give people power over nature, putting an end to disease, poverty, and war.

Other articles to read include: **Chemistry.**

Francis Bacon

Bacon, Roger

Roger Bacon (1214?–1292?) was an important scientific thinker of the Middle Ages. The Middle Ages were a period in the history of Europe that lasted from the 400's through the 1400's. Bacon studied and wrote about astronomy, physics, mathematics, and religion. He was one of the first people to do scientific experiments. For this reason, he is known as the founder of experimental science. Bacon was also one of the first people to study *optics* (the science of light).

Bacon was born in England. He became a Franciscan monk and lived in Paris. The Franciscans would not let Bacon tell others about his work in science. But Pope Clement IV asked Bacon to write down his ideas. Bacon wrote a book and sent it to the pope.

Bacon thought people should study Arabic, Greek, and Hebrew. He believed it would help them understand the Bible better and learn about Arab and Greek scientific ideas. Bacon thought that mathematics was very important to science.

Other articles to read include: **Mathematics; Optics.**

Roger Bacon

Ballistics

Ballistics is the study of the way *projectiles* move and behave. Projectiles include arrows, balls, bombs, bullets, missiles, and other objects that can be thrown or shot from weapons. Soldiers, scientists, and police study ballistics in special laboratories. To understand ballistics, they use chemistry, mathematics, and physics.

Some scientists study how projectiles move inside a weapon. Others study how bullets, balls, or other projectiles move through the air. Some experts study what happens when projectiles hit targets.

Police rely on a special kind of ballistics called *forensic ballistics*. This kind of ballistics often enables the police to show that a specific bullet was fired from a specific gun. This evidence can help the police catch criminals.

Other articles to read include: **Motion.**

Bases are used in medicines called antacids that help treat people with heartburn. ▼

Base

A base, in chemistry, is any substance that makes a salt when it is mixed with an acid. Acids are chemicals that taste sour and cause a burning feeling if they touch the skin. The science of chemistry is the study of bases, acids, salts, and other chemical substances.

A base is also called an *alkali (AL kuh ly)*. When a base is mixed in water, it feels

slippery and tastes bitter. You can find out whether a substance is a base by putting a drop of the substance on red *litmus (LIHT muhs)* paper. Litmus paper is paper treated with a special dye. If the substance is a base, the litmus paper turns blue.

Bases have many uses. Bases that break down grease are used to clear clogs in sinks. Bases are added to many soft soaps to make them dissolve easily in water. Medicines called *antacids* that help fight stomachaches also contain bases.

Some bases are much stronger than others. Tea is a weak base. Strong bases, such as lye, can burn the skin.

Acids *neutralize* bases. That is, adding an acid to a base of equal strength will weaken the base until the acid and base are balanced.

Other articles to read include: **Acid; Litmus.**

Testing acids and bases

When you add an acid to a base of equal strength, the base substance and the acid balance each other out. Scientists say they *neutralize* each other. People can get indigestion pains when there is too much acid in their stomachs. Look at a packet of indigestion tablets. You'll see they contain bicarbonate of soda, also called baking soda or sodium bicarbonate. Why do you think this helps?

Find out if a solution is acidic or basic. The litmus papers are indicators.

What you need:

- 6 glass jars
- 1 teaspoon lemon juice
- 1 teaspoon baking soda
- 1-inch (25-mm) "squeeze" of toothpaste
- 1 teaspoon vinegar
- 1-inch (25-mm) piece of chalk
- water
- spoon
- labels
- marker
- red and blue litmus papers

 Don't drink any liquids unless you know they are safe.

1. Pour 1 inch (25 millimeters) of water into each jar. Mix one ingredient—the lemon juice, baking soda, toothpaste, vinegar, or chalk—into each of the jars. Leave one jar aside with just water.

2. Label each jar.

3. Place a litmus paper in each jar. What happened?

4. Add one of the bases to one of the acids teaspoon by teaspoon. Did the liquid become neutral? If not, why not?*

What's going on:

Acids turn the blue papers red. The red papers stay red in acids. Bases turn the red papers blue. The blue papers stay blue in bases. Neutral substances cause no change in the color of the paper.

*They did not neutralize each other because the acid was stronger than the base.

http://bit.ly/TUVvpz

Becquerel, Antoine Henri

Antoine Henri Becquerel *(ahn TWAHN ahn REE beh KREHL or BEHK uh REHL)* (1852–1908) was a French *physicist.* A physicist is a scientist who studies matter and energy. He shared the 1903 Nobel Prize in physics with Pierre and Marie Curie for his discovery of natural *radioactivity.* Radioactivity is the giving off of particles or energy by certain atoms as they break down.

Becquerel was born in Paris on Dec. 15, 1852. His father and grandfather also were physicists. Becquerel became a physics professor in 1892. He was elected president of the French Academy of Sciences in 1908. Becquerel died on Aug. 25, 1908. The *becquerel,* a unit of radioactivity, is named for him.

Other articles to read include: **Radiation.**

Antoine Henri Becquerel

Beryllium
atomic symbol

Beryllium

Beryllium is a rare, light-gray, metallic *chemical element.* A chemical element is a material that contains only one kind of atom. Beryllium is light and brittle. It resists melting better than most other light metals. Beryllium's chemical symbol is *Be.*

Beryllium never occurs in nature as a pure metal. But it is found in a number of minerals. Beryl and *bertrandite* are the most important sources of beryllium. The German chemist Friedrich Wöhler and the French chemist A. A. Bussy, working independently, separated out the first samples of pure beryllium in 1828.

Beryllium has a number of uses. For instance, beryllium's light weight and its ability to absorb and conduct heat make it useful for specialized parts in missiles, rockets, and satellites. However, a person who inhales beryllium dust may develop *berylliosis,* a lung disease that is sometimes fatal. The United States government has set safety standards to protect workers who work with beryllium from heavy exposure to the metal and its compounds.

Other articles to read include: **Element, Chemical; Metal.**

Binary number

A binary number is written with only two *digits*. Digits are symbols used to write numbers. Binary numbers are usually written using only the digits *0* and *1*. In everyday life, we commonly use the digits *0, 1, 2, 3, 4, 5, 6, 7, 8*, and *9* to write *decimal* numbers. The binary number system is also called *base 2*. The decimal system, on the other hand, is called *base 10*.

Any decimal number can also be written as a binary number. For example, the decimal number *5* is written as *101* in binary. The first *1* is in the "fours" place. The zero is in the "twos" place. And the second *1* is in the "ones" place (4 + 0 + 1 = 5).

Computers use binary numbers to store data and perform calculations. A computer's circuits can be switched either "on" or "off." The switch lets an electric current pass through or not. These two positions work like the two digits in binary numbers. A binary number in a computer can stand for letters and words. It can even represent pictures, sounds, and videos. Modern computers can perform huge numbers of binary calculations at extremely fast speeds.

Gottfried Wilhelm Leibniz, a German philosopher and mathematician, developed the binary number system in the late 1600's. But binary numbers were not widely used until the 1940's, when people developed the first computers.

Other articles to read include: **Decimal system; Digit; Number.**

Biochemists study the chemical processes that take place in living things.

Biochemistry

Biochemistry is the study of the chemical processes that take place inside living things. Studying these processes helps scientists to understand how living things grow and live.

Living things contain tiny particles called *molecules*. Biochemists study the shape of molecules. They also try to learn which chemicals make up different molecules. This research helps biochemists to understand chemical processes.

Chemical processes play an important part in nearly everything that happens in living things. Animals use these processes to turn food into energy. Chemical processes help plants make food using the energy in sunlight. People use chemical processes to digest food and move their muscles.

Biochemical research is useful in many ways. It helps medical scientists find treatments and cures for diseases. Biochemical research also helps farmers grow more and better crops.

Other articles to read include: **Chemistry; Molecule.**

Biogas

Biogas *(BY oh GAS)* is a gas given off by the decaying remains of living things. It forms from such remains when there is not much oxygen present. Biogas comes from buried garbage, sewage, and manure. Dead plants and animals in swampy areas also produce biogas.

Biogas usually contains a mixture of carbon dioxide and *methane (MEHTH ayn)*. Large amounts of methane can be dangerous. A spark near the gas can cause an explosion. But methane can be collected and stored safely. Then it can be burned for energy. Methane is a chief part of natural gas, a widely used fuel. Methane also is used in industry.

Other articles to read include: **Gas; Methane.**

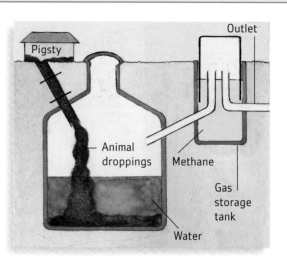

Garbage and sewage can be used to produce biogas. The droppings of farm animals can be collected and put in a tank. The waste gives off methane and other gases. The methane can be collected and used for cooking or heating.

Biophysics

Biophysics *(BY oh FIHZ ihks)* is the study of living things through the use of the tools and methods of physics. Physics is the study of matter and energy.

Many scientists in biophysics study the *molecules* inside cells. Molecules are tiny chemical units made of two or more atoms. Cells are the tiny building blocks that make up living things. In biophysics, scientists try to figure out how molecules work inside cells.

One tool used in biophysics is the *electron microscope*. It lets scientists see the details of cells.

Another tool used in biophysics is the X-ray machine. Scientists use it to shoot X rays at molecules. The rays bend as they pass through the molecules. The way the rays bend gives information about the shape of the molecules.

Other articles to read include: **Physics; X rays.**

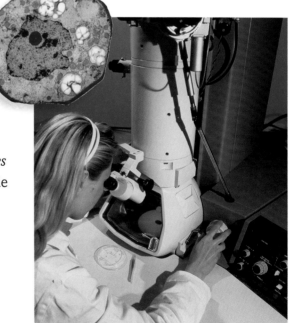

A biophysicist examines a plant cell (inset) through an electron microscope, an important tool in biophysics.

Bleach

Chlorine bleach used in laundering is a chemical bleach.

Bleach is any substance that lightens, brightens, or removes the color from a material. Manufacturers bleach cloth, paper, and other materials. This prepares the materials to be dyed. Homemakers use laundry bleach to clean and brighten clothes. People also use some bleaches to destroy germs.

There are two main kinds of bleaches, *chemical* and *optical.* Chemical bleaches act on the *molecules* (tiny bits of matter) that give a material its color. These bleaches make materials colorless or nearly colorless. Optical bleaches mask yellow stains in a material. These bleaches reflect more blue light. The extra blue color helps hide yellow colors. Optical bleaches are commonly called *fabric brighteners.*

Many ancient peoples bleached fabrics. They sometimes treated the cloth with smoke from burning sulfur. They also used bleaches they made from plants or plant ash. Then they spread the treated cloth on the ground to whiten in the sun. People began manufacturing bleaches in the 1700's.

Other articles to read include: **Chlorine.**

Bohr, Niels

Niels Bohr (1885-1962) was a famous scientist from Denmark. He is known for his ideas about *atoms,* one of the basic units of matter. An atom has particles called *electrons* that whirl around a small *nucleus* (core). Bohr said that electrons could travel around the nucleus only in certain orbits. He thought that the outer orbits—that is, those farther from the nucleus— could hold more electrons than the inner ones. He won the 1922 Nobel Prize in physics chiefly for his work on the structure of atoms.

Niels Bohr

Bohr also thought about how atoms give off light. He said that when an electron jumps from an outer orbit to an inner one, it gives off light. Later, other scientists used Bohr's ideas to figure out a type of physics called *quantum mechanics.* Quantum mechanics explains how the smallest bits of matter behave.

Bohr was born on Oct. 7, 1885, in Copenhagen, Denmark. He earned a Ph.D. degree in physics in 1911. In 1916, Bohr became a professor of physics.

During World War II (1939-1945), forces from Nazi Germany invaded Denmark. Bohr escaped to the United States. There, he helped scientists working on the first atomic bomb. Bohr later encouraged people to use nuclear energy peacefully. He died on Nov. 18, 1962.

Other articles to read include: **Atom; Electron; Light; Matter; Quantum mechanics.**

Boiling point

The boiling point is the temperature at which a liquid bubbles and turns into a *vapor* (gas).

A liquid reaches its boiling point when its *vapor pressure* is the same as the *air pressure*. Air pressure is the downward pressure of the air in the atmosphere. Vapor pressure is the upward pressure of the molecules of vapor near the liquid's surface. The motion of the vapor molecules produces the vapor pressure.

As a liquid is heated, the vapor molecules move faster and push harder against the air above. When the vapor pressure equals the air pressure above, the liquid turns into a gas.

A liquid's boiling point varies with changes in air pressure. The boiling point rises as air pressure increases and falls as air pressure decreases. For example, the boiling point of water at sea level is 212 °F (100 °C). But at 10,000 feet (3,050 meters) above sea level, water boils at about 194 °F (90 °C).

Different substances have different boiling points. The boiling point depends on the force of attraction between molecules in the substance. Some substances, such as gold, have very strong forces. Higher temperatures are needed to break the attraction. Other substances, such as nitrogen, have weaker forces. They boil at lower temperatures.

Other articles to read include: **Gas; Liquid; Temperature; Vapor.**

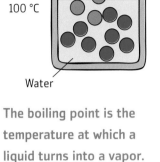

Steam
212 °F
100 °C
Water

The boiling point is the temperature at which a liquid turns into a vapor.

Bond, Chemical

Chemical bonds are invisible connections between tiny bits of matter called *atoms*. Chemical bonds join atoms together to make new kinds of substances.

Chemical bonds form because of the activity of tiny particles called *electrons*. Electrons, which have a negative charge, orbit the *nucleus* (center) of an atom. In one type of chemical bond, an electron that belongs to one atom forms a pair with an electron that belongs to another atom. The atoms then share the electrons, forming a *molecule*. This is called a *covalent* bond. In another type of chemical bond, one atom loses an electron to another atom. Atoms bonded in this way are called ionic compounds. Not all bonds are purely covalent or ionic. Many bonds share characteristics of both types.

Other articles to read include: **Atom; Element, Chemical; Ion.**

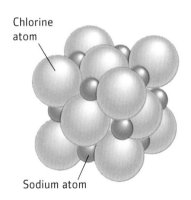

Chlorine atom

Sodium atom

Sodium and chlorine atoms form an ionic bond to become sodium chloride, or table salt.

Boron

| 5 | **B** | 2 3 |

Boron
10.811

Boron atomic symbol

Boron *(BAWR ahn),* a chemical element, is an extremely hard *metalloid.* A chemical element is a material that is made of only one kind of atom. A metalloid has properties of both a metal and a nonmetal.

Boron is found in small amounts throughout Earth's surface. The chief sources of boron and boron compounds are mineral deposits left after the evaporation of lakes and other bodies of water. Major deposits of boron minerals are found in Kazakhstan, Turkey, the United States, and a strip of South America from Peru to Argentina.

Boron is essential to proper plant growth. It also has many industrial uses. Adding boron to steel increases its hardness and strength. A type of boron is used in nuclear reactors. Compounds of boron and oxygen, such as borax and boric acid, are used in heat-resistant glass, detergents and soaps, and medicines.

The color of boron ranges from brown to black. It has the chemical symbol *B.* Boron was first identified as a chemical element in 1808 by the French scientists Joseph Louis Gay-Lussac and Louis Jacques Thenard.

Other articles to read include: **Element, Chemical; Metal.**

Boson

A boson *(BOH son)* is one kind of *subatomic particle.* A subatomic particle is a bit of matter that is smaller than an atom. Scientists divide all subatomic particles into bosons or *fermions.* The matter around us is made up of fermions. Many bosons are associated with such forces as electromagnetism.

The simplest bosons cannot be broken down into smaller parts. These bosons are called *fundamental* bosons or *gauge* bosons. Fundamental bosons carry forces between particles. Scientists have discovered four kinds of fundamental bosons. They are (1) photons, (2) gluons, (3) weak bosons, and (4) the Higgs boson.

Continued on the next page

Photons carry electromagnetic forces. Light is made up of photons.

Gluons carry the *strong nuclear force.* This force holds the *nuclei* (cores) of atoms together.

Weak bosons carry the *weak nuclear force.* This force is involved in the breakdown of certain kinds of subatomic particles.

The *Higgs* boson is responsible for *mass.* Mass is the amount of matter in an object.

Many scientists think that there is only one fundamental boson that has not been found yet. It is the *graviton,* which carries the force of gravity.

Other articles to read include: **Higgs boson; Light; Photon.**

Boyle, Robert

Robert Boyle (1627–1691) was an Irish scientist. Boyle is sometimes called the founder of modern chemistry. He helped create methods for carrying out chemistry experiments.

Boyle is most famous for his experiments with gases. He discovered how gases act under pressure. He also studied the nature of vacuums.

Boyle figured out ways to determine which *chemical elements* make up a substance. Chemical elements are materials that have only one kind of atom. Boyle showed that an older belief about chemical elements was not true. His experiments proved that air, earth, fire, and water are not the basic elements of matter. That belief began in ancient Greece and was accepted for many centuries. Boyle argued that all the basic physical *properties* (characteristics) of materials were due to the movement of atoms, which he called "corpuscles."

Robert Boyle

Boyle belonged to an important group of scientists called the Royal Society of London. He wrote many books about his experiments.

Other articles to read include: **Chemistry; Element, Chemical.**

Braun, Karl Ferdinand

Karl Ferdinand Braun

Karl Ferdinand Braun (1850–1918) was a German *physicist.* A physicist is a scientist who studies matter and energy. Braun helped develop radio. A certain kind of television screen is based on one of his inventions. He shared the 1909 Nobel Prize in physics with the Italian radio pioneer Guglielmo Marconi (1847-1937).

Braun studied electricity and invented several electrical devices. The most important of these was a type of vacuum tube, developed in 1897. The tube formed light rays into a fine beam. The beam could trace out patterns of light. At first, this device was used to display and measure *voltage* (the strength of an electric potential). It was later used to develop the television and the radar screen.

In 1898, Braun began to experiment with broadcasting radio waves. He improved the design of the *aerial* (wire that sends out radio waves). This enabled signals to be broadcast much farther. He also found ways of directing radio waves into a beam, like the beam of a searchlight. Waves directed in this way could travel farther, reaching more listeners. It was for this work that he won the Nobel Prize.

Braun was born in the German city of Fulda in 1850. He died in the United States in 1918.

Other articles to read include: **Radio wave.**

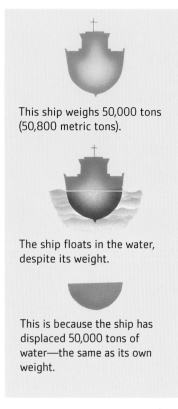

This ship weighs 50,000 tons (50,800 metric tons).

The ship floats in the water, despite its weight.

This is because the ship has displaced 50,000 tons of water—the same as its own weight.

Buoyancy

Buoyancy *(BOY uhn see)* is the ability to float. Boats float on water because of buoyancy. Buoyancy also enables balloons to float in the air.

Imagine putting a hollow rubber ball in a bucket of water. The ball *displaces* (pushes aside) some of the water. The water pushes back against the ball. This pushing action creates buoyancy. It makes the ball float.

Buoyancy depends on an object's *density*—that is, how heavy the object is for its size. An object with a density lower than that of water will float. A ship, even one made of steel, has a lower density than water. That is because the ship has open spaces inside it. If it were a solid mass of steel, its density would be higher than that of water. As a result, it would sink.

Other articles to read include: **Density.**

Calcium

20	Ca	2 8 8 2
	Calcium	
	40.078	

Calcium atomic symbol

Calcium *(KAL see uhm)* is a soft, silvery-white, metallic *chemical element.* A chemical element is a material that has only one kind of atom. Calcium is one of the most common metals on Earth. Calcium is found most widely in such rocks as limestone and marble. In nature, calcium is found only with other chemical elements in substances called *compounds.* Compounds have more than one kind of atom.

People use calcium and calcium compounds to make many things. Calcium is used to make some *alloys.* Alloys are mixtures of different kinds of metals. Calcium compounds are used to make cement, fertilizer, and paint. Calcium compounds are also used in making leather and gasoline.

Calcium is also a nutrient important to all living things. It forms a major part of many animal shells, bones, and teeth.

The ancient Egyptians, Greeks, and Romans used calcium compounds to make mortar, a building material that holds bricks or stones together. In 1808, the English chemist Sir Humphry Davy became the first person to obtain pure calcium.

Other articles to read include: **Alloy; Element, Chemical; Metal.**

Foods rich in calcium

Food	Serving size	Calcium per serving (mg)
Milk		
Skim, low fat, whole	1 cup	300
Lactose-reduced	1 cup	250
Soy, fortified	1 cup	280
Yogurt		
Plain low-fat	1 cup	415
Fruit low-fat	1 cup	343
Frozen	1 cup	200
Ice cream or ice milk	1 cup	190
Cheese		
Swiss	1 ounce	245
Cheddar	1 ounce	205
Mozzarella	1 ounce	185
American	1 ounce	175
Ricotta	1/2 cup	335
Cottage (low-fat)	1/2 cup	80
Sardines, canned (with bones)	3 ounces	325
Broccoli	1 cup	100
Calcium-fortified orange juice	1 cup	350

The foods listed in this table are rich in calcium. Children ages 9 through 18 should consume 1,300 milligrams of calcium per day, according to the United States Food and Nutrition Board.

Calculus

Calculus *(KAL kyuh luhs)* is a branch of mathematics that deals with change. It is often used by engineers, physicists, and other scientists. They rely on calculus to solve many practical problems about objects in motion.

Geometry, another branch of mathematics, often deals with straight lines or simple shapes. Calculus deals with curves. For example, imagine watching a ball thrown in the air. The ball flies in a smooth curve. As it flies, the speed and direction of its movement change constantly. Calculus can be used to figure out the ball's speed at any point along the curve.

Calculus can solve certain problems that other branches of mathematics cannot. For example, the laws of *aerodynamics* are written in calculus. Aerodynamics is the study of forces that push or pull on an object as it moves through the air. The laws of aerodynamics can describe the forces acting on an airplane during flight.

Some ancient problem-solving methods were similar to calculus. But the actual study of calculus began in the 1600's. People used calculus to study the motion of planets. The most important rule of calculus was discovered in the late 1600's by two people. One was the English scientist Sir Isaac Newton. The other was the German philosopher Gottfried W. Leibniz. Newton and Leibniz are called the founders of calculus.

Other articles to read include: **Mathematics; Newton, Sir Isaac.**

Calorie

A calorie is a unit in the metric system for measuring the amount of heat energy in something. The word *calorie* comes from a Latin word that means *heat.*

A calorie is the amount of energy needed to raise the temperature of 1 gram of water by 1 degree Celsius. Many chemical *reactions* (changes) produce heat. Scientists measure the amount of heat produced with an instrument called a *calorimeter.* One of the most important uses of the calorimeter is to measure the

Continued on the next page

amount of heat given off by different foods when they burn. This measurement tells how much energy a certain food yields when it is completely used by the body.

The symbol for the calorie is *cal*. The calorie used to measure the energy content of food—the symbol *Cal*—is equal to 1,000 cal. The larger Cal is commonly called a *food calorie*.

Other articles to read include: **Heat.**

This table shows the calories in some foods, and the minutes it would take a 150-pound (68-kilogram) person to use up those calories with exercise.

Food	Calories	Minutes of walking (2 1/2 mph)	Minutes of bicycle riding (9 mph)
Apple, large	125	34	20
Beans, green canned, 1 cup	25	7	4
Cake, yellow with chocolate frosting, 1 piece	235	64	38
Hamburger sandwich	245	67	39
Milk, lowfat (2% fat), 1 cup	120	33	19
Pizza, cheese 15-inch (38 cm) diameter, 1/8 of pizza	290	79	46

Capillary action

Capillary *(KAP uh LEHR ee)* action is the rising of water in a narrow tube. Capillary action helps raise water from a tree's roots up to its leaves. Tree trunks and branches have many tiny tubes called *capillaries.*

When water enters a capillary, the sides of the capillary pull the water *molecules* to them. Molecules are particles made up of atoms *bonded* (connected) together in certain ways. The sides pull the molecules to them more strongly than gravity can pull the molecules down. As a result, the water molecules "climb" the sides of the capillaries.

Capillary action works in many other things besides trees. For example, a paper towel has many tiny capillaries. These pull on molecules of liquid, such as milk, helping to soak up a spill.

Other articles to read include: **Absorption and adsorption.**

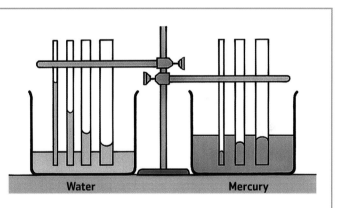

Water   Mercury

Capillary action explains how water can rise in a narrow tube. Glass tubes of different widths are placed in a bowl of water (left) and of mercury (right). Water rises highest in the narrowest tube because water molecules are attracted to the walls of the tube and are pulled up against the force of gravity. But mercury molecules are slightly *repelled* (pushed away) by the walls of the tubes, lowering the mercury levels more in the narrower tubes. So the mercury level is highest in the widest tube.

Carbon

6	C	2 4
Carbon		
12.0107		

Carbon atomic symbol

Carbon is an important *chemical element*. A chemical element is a material made up of only one type of atom.

Carbon is a necessary part of all living things. Carbon atoms can *bond* (join) with atoms of many other chemical elements to form *compounds*. Many of these substances make it possible for living things to build cells and other body parts.

Diamonds are a form of carbon.

Much of the carbon on Earth exists in compounds. Scientists have found more than 1 million carbon compounds. The gas carbon dioxide is a compound of carbon and oxygen. Hydrocarbons are another type of carbon compound. These compounds of carbon and hydrogen are the chief elements in petroleum fuels and natural gas.

Pure carbon exists in nature in four forms. They are *diamond, graphite, amorphous* or *"glassy" carbons,* and *fullerenes.* Diamond is the hardest substance found in nature. Graphite is a soft mineral used in pencils. It consists of layers of thin, tough sheets called *graphene.* Charcoal is a type of amorphous carbon. Fullerenes are hollow structures with many carbon atoms. The best known fullerene is the buckminsterfullerene. It consists of 60 carbon atoms bonded together in the shape of a soccer ball. This structure is also known as a *buckyball.*

Other articles to read include: **Element, Chemical; Hydrocarbon.**

Anders Celsius

Celsius, Anders

Anders Celsius *(SEHL see uhs)* (1701–1744) was a Swedish astronomer who developed the *Celsius temperature scale.* An *astronomer* is a scientist who studies objects in the universe. The Celsius scale is used to determine temperature in the metric system of measurement.

In 1736, Celsius joined an expedition to Lapland that helped to show that Earth is flattened around the North and South poles. The fame he earned helped him to raise money to build an observatory in Uppsala, Sweden. Celsius also first linked *auroras* to disturbances in Earth's *magnetic field.* Auroras are displays of colored light in the sky. Earth's magnetic field is the pattern of magnetic forces surrounding the planet.

Other articles to read include: **Celsius scale; Magnetic field; Temperature.**

Celsius scale

The Celsius *(SEHL see uhs)* scale is a way of measuring temperature. The Celsius scale is part of the international system of measurement commonly called the metric system. People in most countries use the Celsius scale. People in the United States often use a different temperature scale called the Fahrenheit *(FAR uhn hyt)* scale.

The Celsius scale is based on the freezing point and the boiling point of water. The freezing point is the temperature at which water turns to ice. The boiling point is the temperature at which water turns to *vapor* (gas). The Celsius scale divides the range between them into 100 equal parts. Each of these parts is called a degree.

The symbol for degrees Celsius is $°C$. On the Celcius scale, 0 °C is the freezing point of water. The boiling point of water is 100 °C.

The Celsius scale is named for its inventor, the Swedish astronomer Anders Celsius (1701-1744).

Other articles to read include: **Celsius, Anders; Temperature.**

This thermometer displays the Celsius temperature scale.

Centrifugal and centripetal forces

Centrifugal *(sehn TRIHF yuh guhl* or *sehn TRIHF uh guhl)* force and centripetal *(sehn TRIHP uh tuhl)* force are terms sometimes used to describe the motion of objects traveling in a circle.

Consider an object in motion. It tends to keep moving in a straight line. To move in a circle, it must constantly be pulled toward the circle's center. This inward pull is called a *centripetal force.*

Imagine a rock tied to a stone. To whirl the rock around, a person must hold onto the string. The string maintains a centripetal force. If the person lets go of the string, the rock will fly off in a straight line. In the same way, Earth's gravity maintains a centripetal force on artificial satellites. This keeps the satellites from flying into space.

Continued on the next page

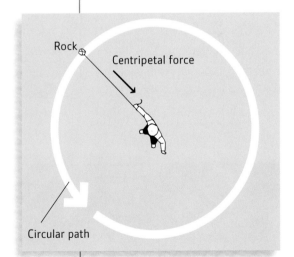

Rock
Centripetal force
Circular path

Centripetal force makes an object move in a circular path. The person in this drawing maintains a centripetal force on the rock by pulling the string.

Centrifugal and centripetal forces
Continued from the previous page

When you ride a merry-go-round, an outward pull sometimes called centrifugal force pulls you away from its center.

Now imagine standing on a merry-go-round. A centripetal force keeps you from flying off. This force is held by friction rubbing between your shoes and the merry-go-round. But your body still feels a tendency to fly off. This tendency is felt as an outward pull. People sometimes call this outward pull *centrifugal force*. But the pull is not really a force. It is just the tendency to keep moving in a straight line. This tendency is called *inertia*.

Centripetal force acts in other ways. For example, a speeding automobile tends to move in a straight line. Centripetal force must act on the car to make it travel around a curve. This force comes from the friction between the tires and the pavement.

Other articles to read include: **Force; Gravitation; Motion.**

CERN

CERN houses the world's largest particle accelerator. This device speeds up the movement of tiny bits of matter and collides them to reveal information about the nature of matter.

CERN is a major research center for the study of *subatomic particles*. Subatomic particles are tiny bits of matter smaller than atoms. Scientists at CERN conduct experiments using *particle accelerators*. These huge machines produce beams of subatomic particles at extremely high energies. CERN houses the world's largest accelerator, the Large Hadron Collider (LHC). This ring-shaped machine measures 17 miles (27 kilometers) in circumference.

CERN is near Geneva, Switzerland. It is run by a group of European nations called the European Organization for Nuclear Research. The name *CERN* comes from this group's original name in French. CERN was founded in 1954.

Other articles to read include: **Atom; Matter.**

Chain reaction

A chain reaction is a process in *physics*. Physics is the science of matter and energy. In a chain reaction, the *chemical elements* uranium or plutonium release energy. A chemical element is a substance with only one kind of atom. The energy in a chain reaction comes from splitting the *nuclei* (cores) of atoms. The splitting of one nucleus leads to the splitting of another, and so on. This is why the reaction is called a "chain."

A falling row of dominoes demonstrates the concept of a chain reaction. As a domino falls, it knocks down the piece behind it.

A chain reaction takes place in a device called a *nuclear reactor*. In some reactors, a uranium nucleus is struck by a subatomic particle called a *neutron*. This causes the nucleus to split. When it splits, it gives off more neutrons. These neutrons cause other nuclei to split. Energy is released, mainly in the form of heat. In nuclear physics, splitting a nucleus is called *fission*. In a chain reaction, trillions of atoms can split within a fraction of a second.

Other articles to read include: **Nuclear energy; Radiation.**

Neutron

Uranium atom

Uranium atom

Neutron

Energy released

Neutron

One type of chain reaction is used to make electric energy in nuclear power plants. When the nucleus of a uranium atom is split, neutrons are released. The neutrons hit other atoms, causing them to split, and so on. Most of the energy released takes the form of heat.

Chandrasekhar, Subrahmanyan

Subrahmanyan Chandrasekhar

Subrahmanyan Chandrasekhar *(SU brah MAN yuhn SHAHN druh SAY kahr)* (1910–1995) was an American astrophysicist *(as troh FIHZ uh sihst)*. An astrophysicist is a scientist who studies objects in space. Chandrasekhar shared the 1983 Nobel Prize in physics with the American astrophysicist William A. Fowler. They won for research on how stars change and eventually die.

Chandrasekhar is best known for his work on *white dwarfs.* A white dwarf is a small, heavy star that has run out of fuel. Some white dwarfs grow larger by pulling matter away from other nearby stars. Chandrasekhar discovered that white dwarfs that grow larger than 1.4 times the size of our sun collapse from their own gravitation. They then become exploding stars called *supernovae* (the plural of supernova). Eventually, they become *neutron (NOO tron) stars.* A neutron star is a tiny star made up of subatomic particles called *neutrons.*

Chandrasekhar went by the nickname Chandra *(SHAHN druh).* He was born in Lahore, in what is now Pakistan. A space telescope called the Chandra X-ray Observatory was named in his honor. NASA launched the telescope on July 23, 1999.

Other articles to read include: **Neutron.**

Chaos theory

Chaos *(KAY os)* theory is the study of things that behave in unexpected ways. Such things are called *chaotic systems.* One example is the weather. Scientists have difficulty knowing what the weather will do. Studying chaos theory can help them understand the chances certain weather events might happen. Scientists once thought that they could learn exactly how every system works. They thought that they just needed more information to make predictions. But the science of chaos showed that it is difficult to predict the long-term behavior of very complex systems.

The game of pool is an example of a chaotic system. Imagine a player striking one ball. It is fairly easy to predict in which direction the ball will go and where the ball will stop. However, each time the ball strikes another object, such as another ball or the

Continued on the next page

table's bumpers, it becomes increasingly difficult to determine where the ball will go next.

A common game of pool begins with 15 balls arranged in a triangle. One player strikes the triangle of balls with another ball—the cue ball. The cue ball sets off a string of collisions among the other balls. Tiny variations in the first strike can change the sequence of collisions in very complex ways. For this reason, it is impossible to predict in which direction all 16 balls will go and where they will stop. This complexity is typical of a chaotic system.

Scientists can sometimes predict how chaotic systems will behave over a short period. For example, weather forecasters can make useful five-day forecasts for many locations. But chaos prevents them from predicting the weather a year into the future.

Other articles to read include: **Probability.**

Chemical

A chemical is any of the many materials that make up living and nonliving things. All chemicals are made of *chemical elements (EHL uh muhnts).* Chemical elements are substances that have only one kind of atom. An atom is a tiny piece of matter. Calcium, gold, and nitrogen are examples of chemical elements. Two or more chemical elements can be combined to form a *chemical compound.*

There are natural and artificial chemicals. For example, water is a natural chemical compound. It is made up of the chemical elements hydrogen and oxygen. Table salt is another natural chemical compound. It contains the chemical elements sodium and chlorine. Your body contains many kinds of natural chemicals. Coal, gas, and oil are natural chemicals that formed from dead plants and animals over millions of years.

Chemists combine natural chemicals to make many kinds of artificial chemicals. Cleaning supplies, dyes, paint, plastics, and many medicines are examples of artificial chemicals.

Other articles to read include: **Compound; Element, Chemical.**

Water is a natural chemical compound. It consists of the chemical elements hydrogen and oxygen.

Paint is an artificial chemical compound. It is a combination of many natural and other artificial chemicals.

Chemical reaction

A chemical reaction occurs when one or more substances are changed into different substances. Chemical reactions involve tiny pieces of matter called *atoms* and *molecules*.

A molecule consists of two or more atoms held together by an attraction called a *chemical bond*. Bonds hold together every substance in the universe that is made of atoms. Bonds develop from the activity of *electrons* (negatively charged particles) that whirl about the positively charged *nucleus* (core) of an atom.

Fireworks explode in fast chemical reactions triggered by a spark. The spark ignites a chemical reaction that produces heat. The heat quickly causes a chain reaction that ignites other materials in the fireworks.

During a chemical reaction, chemical bonds can be broken, and new bonds can form. The atoms that form molecules rearrange themselves to form new molecules. Many substances, including glass, rock, platinum, and water, strongly resist chemical reactions. However, all substances can react chemically under certain conditions.

Chemical reactions take place everywhere. Some chemical reactions, such as the explosion of fireworks, are fast. Other chemical reactions, such as the rusting of metal, are slow. Living things use many different chemical reactions to grow and live. Burning such fuels as coal, gasoline, or natural gas is a special kind of chemical reaction called a *combustion reaction*.

Scientists describe chemical reactions using special letters and symbols. For example, the following describes the burning of *methane*, a major part of natural gas:

$$CH_4 \text{ (methane)} + 2O_2 \text{ (oxygen)} \rightarrow$$
$$CO_2 \text{ (carbon dioxide)} + 2H_2O \text{ (water)}$$

Rust is made by a slow chemical reaction that does not need a spark to form. The reaction requires only oxygen, water, and iron. But adding heat can speed the process.

This means that one molecule of methane and two molecules of oxygen react together to form one molecule of carbon dioxide gas and two molecules of water.

Other articles to read include: **Atom; Combustion; Molecule; Rust.**

Chemical reactions: Changing change

Mixing certain chemicals together may cause them to change into different chemicals. This process is known as a chemical reaction. A simple reaction of two chemicals may produce one or many new chemicals. The new chemicals have different properties than the original chemicals.

Often a chemical reaction needs help to get started. Heat is a common way trigger a reaction. Sometimes a chemical called a catalyst is added. It may help the reaction to start, speed up, or even produce different chemicals than what would be made without them.

In each of the next two experiments, decide whether a chemical change is involved. Be sure to examine your materials carefully before you begin each experiment.

1. Fold the paper towel in half and then in half again to form a square with four layers.

2. Place the folded towel on the saucer, and pour enough vinegar on the towel to wet it thoroughly.

3. Place the pennies on the vinegar-soaked towel. Draw a picture of your setup.

4. Wait a day. Then examine the pennies and towel and draw what you see. Has there been a chemical change? What makes you think so? Write down your conclusions.

http://bit.ly/VJhnk9

What you need:

- a paper towel
- a saucer
- vinegar
- three or more pennies
- paper
- pen or pencil

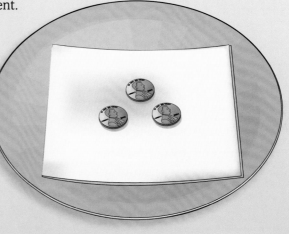

What's going on:

The green coating that has formed on the pennies shows a chemical change has occurred. The green coating is copper acetate, which is formed when copper atoms in the pennies join with acid in the vinegar.

Chemical reactions: The heat of change

1. Place the thermometer inside the jar. Close the lid and wait five minutes. Record the temperature inside the jar.

2. Pull or cut the steel wool pad into two unequal parts. Set the smaller part aside in a dry place. Soak the larger part of the pad in a measuring cup or bowl of vinegar for two minutes.

3. Squeeze out the excess liquid from the pad. Then wrap the damp pad around the bulb of the thermometer.

4. Place the thermometer and damp pad inside the jar. Close the lid. Wait five minutes and then record the temperature. Compare it with the earlier temperature reading.

5. Open the lid and wait two or three days. Then examine the steel wool. Compare it with the untouched part of the pad. Has there been a chemical change? Write down how you know.

What you need:

- a cooking or outdoor thermometer
- a clear glass jar with a lid (The closed jar must be big enough to hold the thermometer.)
- paper
- pen or pencil
- scissors (optional)
- a steel wool pad without soap
- A measuring cup or bowl big enough to hold the steel wool pad
- vinegar

What's going on:

A chemical reaction between iron in the steel wool and oxygen has caused rust to form on the steel wool in the jar. This reaction is made possible when the vinegar removes the protective coating from the steel wool. The thermometer shows that the heat was released by the reaction.

http://bit.ly/WUOHKo

Chemistry

Chemistry is the scientific study of the substances that make up our world and the rest of the universe. These substances are called *chemicals*. Scientists who study chemistry are called *chemists*. Chemists try to understand and explain the *properties* (characteristics) of chemicals. They study how chemicals act under different conditions, such as at different temperatures. Chemists also study how two or more chemicals behave when mixed together. For example, chemists may experiment with combining certain chemicals to make a new chemical substance.

Chemists work to understand chemical reactions, the processes by which one or more substances are changed into different substances.

One of the main goals of chemists is to understand *chemical reactions*. These reactions take place constantly in all living things, including the human body. For example, chemicals in the food we eat go through many chemical reactions in the body. These reactions give you energy to work and play. Chemical reactions also take place in the air, in the soil, and even deep inside Earth. The formation of rust on a metal bridge or car is a chemical reaction. It occurs when iron combines with oxygen from the air. Chemical reactions take place as wood burns and becomes ashes and gases.

Chemists have created many useful substances not found in nature. Products resulting from chemical research include many artificial fibers, drugs, dyes, fertilizers, and plastics.

People have been watching and making use of chemical reactions for more than 1½ million years. Fire was one of the first chemical reactions that humans learned to purposely produce and control.

Other articles to read include: **Chemical; Chemical reaction.**

High-school students conduct an experiment in chemistry class.

A worker checks the chlorine level in water from a swimming pool. The chemical is added to the water to kill bacteria.

Old refrigerators that used chlorofluorocarbons can be recycled. ▼

Chlorine

17	**Cl**	2 8 7
Chlorine		
35.453		

Chlorine atomic symbol

Chlorine *(KLAWR een)* is a poisonous, yellowish-green gas at room temperature. It has a strong, unpleasant odor. Chlorine gas will hurt your nose, throat, and lungs.

Chlorine is a *chemical element.* A chemical element is a material that has only one kind of atom. In nature, chlorine is never a gas. It is always combined with other chemical elements. It is found mainly in seawater, salt lakes, and deposits of rock salt. Chlorine combined with the chemical element sodium forms sodium chloride, or table salt. Manufacturers make chlorine gas chiefly by passing an electric current through a solution of sodium chloride in water.

Chlorine has many other uses. Chlorine can kill germs. People put chlorine in drinking water and swimming pools to make the water safe. Chlorine is also used to make bleach and germ-killing cleaners. Chlorine is part of the chemical mixtures used to make paper and plastics.

Other articles to read include: **Element, Chemical; Bleach; Disinfectant; Gas.**

Chlorofluorocarbon

Chlorofluorocarbon *(KLAWR uh FLOOR uh KAHR buhn)* is a chemical used in refrigeration and the making of plastics. Chlorofluorocarbons (CFC's) are not found in nature. They are made by people. Chlorofluorocarbons contain the *chemical elements chlorine, fluorine, and carbon.* A chemical element is a substance that has only one kind of atom. The two most common CFC's are called CFC-11 and CFC-12. They are used in air conditioners and refrigerators to cool the air. They are also used to make foam for furniture and insulation.

CFC-11 and CFC-12 are normally not poisonous or flammable. They turn easily from liquid to gas or from gas to liquid. This ability makes them useful as *propellants.* Propellants are chemicals in aerosol spray products. They help shoot material out of a container.

CFC's harm the environment by breaking down ozone in Earth's atmosphere. Ozone is a gas that blocks harmful ultraviolet rays from the sun from reaching Earth's surface. The United States and most other countries now have laws against CFC's for most uses.

Other articles to read include: **Carbon; Chlorine; Fluorine.**

Chromium

27	**Ch**	2 8 13 1
Chromium 51.9961		

Chromium
atomic symbol

Chromium *(KROH mee uhm)* is a *chemical element* also known as *chrome.* It is a soft, gray metal. A chemical element is a material that has only one kind of atom. Chromium has the chemical symbol Cr. In nature, chromium is almost always found combined with iron and oxygen in a mineral called chromite.

Chromium shines brightly when polished. It is often used to coat other metals to make them shiny. For example, some old cars have door handles and bumpers coated with chromium.

Chromium can be added to steel to make it harder. Chromium steel is used for armor plates on ships and tanks. It is also used to make hard cutting tools. Steel with a certain amount of chromium is called *stainless steel.* Stainless steel does not rust easily. It is often used to make knives, forks, spoons, and other kitchen items.

Other articles to read include: **Element, Chemical; Metal.**

Forks and other eating utensils are often made of stainless steel. Stainless steel is steel made with a lot of chromium.

Circle

A circle is a closed curve—that is, a curve whose ends meet. Every point on a circle is the same distance from the circle's center.

You can draw a circle with an instrument called a *compass.* Place the compass's pointed tip on a piece of paper. That point is the circle's center. Then rotate the compass's pencil. The pencil will draw a circle.

A circle has a number of important parts. A circle's *circumference* is the length of its outer curve. A circle's *radius* is a straight line that connects the circle's center to its outer curve. A circle's *diameter* is a line that goes all the way through the circle across its center. The diameter is twice as long as the radius.

When you divide a circle's circumference by its diameter, the result is a special number called *pi.* Pi is the same for every circle. The number pi is close to the number 3.14159. But you cannot write pi exactly as a decimal number. The digits would go on forever. The symbol π stands for pi.

Other articles to read include: **Diameter; Geometric shapes; Radius.**

A compass is a tool for drawing a circle.

Cobalt is a hard, silver-white chemical element.

Cobalt

27	**Co**	2 8 15 2
Cobalt 58.933200		

Cobalt atomic symbol

Cobalt is a silvery-white *chemical element*. A chemical element is a material that has only one kind of atom. Cobalt is a metal. It is similar to iron in some ways. Both are hard and can be attracted by a magnet. Cobalt is rare on Earth.

Cobalt is used mainly to make *alloys* (mixtures of metals). It can be mixed with iron, aluminum, nickel, and other metals. Some of these alloys are very hard. Cobalt alloys are used to make saws and drills that can cut through metal. Other cobalt alloys can keep their shape at high temperatures. For this reason, they are used inside jet engines.

Cobalt can also turn things a bright blue color. It has been used in blue glass, pottery, and paint for thousands of years.

Other articles to read include: **Alloy; Element, Chemical; Metal.**

Color

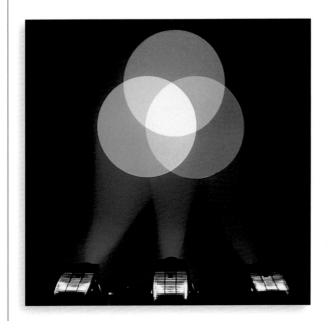

Red, green, and blue are the primary colors in light. They can be combined in various ways to form different colors. Combining all three primary colors in light makes white light.

Color fills the world with beauty. Blue skies, green grass, and red flowers help make the world a more interesting place. Color plays an important part in nature. The bright colors of flowers draw insects to them. The insects help the plants make seeds and fruits. The color of some animals helps them to hide from *predators* (hunting animals). For example, Arctic hares have brownish fur in summer but white fur in winter. The white fur makes it harder for predators to see them in the snow.

People use color in many ways. Color helps us to *communicate* (share information). In sports, for example, players wear uniforms of different colors to show which team they play for. A red traffic light tells drivers to stop.

When we see color, we are really seeing light. Light travels in waves. These waves are somewhat like the waves in water. Some light travels in short waves. Other light travels in long waves.

Continued on the next page

Ultraviolet		Visible spectrum				Infrared
Nanometers	400	450	500	550	600 700	

A band of colors called the *visible spectrum* forms when light passes through a *prism* (a specially shaped glass object). The visible spectrum is the range of light we can see. A prism bends the shortest light waves the most. They appear violet. It bends the longest waves the least. They appear red. All other colors lie in-between. Other forms of light, including ultraviolet and infrared light, are outside the visible spectrum and are invisible to people. The length of light waves is measured in nanometers. One nanometer is a billionth of a meter, or about 1/25,000,000 of an inch.

Prism ———

White light ———

We see these different lengths of waves as different colors. The shortest waves of light we can see make the color violet. The longest waves of light we can see make the color red.

Basic colors called *primary colors* can be mixed together to create all other colors. The primary colors in *pigments* (colors in paints) are red, yellow, and blue. They create another color by *absorbing* (taking in) light waves. For example, you can combine blue and yellow pigments to form green. The blue and yellow pigments each absorb some of the light's waves. The waves that remain appear green.

The primary colors in light are red, green, and blue. They form new colors by adding light of different wavelengths. For example, red light and blue light form purple light.

We can see colors because of the way our eyes and brain work together. When we look at something, light from the object enters our eyes. The light makes an image of the object on the retina *(REHT uh nuh)*. The retina is a thin layer of cells that covers the back and sides of the inside of the eyeball. The retina takes in the light and turns it into electrical signals. These signals travel to nerve cells in the brain. The brain then tells us which colors we are seeing. Scientists are still trying to learn how the brain does this.

Other articles to read include: **Electromagnetic spectrum; Light.**

To see an afterimage, stare at the center of the flag for about 30 seconds. Then look at a sheet of white paper. You will see an image of the flag with its proper colors.

Combustion

Combustion is a word scientists use for *burning*. Combustion takes place when chemicals react with one another to give off heat and light in the form of fire. In most cases, combustion occurs rapidly when oxygen is combined with a fuel, such as coal or wood. The fuel may begin as a solid or liquid. But it must turn to a vapor gas before it can burn.

A spark usually starts the combustion between oxygen and fuel. For example, striking a match produces heat. The heat makes a spark. The spark can be used to start the combustion of charcoal in a barbecue grill. The charcoal continues to burn as it mixes with oxygen in the air. The fire goes out if the grill is closed, because air cannot reach the coals.

Some fuels can begin to burn without being started by a spark or flame. This is called *spontaneous combustion*. It can take place in a pile of oily rags. The chemicals inside the rags mix together and make heat. If the heat cannot escape, the rags get so hot that they finally start to burn. In addition, certain chemicals will begin to burn if exposed to other chemicals. For example, some metals will begin to burn violently when dropped into an acid.

Combustion is very important in our lives. We burn fuel to heat our homes and schools. Many machines turn combustion into power. For example, the engine in a car burns fuel to make the car move.

Combustion can also be dangerous. A forest fire may grow out of control. Forest fires are hard to put out because there is so much fuel and oxygen. The trees are the fuel, and oxygen is in the air. Wind may bring more oxygen to the fire.

Other articles to read include: **Ash; Chemical reaction; Fire.**

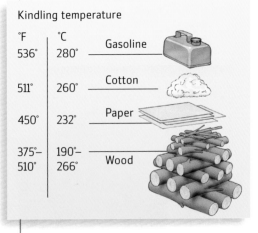

Kindling temperature

°F	°C	
536°	280°	Gasoline
511°	260°	Cotton
450°	232°	Paper
375°–510°	190°–266°	Wood

▲ Combustion is another word for burning. Materials need to be heated to a certain temperature before they burn. The lowest temperature at which an object begins to burn is called the kindling temperature. This temperature differs from one material to another.

Compound

A compound is a material made of two or more different kinds of atoms *bonded* (connected) together. There are millions of different compounds.

Water is a compound containing the chemical elements hydrogen and oxygen. Each water molecule is made of two hydrogen atoms bonded to one oxygen atom. The chemical formula for water is H_2O. Every kind of compound has its own chemical formula. Other common compounds include salt and sugar.

Other articles to read include: **Bond, Chemical; Molecule.**

Condensation

Condensation takes place when a *vapor* (gas) turns into a liquid by cooling.

Clouds form because of the condensation of water vapor in the air. Warm air can hold more water vapor than cool air can. As air rises higher above Earth's surface, it cools. Water vapor is invisible. But as it cools, it condenses into *droplets* (tiny drops of water). Masses of such droplets are visible as clouds.

Dew is another example of condensation. Dew forms when the surfaces of plants or other objects become colder than the air. Water vapor in the air condenses into droplets on the cool surfaces.

Other articles to read include: **Gas; Liquid; Vapor.**

Condensation collects on the inside of a window if the surface is cooler than the air inside the building. The condensation comes from water vapor in the air.

Conduction

Conduction *(kuhn DUHK shuhn)* is the movement of heat through a material. It is one of three ways that heat moves. The other ways are called *convection* and *radiation*. In conduction, the heat moves through the material. But it does not carry the material with it.

Imagine putting one end of a metal rod into a fire. Over time, the other end of the rod will heat up. This is an example of conduction. The rod is made up of tiny bits of matter called *atoms*. Atoms are always moving. When they get hot, they move faster. As one end of the rod gets hot, its atoms start to move faster. They bump into the atoms next to them. This makes those atoms move faster. The heat passes from one atom to another in this way. Eventually, the heat reaches the other end of the rod.

Other articles to read include: **Convection; Heat; Radiation.**

Conduction carries heat through an object. For example, heat from a burner makes the atoms on the underside of a frying pan vibrate faster. These atoms then strike atoms above them. In this way, heat passes through the pan to the food inside it.

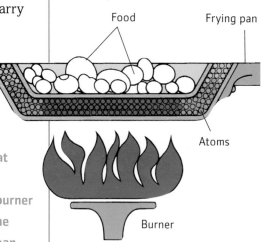

Food   Frying pan

Atoms

Burner

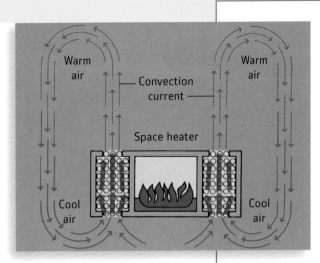

Convection carries heat by circulating a heated material. A space heater, for example, warms the air around it. This heated air rises and is replaced by cooler air. The movement of the air creates a *convection current* that carries hot air through a room.

Convection

Convection is one way that heat moves from one place to another. The other two ways are called *conduction* and *radiation*. In convection, heat is carried by a moving gas or liquid.

A hot stove warms a room by convection. The hot air near the stove is lighter than cool air. As a result, the hot air rises. The cooler air moves next to the stove. That air also gets hot and rises. Hot air constantly moves away from the stove. This motion carries the stove's heat around the room.

Convection also occurs in cold water heated on a stove. The water on the bottom of the pan warms up and expands. It becomes lighter and rises to the top of the pan. The cold water sinks and replaces the warmer water. Eventually, this water becomes heated and rises. This movement of water, called a convection current, spreads the heat through the water.

Other articles to read include: **Conduction; Heat; Radiation.**

This rock contains both pure, gleaming copper *(left)* and reddish copper ore, a mixture of copper and other materials, *(right)*.

Copper

Copper atomic symbol

Copper is a reddish-orange metal. It is a *chemical element*. A chemical element is a material with only one kind of *atom*. An atom is a small bit of matter.

Copper is one of the most useful materials ever discovered. Electricity moves through copper very easily. Because of this, copper is used to make wires for electrical equipment. Copper also heats up easily. That makes it a good material for kitchen pots and pans and for *radiators* (devices that heat rooms). Copper is easy to shape. It can be used to make *sculptures* (modeled objects of art). Copper does not rust, so it lasts for a long time.

Copper is found throughout the world. Mountain ranges in North and South America are the largest sources of copper.

Other articles to read include: **Corrosion; Element, Chemical; Metal.**

Corrosion

Corrosion *(kuh ROH zhuhn)* is the destruction of a material by the chemical action of a gas or liquid. Corrosion occurs mainly in metals. *Rust* is the most familiar form of corrosion. This reddish-brown substance forms on iron and steel that is exposed to water or moist air.

Not all corrosion is harmful. Moist air corrodes aluminum quickly to make a chemical called *aluminum oxide (OK syd)* . This layer of corrosion protects the metal against further damage from air or water.

The type and strength of corrosion depend on the metal and the substance causing the reaction. Other factors that affect corrosion include cracks in the metal and the temperature of the material. Corrosion tends to be stronger if the corrosive material hits the metal at a high speed.

Other articles to read include: **Metal; Rust.**

Corrosion causes a greenish film on copper surfaces.

Cosmic microwave background radiation

The cosmic microwave background (CMB) radiation is energy left over from the early universe. Scientists think the energy formed soon after the *big bang.* The big bang is the event that marked the beginning of our universe about 13.8 billion years ago. The CMB is made up of *microwaves,* a type of invisible energy similar to visible light.

The American physicists Arno Penzias and Robert W. Wilson discovered the CMB radiation in the 1960's. They were using a type of telescope that can detect microwaves. They noticed a weak signal coming from every direction in the sky. After discussing the signal with other scientists, Penzias and Wilson concluded that they were detecting energy left over from the early universe. They each shared half of the 1978 Nobel Prize in physics for the discovery.

Several space telescopes have studied the CMB radiation. One of these probes, called Planck, has made a detailed map of this energy. Scientists use this map to help understand how the universe grew and changed over time.

Other articles to read include: **Microwave; Radiation.**

Crystal

A crystal is a solid material made up of *atoms* arranged in a repeating pattern or other well-organized structure. Atoms are tiny bits of matter. Many nonliving things are made of crystals. Diamonds, sand, snowflakes, and sugar are all crystals.

The atoms in crystals are arranged in a particular pattern. The pattern gives each crystal a certain shape. There are many basic patterns of crystals. Most crystals have smooth, flat surfaces with sharp edges.

Different kinds of crystals look different from one another. For example, ice crystals are arranged in patterns with six sides. But salt crystals look like tiny square boxes. A small number of substances can produce more than one type of crystal.

Crystals are used in many ways. Diamonds and other crystal gems are used to make jewelry. Quartz crystals are used to change electric signals into vibrations and vice versa in radios, watches, and other electronic devices. Some crystals, including quartz, produce an electric charge when squeezed.

Other articles to read include: **Atom.**

The atoms in different crystals join together to form different patterns. There are seven basic patterns of crystals.

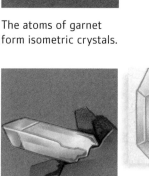

The atoms of garnet form isometric crystals.

The atoms of zircon form tetragonal crystals.

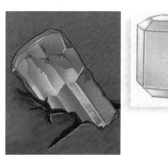

The atoms of beryl form hexagonal crystals.

The atoms of gypsum form monoclinic crystals.

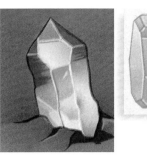

The atoms of quartz form rhombohedral crystals.

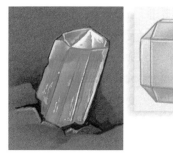

The atoms of topaz form orthorhombic crystals.

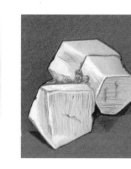

The atoms of feldspar form triclinic crystals.

Grow your own crystals

You can grow crystals by evaporating water in which Epsom salts have been dissolved. After a few days in a warm room, the crystals will grow.

What you need:

- hot water
- a spoon
- a shallow dish
- a few drops of food coloring
- Epsom salts (magnesium sulfate)
- an oven-proof jar
- a small bowl

1. Put the spoon into the jar and fill the jar with hot water.

2. Add a few spoonfuls of Epsom salts to the water and stir the mixture. Add some more Epsom salts and stir again.

3. Fill the bowl with hot water and stand the jar in it. Keep adding more Epsom salts to the jar and keep stirring until the Epsom salts stop dissolving in the water. Allow the liquid to cool.

4. Place the shallow dish in a place where it will not be disturbed. Pour the mixture into the dish to a depth of about ½ inch (1.25 centimeters). Add a few drops of food coloring. Observe how crystals form as the water evaporates. After a few days, you will have a dish of beautifully colored crystals.

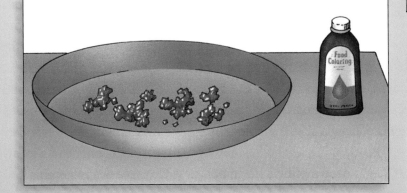

 Have a teacher or other adult help you pour the hot water.

http://bit.ly/128aPhF

Curie, Marie Skłodowska

Marie Skłodowska Curie *(ma REE sklaw DAWF skah KYOO ree)* (1867-1934) was a Polish-born French scientist. She became famous for her work with radioactivity *(RAY dee oh ak TIHV uh tee).* Radioactivity is the giving off of particles and energy by the *nucleus* (core) of an atom. In 1903, Curie became the first woman to win a Nobel Prize. In 1911, she became the first person to win a second Nobel Prize.

Curie worked with her husband, Pierre. Together they studied the radiation given off by such *chemical elements* as uranium and thorium. A chemical element is a material made up of only one kind of atom. The Curies' work led to the discovery of two new chemical elements.The Curies named the elements radium and polonium. Marie and Pierre received the Nobel Prize in physics for their studies of radiation. Marie received the Nobel Prize in chemistry for her discovery of radium and polonium and for her work studying the chemical properties of radium.

Marie and Pierre Curie shared a Nobel Prize in physics for their research on radiation. Marie Curie was the first woman to win a Nobel Prize. She was also the first scientist to win a second Nobel Prize.

Marie was born Marya Skłodowska in Warsaw, Poland. As a young woman in Paris, she decided to use the French spelling of her name, Marie. She died on July 4, 1934, of leukemia, a type of cancer. Years of exposure to radiation probably caused the illness.

Other articles to read include: **Curie, Pierre; Radiation; Uranium.**

Curie, Pierre

Pierre Curie *(pyair KYOO ree)* (1859-1906) was a French scientist. He was known for his work with radioactivity. Radioactivity is the giving off of particles and energy by the *nucleus* (core) of an atom. Pierre worked with his wife, Marie. In 1903, the Curies won the Nobel Prize in physics for their studies of radiation. They studied the radiation given off by such *chemical elements* as uranium and thorium. A chemical element is a material made of only one kind of atom. In 1898, the Curies discovered two radioactive elements, polonium and radium. The French chemist Gustave Bémont helped in the discovery of radium.

Curie was born in Paris, France. He was mostly schooled at home. His lack of a formal education slowed his rise through the scientific establishment. Nevertheless, he became a science teacher at the University of Paris. In 1880, Pierre and his brother Jacques discovered a property known as *piezoelectricity* in crystals. Piezoelectricity is the ability of some materials to convert mechanical energy to electric energy and vice versa.

Other articles to read include: **Curie, Marie Skłodowska; Radiation; Uranium.**

Dark energy

Dark energy is a mysterious form of energy. Scientists think it is responsible for increasing the speed at which the universe is expanding.

In 1929, the American astronomer Edwin P. Hubble found that the universe is expanding. Scientists used this information to propose that the universe was once very tiny. Eventually, this information led to the idea of the *big bang*. The big bang is thought to be a cosmic explosion that began the expansion of the universe billions of years ago. According to scientific theory, the universe has been expanding ever since.

In the 1990's, astronomers discovered that the universe is not expanding steadily. Rather, it is expanding at an ever-faster rate. They concluded that some force was causing the expansion to speed up. Astronomers called this force *dark energy.* Some scientists believe that dark energy makes up 70 percent of all the matter and energy in the universe.

Other articles to read include: **Energy; Force.**

The loudness of sound is measured in decibels. This chart shows the loudness of some sounds.

Decibel

The decibel *(DEHS uh behl)* is a unit for measuring the *intensity* (strength) of sound. Its symbol is *dB*. A decibel equals one-tenth of a *bel*. A bel is the basic scientific unit of sound intensity. The bel was named after American inventor and educator Alexander Graham Bell, who invented the telephone.

A sound of 0 dB is the weakest sound a person without hearing difficulties can hear. The sound of whispering measures about 20 dB. The noise near a jumbo jet taking off measures about 140 dB. A sound of more than 140 dB is painful to the ears. It can seriously damage hearing. Each increase of 10 decibels represents a tenfold increase in power.

Other articles to read include: **Sound.**

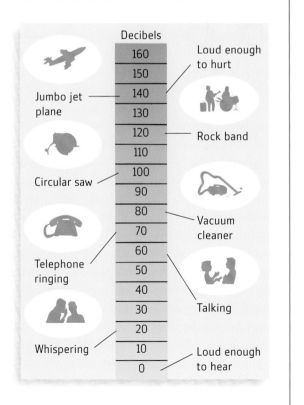

Decibels	
160	Loud enough to hurt
150	
140	Jumbo jet plane
130	
120	Rock band
110	
100	Circular saw
90	
80	
70	Vacuum cleaner
60	
50	Telephone ringing
40	
30	Talking
20	
10	Whispering
0	Loud enough to hear

Decimal system

The decimal system is a system for writing numbers. Under this system, any number can be written using the 10 basic symbols *1, 2, 3, 4, 5, 6, 7, 8, 9,* and *0.* These symbols are called *numerals.* The word *decimal* comes from a Latin word that means *ten.*

The value of a numeral in the decimal system depends on its place in the number. For this reason, the decimal system is known as a *place-value system.* The number farthest to the right occupies the *ones place.* The number in the second place—to the left of the first number—occupies the *tens place.* The number in the third place—to the left of the second number—occupies the *hundreds place.* The number in the fourth place occupies the thousands place, and so on.

The value of each place is 10 times greater than the value of the place just to its right. Thus, the numerals on the left of a number represent larger values than do numerals farther to the right. For example, the numeral *2* in the number *328* stands for 20. In the number *287,* however, the numeral *2* stands for 200, which is 10 times greater than 20.

The decimal system uses a special symbol called the *decimal point* to write numbers smaller than one. For example, the number *0.5* means the same thing as *one-half.* The decimal point is read as "point." The number *7.5* is read as "seven point five." This means the same thing as *seven-and-a-half.*

Mathematicians in India created the decimal system about 2,000 years ago. Arabs learned this system after conquering parts of India in the A.D. 700's. They spread it throughout the Middle East and northern Africa.

Many people in Europe began using the decimal system during the 1400's. Before that time, Europeans wrote numbers with a system called *Roman numerals.* Roman numerals are written as a group of letters. You cannot change the values of these letters by changing their place in the same way you can using the decimal system. This made it very difficult to write large numbers. For example, the number *3,673* is written as *MMMDCLXXIII* in Roman numerals. Roman numerals were also hard to add, subtract, multiply, and divide.

Other articles to read include: **Digit; Number; Zero.**

In the decimal system, the value of each place is 10 times greater than the value of the place to its right. In the numbers below, the symbol 2 in 238 is greater than the 2 in the number 832, because the 2 in 238 is farther to the left than the 2 in 832.

2 3 8
hundreds   tens   ones

8 3 2
hundreds   tens   ones

Degree

The degree is a name given to several small units of measurement. Degrees can be used to measure temperature. Thermometers usually measure temperature in two kinds of degrees. These are called degrees Fahrenheit *(FAR uhn hyt)* and degrees Celsius *(SEHL see uhs)*. The symbol for a degree looks like this: °.

The degree is also used in geometry to measure *angles*. An angle is the slant between two lines that touch. The angle between a wall and the floor is 90 degrees. A narrower angle measures fewer degrees. A wider angle measures more degrees. Degrees can be used to measure parts of a circle. There are 360 degrees in a circle.

Other articles to read include: **Angle; Celsius scale; Fahrenheit scale; Temperature.**

A thermometer usually measures temperature using two scales: Fahrenheit and Celsius. A third scale, called the Kelvin scale, is often used by scientists.

Democritus

Democritus *(dih MOK rih tuhs)* (460?–370? B.C.) was a *philosopher* in ancient Greece. Philosophy *(fuh LOS uh fee)* is the study of truth and knowledge. Democritus was one of the first people to argue that everything is made of tiny, invisible particles. He said that these particles cannot be divided into anything smaller. He called the particles *atoms*, which means *uncuttable* in Greek. Modern scientists still use the term *atoms* for the simplest particles of chemical elements.

Democritus believed there were only two things in the universe: atoms and nothingness. He wrote that everything we know comes from our *senses* (sight, smell, taste, hearing, and touch). He said that our experiences are caused by atoms acting on the senses. But he also said that true knowledge comes only from the mind—not the senses. Democritus wrote about many other subjects, including mathematics and literature.

Other articles to read include: **Atom, Element, Chemical.**

Democritus

Density

Density is the amount of matter in a certain space. The amount of matter in an object or substance is called its *mass*. Mass is related to weight, but they are not the exact same thing. In everyday activities, mass is the same as weight. But *mass* actually describes the force needed to move an object. Weight is the force of gravity on an object.

Imagine a block of wood and a block of iron. Both of the blocks are the same size. But the block of iron feels heavier. This is because it has more mass than the wood block. The iron has greater mass in the same amount of space. So, we can say that the iron has a higher density. The wood has less mass in the same space. Thus, it has a lower density.

You can figure out a material's density if you know its mass and *volume*. Volume is the amount of space something takes up. You can divide a material's mass by its volume to get its density.

All materials have density. This density can change. Many materials become less dense when you heat them.

Other articles to read include: **Mass; Matter.**

Different liquids have different densities. Syrup falls to the bottom of the jar because it is denser than water and oil.

Cooking oil

Water

Syrup

Desalination

Desalination *(dee SAL uhn AY shuhn)* is the process of removing salt, usually from seawater. Water in the ocean is salty. But human beings and other animals can drink only fresh water. Most plants also need fresh water. People use desalination to prepare seawater for drinking or farming.

Continued on the next page

The Barka desalination plant near Muscat, the capital of the Middle Eastern country of Oman, produces fresh water using reverse osmosis.

There are several methods of desalination. In *distillation,* seawater is boiled. As the water turns to steam, the salt is left behind. When the steam cools, it becomes liquid water again. The now-fresh water can be collected and used. This process has been used for thousands of years.

In *reverse osmosis,* salt water is forced under pressure through a special barrier that blocks the salt. Fresh water collects on the other side of the barrier.

Electrodialysis is used chiefly to desalt *brackish* (slightly salty) ground water and water from *estuaries* (river mouths). In electrodialysis, electric currents are used to separate salt from water. All desalination methods are costly, mostly because desalting plants use large amounts of energy, which is expensive to produce.

Other articles to read include: **Distillation.**

Descartes, René

René Descartes *(ruh NAY day KAHRT)* (1596–1650) was a French scientist, mathematician, and *philosopher.* A philosopher *(fuh LOS uh fuhr)* is a person who studies the truth of knowledge and seeks to understand the mysteries and reality of existence.

René Descartes

Descartes lived at a time of great changes in science. His philosophy helped scientists develop and test new ideas using scientific and mathematical principles. For this reason, Descartes has been called the father of modern philosophy.

Descartes claimed that the world consists of two basic substances—matter and spirit. Matter is the physical universe and includes our bodies. The human mind, or spirit, interacts with the body but is completely separate from it. As a young man, Descartes was concerned with the question, "How do I know what is real—that is, what exists?" He summed up this thinking in the famous statement, "I think, therefore I am."

Descartes also invented a type of geometry. In addition, he developed a description of the universe using matter and motion. Descartes was one of the first people to try to determine the simple laws of motion that control all physical change.

Other articles to read include: **Matter.**

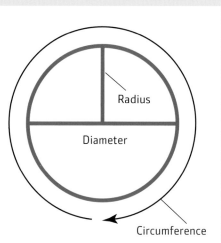

The distance across a circle, going through the center, is called the diameter. The radius is the distance from the center of the circle to any point on the circle's edge. The distance around the edge of a circle is called the circumference.

Diameter

Diameter *(dy AM uh tuhr)* is a line drawn across the center of a circle. The word *diameter* can also mean the measure of this line. People often describe the size of a circle by its diameter. The diameter is the circle's "width."

The diameter of a circle is always twice as long as its *radius (RAY dee uhs)*. The radius is the distance from the circle's center to any point on the circle's edge.

A *sphere* (ball-shaped object) can also be measured by its diameter. A basketball has a diameter of about 9 inches (23 centimeters). Earth's diameter is nearly 8,000 miles (13,000 kilometers).

Other articles to read include: **Circle; Radius.**

Diffusion

Diffusion *(dih FYOO zhuhn)* is the mixing of one substance with another without stirring or shaking. Diffusion happens because *atoms* and *molecules* are always in motion. Atoms and molecules are tiny bits of matter.

Diffusion can be seen by gently adding ink to a glass of water. At first, the dark ink holds together in the water. However, as the molecules of ink move around, the ink spreads out. The water molecules also move around. They become mixed with the ink.

In gases and liquids, atoms and molecules move around freely. Diffusion happens easily in these substances. In solids, atoms and molecules move very little. For this reason, diffusion rarely happens in solids.

Other articles to read include: **Atom; Molecule.**

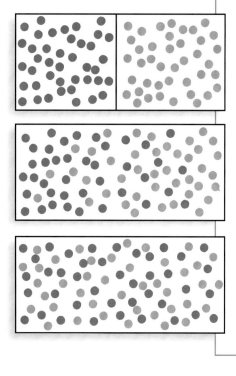

In diffusion, the molecules of two different gases or liquids mix because of the natural, constant movement of the molecules in these substances.

Digit

A digit *(DIHJ iht)* is any *numeral* from 0 to 9. A numeral is symbol that stands for a number. We often use the word *digit* to mean a particular numeral. For example, the number 3,954 has four digits or numerals.

Arabic numerals are the most common symbols used for numbers. With Arabic numerals, the position of a digit tells us its value. For example, the Arabic numeral for the number *two hundred and thirty-seven* is *237*. The number means 2 hundreds plus 3 tens plus 7 ones.

The word *digit* comes from the Latin word *digitus,* meaning *finger.* This is because people began to count by using their 10 fingers. For this reason, almost everyone in the world calculates using groups of 10.

Other articles to read include: **Decimal system; Number.**

The word *digit* comes from the Latin word *digitus,* meaning *finger.* This is because people first used their fingers for counting. The early Roman numerals for one, two, three, and four look like fingers held straight up. The Roman numeral for five looks like the space between your thumb and first finger when your hand is spread open. The Roman numeral for 10 looks like two crossed hands.

I 🖐 II 🖐 III 🖐 IIII 🖐 V 🖐 X 🖐

Disinfectant

A disinfectant is a chemical used to kill germs on the surfaces of such nonliving things as medical instruments and floors. Different chemicals, called *antiseptics,* are used to kill germs on people and other animals.

There are many different kinds of disinfectants. Some are used to kill germs in public water supplies. This helps to prevent the spread of disease. Other kinds of disinfectants are used in the home to clean floors, walls, and other surfaces. People often use disinfectants in the kitchen and bathrooms. More powerful disinfectants are used in hospitals and other health care places. These disinfectants can kill many germs that cause dangerous diseases.

Chemicals called *detergents* are added to many disinfectants. Detergents make a disinfectant also work as a cleaner.

Other articles to read include: **Alcohol; Ammonia; Iodine.**

People often use disinfectants in the bathroom to kill germs.

Distillation

Distillation *(dihs tuh LAY shuhn)* is a process for making substances pure. In distillation, a mixture of substances is usually heated. Most liquids boil at different temperatures. By heating the mixture slowly, each substance can be made to boil into a *vapor* (gas) one at a time. The vapor of each substance that forms is collected in different containers and then cooled. As the vapor cools, it returns to a liquid. The distilled liquids have been separated from the mixture. Distillation is important in many industries.

Simple distillation can separate salt and water from seawater. Boiling the water away will leave the solid salt. Distillation can also be used to separate oxygen from other gases in the air. When gases are distilled, cold is used instead of heat. Slowly lowering the temperature of the gases turns the mixture into separate liquids.

Other articles to read include: **Desalination; Vapor.**

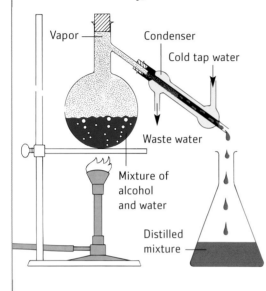

▲ Simple distillation separates substances in a liquid. When a mixture of alcohol and water is heated to a boil in a flask, the mixture turns into vapor. The vapor has a higher percentage of alcohol than the liquid mixture did because alcohol boils at a lower temperature than water. The vapor liquefies in a tube called a condenser and flows into another container.

Division

Division is a way of separating a group of things into equal parts. It is one of the four basic operations in arithmetic. The others are addition, subtraction, and multiplication.

Imagine that you have 18 marbles that you want to share with two friends. You want each of you to get the same number of marbles. So you would divide the marbles into three equal groups. Each of you would then get six marbles.

Division is important in math. You could write the marble problem as a math equation. It would be $18 \div 3 = 6$, or eighteen divided by three equals six. The math symbol for division is $\div$.

Most people learn division by memorizing the division facts. The division facts are 64 simple division problems and their answers. You can use the division facts to solve any division problem without counting.

In an example of division, a group of 18 things can be separated into three equal groups of 6 things each.

Other articles to read include: **Addition; Multiplication; Number; Subtraction.**

Doppler effect

The Doppler effect is a change in the *pitch* of a sound caused by movement. Pitch is the highness or lowness of a sound as we hear it. The Doppler effect happens when the source of the sound moves. The source may move toward the listener. This motion causes the pitch to get higher. The source may move away. This motion makes the pitch lower.

For example, the pitch of a train whistle seems higher as the train approaches. The pitch becomes lower after the train passes the listener. The actual pitch given off by the whistle never changes. But the listener hears a shift in pitch because sound is carried in waves. The pitch of a sound is related to its *wavelength*. Wavelength is the distance between neighboring *crests* (peaks) of a sound wave. As the train moves toward the listener, the crests pile up in front of the whistle. This results in a shorter wavelength and thus a higher pitch. As the train moves away, the crests spread out behind the whistle. This results in a longer wavelength and a lower pitch.

The Doppler effect also works with light. It causes light to change color. If the source of the light is moving away from the viewer, the light becomes redder. If the source is approaching the viewer, the light becomes bluer.

Other articles to read include: **Light; Sound; Wavelength.**

The sound waves of an approaching train are squeezed together, giving them a high pitch. The sound waves of a train moving away are stretched out and have a lower pitch.

Dry ice

Dry ice is solid *carbon dioxide*. In nature, carbon dioxide is usually a gas. It becomes a solid at very low temperatures. At room temperature, dry ice will turn directly back into a gas. It will not melt into a liquid first. The turning of a solid directly into a gas is called *sublimation*.

Dry ice is manufactured in snowlike flakes or in blocks. It is used to keep food cold in shipping or storage. It is also used in films and at rock concerts to produce swirling clouds of mist. Chemists use dry ice to cool chemicals during certain reactions.

Dry ice has a temperature of −109.3 °F (−78.5 °C). This is much colder than the temperature of ordinary water ice. Dry ice must be handled carefully because it can easily cause frostbite.

Other articles to read include: **Carbon; Ice; Sublimation.**

Dry ice forms bubbles of carbon dioxide gas when it is dropped in water. (Handling dry ice without protection can cause frostbite.)

Ee

Echo

An echo *(EK oh)* is a sound that bounces back to its source after hitting an object. When we shout, the sound of our voice travels through the air as sound waves. Sound waves are invisible waves that travel in all directions. Some of the waves from the shout go straight to our ears, and we hear our shout. Some of the waves may also hit a large object, such as the side of a building. These waves may bounce back and reach our ears a second time. That second sound is an echo.

Sometimes we do not hear echoes because they are not loud enough. At other times, we may hear more than one echo. That is called *repeated echoing.* It usually occurs in valleys and canyons where there are many places for a sound to bounce off.

Other articles to read include: **Reflection; Sound.**

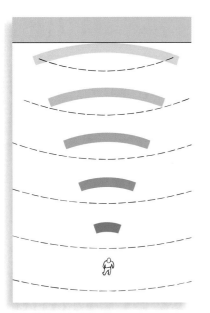

An echo is a sound that bounces off a large object and travels back to your ears.

Albert Einstein is famous for his theories of relativity.

Einstein, Albert

Albert Einstein (1879–1955) was one of the greatest and most famous scientists of all time. Einstein made important contributions to scientists' understanding of *matter* (physical substance) and energy. He helped to solve some major mysteries of the universe.

Einstein is most famous for his two theories of relativity *(REHL uh TIHV uh tee).* One theory explains that the speed of light is the same for all observers. The other theory was a new explanation for *gravity,* the force of attraction among objects with *mass* (amount of matter).

Einstein was born in 1879 in Ulm, Germany. He received most of his education in Switzerland. He was especially interested in *physics* (the study of matter and energy). Einstein earned a Ph.D. (doctor of philosophy) degree in physics from the University of Zurich in 1905.

From 1902 to 1909, Einstein worked at a patent office in Bern, Switzerland. A *patent* is a legal document that

Continued on the next page

gives an inventor sole ownership of an invention. Einstein's job left him with plenty of time to work on physics. He published several important papers on his ideas in physics during those years, including a paper on one of his theories of relativity. Those papers made him well known. Beginning in 1909, Einstein became a professor of physics. He taught at various universities in Europe.

Einstein moved back to Germany in 1914. There he continued to teach and to do research. He won the Nobel Prize in physics in 1921. In 1933, Einstein moved to the United States. He left Germany because Adolf Hitler and his Nazi party gained control of the government. The Nazis had an official policy of *anti-Semitism* (prejudice against Jews). Einstein was of Jewish descent. He became an American citizen in 1940.

Other articles to read include: **Gravitation; Relativity.**

Electricity

Electricity is a source of energy that can be used to make light and heat and do useful work. Electric power plants produce large amounts of energy that light people's homes and drive machines in factories. But electricity is also found throughout nature. It is, in fact, a part of all the *matter* (physical substance) in the universe. Atoms and molecules of matter are held together by electric forces. In the human body, electrical signals travel along nerves to carry information to and from the brain. Electrical signals even tell the heart when to beat. Storms release electricity in the form of lightning.

Electricity is related to *magnetism*. Electricity and magnetism together make up a kind of energy called *electromagnetic energy*. Light is a form of electromagnetic energy. So are X rays.

Electric power lights up the skyline at night in Kowloon, Hong Kong.

Continued on the next page

Electricity *Continued from the previous page*

Electricity comes from particles that make up atoms, called *electrons* and *protons*. These particles have a property called *electric charge*. Electrons have a *negative charge*. Protons have a *positive charge*. The opposite charges of the electron and proton have exactly the same strength.

Charges of the same kind *repel* (push away) each other. Opposite charges attract each other. Charges repel or attract other charges even when they are not touching. That is because they are surrounded by invisible areas of force called *electric fields*.

In most objects, there are equal numbers of positive and negative charges. The overall electric charge of the object is then *neutral* (zero). That is because the positive and negative charges balance each other. But if some charges are added or stripped away, that balance can be lost. The object then has either a positive or negative charge. These extra charges make up what is called *static electricity*.

Electric charges can flow through a wire. A flow of charges is called a *current*. Electric currents are produced by electric power companies with large machines called *generators*. An electric current carries the energy that powers the lights and appliances in a home.

Electric charges flow more easily through some materials than others. Such materials, which include many metals, are called *conductors*. Materials that do not carry electric charges well are called *insulators*. Rubber and plastic are both good insulators. Most electrical cords are made from metal wire covered with an insulating material. The insulator makes it possible to touch the wire while it is carrying a current without getting an electric shock.

There are two kinds of electric current used for power: *direct current* (DC) and *alternating current* (AC). A direct current is one that flows steadily in one direction. A battery produces direct current. The current that is used in homes and factories is alternating current. It constantly changes direction.

Although the currents used for power move in two ways, the energy they carry does not. The energy carried by either an AC or DC current always moves forward. It is the energy transported by electric

Using electricity safely

Don't touch things that use electric energy when you are wet.

Dry your hands before you use any electrical equipment.

Do not plug too many devices into an outlet.

Cover unused outlets with safety plugs.

Do not fly kites or climb trees near power lines. If a line is down, stay away.

Stay indoors if there is lightning. Use the phone only in an emergency.

Continued on the next page

charges, not the charges themselves, that makes things work. If a current in a wire stops, the charges in the metal continue to exist. But the charges are no longer carrying energy.

Static electricity was first studied by the ancient Greeks. The first real understanding of electricity was gained by scientists in the 1700's. The connection between electricity and magnetism was discovered in the 1800's. James Clerk Maxwell, a Scottish scientist, worked out the mathematics explaining this relationship. In 1897, the English physicist Joseph John Thomson proved the existence of electrons, as proposed by the Irish physicist G. Johnstone Stoney. Thomson also showed that all atoms contain electrons.

Other articles to read include: **Electron; Energy; Magnetism; Nuclear energy.**

Electromagnetic spectrum

The electromagnetic spectrum is the entire range of the different types of *electromagnetic waves*. Electromagnetic waves are moving patterns of electric and magnetic energy. They are made by the back-and-forth movement of electric charges.

The electromagnetic spectrum is made up of all the forms of *radiant energy* (the energy of light). There are many different kinds of radiant energy. People can see only a tiny part of the electromagnetic spectrum. This part is called *visible light* or the *visible spectrum*. A rainbow is a representation of the visible spectrum. The radiant energy we cannot see is called the *invisible spectrum*. The electromagnetic spectrum is a combination of the visible spectrum and the invisible spectrum.

The electromagnetic spectrum includes gamma rays, X rays, ultraviolet radiation, visible light, infrared radiation, microwaves, and radio waves. Gamma rays have the shortest *wavelength* and the highest energy. Wavelength is the distance between neighboring *crests* (peaks) of a wave. Radio waves have the longest wavelength and the lowest energy.

Other articles to read include:

Energy; Light; Magnetism; Wavelength.

The electromagnetic spectrum is the entire range of the different types of electromagnetic waves. At one end of the spectrum are gamma rays, which have the shortest wavelength. At the other end of the spectrum are radio waves, which have the longest wavelength.

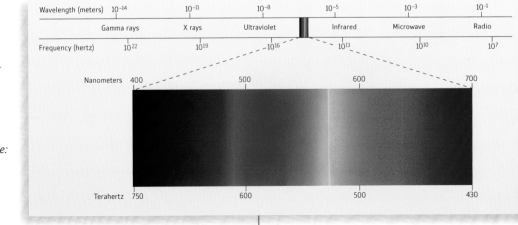

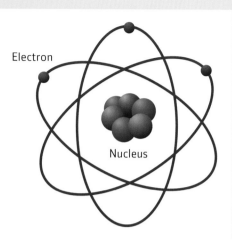

Electron

Nucleus

Electrons whirl around the *nucleus* (center) of an atom at fantastic speeds.

Electron

The electron *(ih LEHK tron)* is one of three basic particles that make up an *atom* (tiny bit of matter). The other basic particles are *protons* and *neutrons.* Electrons account for most of the space taken up by an atom. But they make up only a tiny fraction of an atom's *mass* (amount of matter). Electrons are *fundamental units of matter*—that is, they are not made up of smaller units.

Electrons carry a negative electric charge. They orbit around an atom's *nucleus (NOO klee uhs)* (core) in layers called *shells.* Every atom normally has at least one electron orbiting its nucleus. The chemical behavior of an atom depends greatly on the number of electrons in its outermost shell.

Atoms can gain or lose electrons. Atoms that gain electrons have a negative charge. Those that lose electrons have a positive charge.

Atoms can absorb energy from outside themselves, becoming *excited.* The movement of many electrons is an electric current. Excited electrons also provide the energy to give off light. Electrons are the lightest particles that have an electric charge.

Other articles to read include: **Atom; Neutron; Nucleus; Proton.**

Sulfur

Gold

Iron

A chemical element is a substance made up of only one kind of atom. Sulfur, gold, and iron are all chemical elements.

Element, Chemical

A chemical element is a substance made up of just one kind of *atom.* An atom is a tiny bit of matter. Chemical elements cannot be broken down into simpler substances. But they can join together to form other substances. For example, water is made of two chemical elements—hydrogen and oxygen—joined together. Such combinations are called *compounds.*

There are three basic kinds of chemical elements: *metals, nonmetals,* and *noble gases.* Gold is an example of a metallic element. The main gases that make up the air around us—oxygen and nitrogen—are examples of nonmetallic elements. Noble gases are gases, such as helium, that do not combine easily with other elements.

Continued on the next page

Scientists have found about 120 chemical elements. Most of them occur in nature. But scientists have created more than 20 new elements using special equipment.

Chemical elements have symbols and numbers as well as names. The symbol for oxygen is *O.* The symbol for the metal cobalt is *Co.* An element's number, called its *atomic number,* tells something about its atoms. Cobalt's atomic number is 27, because a cobalt atom contains 27 *protons.* A proton is a particle of matter found within an atom's *nucleus* (core). The nucleus of an oxygen atom has 8 protons, so oxygen's atomic number is 8.

Scientists have created a chart that shows the chemical elements with their symbols, numbers, and other information. This chart is called the *periodic table.* The Russian chemist Dmitri Mendeleev created what scholars widely consider to be the first modern periodic table, published in 1869. The periodic table expands as scientists create new elements.

Other articles to read include: **Atom; Chemical reaction; Compound.**

Each entry in the periodic table lists basic information about one chemical element.

Chemical symbol

Atomic number —— | 27 **Co** | 2 8 15 2

Name —— Cobalt 58.933200

Number of *electrons* (negatively charged particles) found in each *shell* (level) surrounding the *nucleus* (core)

Atomic mass number

The known chemical elements are arranged according to their characteristics in a chart called the periodic table.

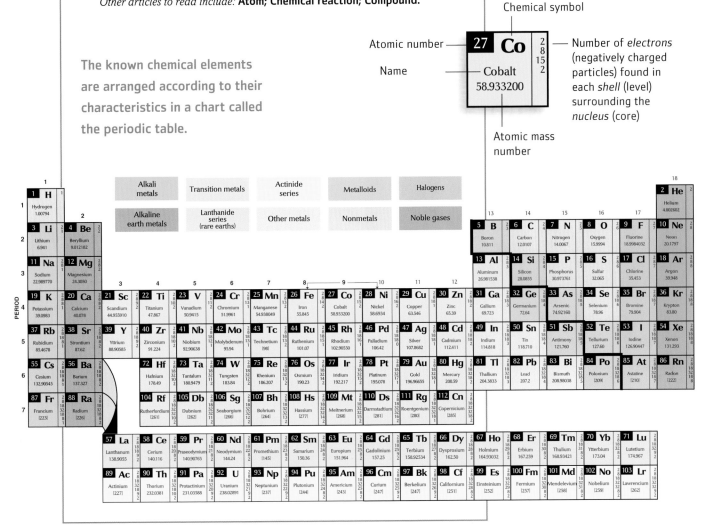

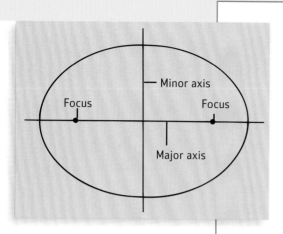

An ellipse, in geometry, is an oval figure that has the shape of a flattened hoop.

Ellipse

An ellipse *(ih LIHPS)* is a figure with a shape like a flattened hoop. It can be drawn using a string. The string is attached to two points, called *foci (FOH sy)* (the plural of focus). Each focus lies toward one end of the ellipse. The string must be longer than the distance between the foci. A pencil is then held in the string. The pencil is pulled all the way around the foci, keeping the string tight. The result is an ellipse. A line passing through the foci is called the *major axis.* A line passing through the middle of the major axis is called the *minor axis.*

In the 1600's, German astronomer Johannes Kepler discovered that the planets of the solar system travel in elliptical orbits. The sun is at one focus of a planet's orbit.

Other articles to read include: **Geometric shapes.**

Wind turbines change the energy of wind to electric energy.

Energy

Energy is the ability to do work. There are many kinds of energy. Most of the energy on Earth comes, in one way or another, from the sun. This energy travels to Earth in the sun's rays. Plants, algae, and certain microscopic living things use the sun's rays to make food. Animals and human beings feed on these living things and on other animals. They use the energy in this food to move and live. All living things need energy to stay alive.

The earliest human ancestors had only the energy of their bodies to do work. Later, people learned how to use the energy of fire. They made fire by burning wood or other fuels. The heat energy of fire warmed them and cooked their food. People tamed animals and used their energy to travel, to pull plows, and to carry things. People discovered how to make sails that used the energy of the wind to move boats. People also learned how to use

Continued on the next page

the energy of water to turn mills that ground grain into flour.

Today, people still use the energy of sunlight, water, wind, and fire. Another kind of energy comes from splitting or joining atoms to create new atoms. That kind of energy is called *nuclear energy.* People have many other ways to release energy. They burn coal to turn water into steam. Then they use the steam to generate electric energy. They use this electric energy to power lights, appliances, and heating systems. They also turn this electric energy into radio waves that carry information and ideas for thousands of miles. People release the energy in gasoline by burning it to power automobiles.

Energy has two forms. They are kinetic *(kih NEHT ihk)* energy and *potential energy.* Kinetic energy is the energy of movement. Potential energy is the result of something's position or other condition. It can be thought of as "stored" energy. Kinetic and potential energy can change from one form to the other. For example, a girl who swings backward on a swing set has potential energy at the top of her swing. This energy comes from her position. As she swings down, this potential energy is converted into the kinetic energy of her motion.

Scientists believe that the amount of energy in the universe never changes. We cannot make energy or destroy it. We can only change it from one kind into another.

Other articles to read include: **Electricity; Fuel; Kinetic energy; Nuclear energy; Potential energy.**

Energy can come from burning fuel. Coal is a fuel used to produce heat and electric power.

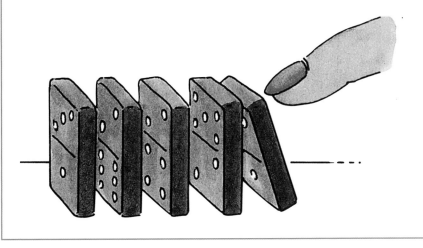

Line up some dominoes as shown. Give one of the end dominoes energy by nudging it so that it tips over onto the domino next to it. Watch the energy pass from one domino to the next as they topple over.

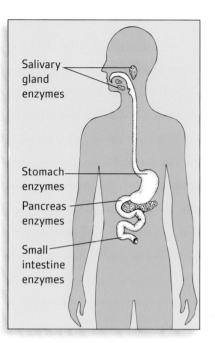

Enzymes in the digestive system break down food for use in the body. Each enzyme performs a special job.

Enzyme

An enzyme *(EHN zym)* is a chemical that plays a key role in the chemistry of life. Enzymes help in the breaking down and joining together of other chemicals in *chemical reactions* (interactions among chemicals). Without enzymes, life would not be possible because these reactions would occur too slowly. Enzymes speed up reactions by attaching to other chemicals, creating more complex substances.

Enzymes perform many important jobs in the bodies of all living things. For example, enzymes play a key role in *digestion* (the breaking down of food). They also help convert chemicals in the body into forms that the body can use more easily. Every living cell makes enzymes. The cells of the human body produce thousands of enzymes.

Other articles to read include: **Chemical reaction.**

Eratosthenes figured out a way to measure the distance around Earth.

Eratosthenes

Eratosthenes *(ehr uh TOS thuh neez)* (276?–195? B.C.) was a Greek mathematician. He found a way to measure Earth's *circumference* (distance around the middle) without leaving northern Africa, where he lived.

Like other Greek scientists of his time, Eratosthenes knew that Earth is round. He observed that at noon on a certain day, a post in one town would cast no shadow. But in another town, the post would cast a shadow. Eratosthenes measured the angle of this shadow. He used this to figure out the angle between the two towns, as measured from Earth's center.

Eratosthenes then measured the distance between the towns. Finally, he multiplied this distance by the number of times that the angle went into 360 degrees, the measure of a complete circle. The result was the distance around the entire Earth. Eratosthenes's distance was not exactly right. But it was surprisingly close for his time. His measurement of Earth's circumference was between 28,000 and 29,000 miles (45,000 and 47,000 kilometers). The actual value is 24,860 miles (40,008 kilometers).

Ethylene

Ethylene *(EHTH uh leen)* is a colorless gas with a faint, sweet smell. Ethylene is *flammable* (easily set on fire). It is slightly lighter than air. Ethylene mixed with air is explosive. Ethylene is one of the most important chemicals used by industry.

Ethylene is a *hydrocarbon*, a compound of carbon and hydrogen atoms. *Molecules* (tiny units) of ethylene can be joined together in long chains. Such chains are called *polymers (POL ih muhrz*). Ethylene makes a polymer called *polyethylene (POL ee EHTH uh leen)*. Polyethylene is a plastic. It is used to make bottles and containers. Ethylene is also used to ripen fruit.

Other articles to read include: **Gas; Hydrocarbon.**

Ethylene is a hydrocarbon. Ethylene molecules can be joined together with the help of a special chemical called a catalyst to form longer molecules called *polymers.*

Hydrogen atom ⎯⎯

Carbon atom ⎯

Single ethylene molecule

Euclid

Euclid *(YOO klihd)* (330?–270? B.C.) was a Greek mathematician. He is often called the *father of geometry*. Geometry is the study of lines, angles, curves, and shapes.

Euclid's greatest contribution to geometry was a work called *Elements*. In this work, Euclid organized geometric ideas that already existed into 13 books. He also wrote sections of *Elements*. It became one of the most important works on scientific thinking ever written.

In addition to being important in mathematics, geometry has many practical uses. Engineers and designers use geometry to make buildings, bridges, airplanes, and other objects. Astronomers use geometry to measure the universe. All these fields make use of ideas and principles set down by Euclid.

Euclid wrote on most branches of mathematics that were known in his time. But only a few of his other writings have survived. Almost nothing is known about Euclid's life.

Other articles to read include: **Geometry.**

Euclid

Evaporation plays a role in the formation of fog. Water evaporating from a lake turns to water vapor. If the air cools, the water vapor changes to tiny water droplets that create fog.

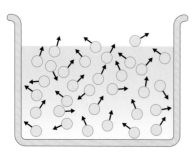

Water evaporates slowly as it turns into a gas and mixes with the air.

Water evaporates quickly when it is heated. As the water boils, it turns into steam.

Evaporation

Evaporation *(ih VAP uh RAY shuhn)* occurs when a liquid or a solid changes into a gas. During this process, the liquid absorbs energy in the form of heat.

The *molecules* of all substances have a certain amount of *kinetic energy* (energy of motion). Molecules are tiny units of matter made of atoms. This kinetic energy is provided by heat from the surroundings, including other nearby molecules. The more energy the molecules have, the faster they move. When they move fast enough, they may start to break the bonds that hold them together. Some of the molecules may begin to move away into the air. The substance starts to turn into a gas. Some liquids, such as alcohol, evaporate quickly at room temperature. Others, including water, evaporate more slowly.

If you put some water into an open pan and leave it in a warm room, the water will slowly disappear. The pan will be dry and empty because the water evaporated. When water evaporates, it turns into a gas, called *vapor*. It can take several days for water to disappear this way.

Adding heat makes things evaporate faster. For example, if you put the pan of water on the stove and then turned on the heat, the water would soon begin to boil. You might see steam rise off the top of the water. Steam is water turning into vapor.

Evaporation is important to life on Earth. The heat of the sun evaporates water from Earth's surface. The evaporated water goes high into the air. Then it cools down and forms clouds. The liquid water falls from the sky as rain or snow. Evaporation is important for people, too. When we sweat, water on our skin evaporates. The evaporation makes the skin feel cooler.

A solid may also change directly into a gas. This process is called sublimation *(SUHB luh MAY shuhn)*. The vaporization of *dry ice* (solid carbon dioxide) is an example of sublimation.

Other articles to read include: **Boiling point; Sublimation; Vapor.**

Expansion

Expansion is an increase in the size of a substance without any more of the substance being added. Most substances expand when they are heated and *contract* (become smaller) when they are cooled. Water is one of the few substances that expand slightly when they become a solid. Gases naturally expand to fill their containers. But gases also expand when heated and contract when cooled.

Expansion results from a change in energy, usually temperature. *Thermal energy* (heat) causes the *atoms* (tiny bits of matter) in a substance to vibrate. Raising the temperature increases these vibrations. In a gas, raising the temperature also increases the speed at which the atoms or *molecules* move about. Molecules are groups of atoms. The increased movement forces the atoms or molecules farther apart, resulting in expansion.

Different materials expand by different amounts under the same change in temperature. The atoms of some kinds of molecules vibrate more easily than those in other kinds. For this reason, they push the atoms and molecules around them farther away. For example, aluminum expands twice as much as iron under the same temperature change.

Other articles to read include: **Gas; Heat.**

Explosion

An explosion is a rapid production of hot gases. It is caused when chemicals burn at extremely high speed. In an explosion, gases move outward at very high speeds and pressures. As they do so, they cause a loud booming sound. The pressure of an explosion can cause great destruction.

A material that produces an explosion is called an *explosive.* Explosives can be solids, liquids, or gases. All explosives consist of a fuel and a substance called an oxidizer *(OK suh DY zuhr).* The oxidizer supplies the chemical element oxygen. Fuels need oxygen to burn. Dynamite and TNT are two well-known explosives.

Explosives are used for many tasks. Some explosives are used for blasting away rock to build roads or tunnels. Explosives are used widely as weapons. They are packed into bombs and missiles.

Other articles to read include: **Combustion; Fuel.**

A material that produces an explosion is called an *explosive.* Gunpowder, an explosive, caused this explosion.

Ff

Fahrenheit, Gabriel Daniel

Gabriel Daniel Fahrenheit *(FAR uhn hyt)* (1686–1736) was a German scientist. He developed the *Fahrenheit temperature scale.* Fahrenheit also made the thermometer more accurate by using the liquid metal mercury instead of a mixture of alcohol and water in the thermometer tube. Pure mercury, unlike a mixture of alcohol and water, always has the same *composition* (makeup). Mercury thermometers thus give more reliable measurements.

The Fahrenheit scale is divided into many equal parts called *degrees.* The symbol for degrees Fahrenheit is: °F. For his scale, Fahrenheit determined three fixed temperatures. They were 0° for the freezing point of ice, salt, and water; 32° for the freezing point of pure water; and 212° for the boiling point of water.

People in the United States usually use the Fahrenheit scale to measure temperature. People in most other countries use the Celsius scale.

Other articles to read include: **Fahrenheit scale; Temperature.**

Fahrenheit scale

The Fahrenheit *(FAR uhn hyt)* temperature scale is a set of numbers used to measure temperature. The scale was developed by Gabriel Daniel Fahrenheit, a German scientist, in the early 1700's. The Fahrenheit scale is generally used to measure temperature in the United States. A different scale, called the *Celsius temperature scale,* is used in most other countries. The Celsius scale is part of the metric system.

The Fahrenheit scale is divided into many equal parts called *degrees.* The symbol for degrees Fahrenheit is: °F. On this scale, 32 °F is the freezing point of water. This is the temperature at which water turns into ice. The boiling point of water is 212 °F. This is the temperature at which water turns into steam.

The Fahrenheit scale is shown on the left side of this thermometer. The Celsius scale is shown on the right side.

Other articles to read include: **Celsius scale; Fahrenheit, Gabriel Daniel; Temperature.**

Falling bodies, Law of

The law of falling bodies is actually several *laws* (rules). They tell what happens to an object when it is allowed to fall without anything stopping it.

One law describes what happens when two objects of different *mass* (amount of matter) are dropped from the same height at the same time. People once thought that the heavier object would hit the ground first. The Italian scientist Galileo did not believe this was true. He reasoned that all objects—whether a brick or a feather—tend to fall at the same speed. The objects might hit the ground at different times, but this was only because of the *resistance* of the air. Resistance is the force with which a fluid, such as air, pushes against something trying to move through it. Galileo's reasoning was later proved correct.

The force that draws objects toward Earth or any other massive object is called *gravity*. Gravity acts on all objects alike, regardless of shape, size, or *density* (the amount of matter in a certain space). Earth attracts objects toward its center, so all objects near Earth are pulled toward that point.

Other articles to read include: **Gravitation; Motion.**

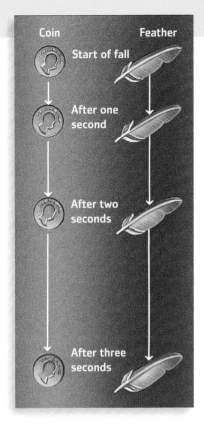

Bodies falling freely in a *vacuum* (a space that has little matter in it) due to gravity descend at the same speed regardless of their size, shape, or weight.

Faraday, Michael

Michael Faraday *(FAIR uh day)* (1791–1867) was one of the greatest English chemists and *physicists*. A physicist is a scientist who studies *matter* (physical substance) and energy.

In 1823, Faraday figured out that a gas can be changed into a liquid and even into a solid by cooling and squeezing it. In 1831, he discovered that moving a magnet through a coil of copper wire caused an *electric current* to flow in the wire. An electric current is the flow of *electrons (ih LEHK tronz)*. Electrons are tiny, invisible particles in an atom that carry an electric charge. The electric generator and the electric motor are based on this principle.

Faraday also became a popular lecturer. He gave scientific lectures for children every Christmas. The most famous of these lectures is called "The Chemical History of a Candle."

Other articles to read include: **Electricity.**

Michael Faraday

Fermentation

Fermentation *(FUR mehn TAY shuhn)* is a process in which tiny organisms called *microbes* break down materials into certain chemicals. Microbes include bacteria, molds, and yeast. Many food products require fermentation, including bread and cheese. Fermentation is also used to make alcoholic beverages, including beer and wine, and to make ethanol fuel. Certain molds ferment mixtures of sugars and other chemicals to produce the antibiotic penicillin.

Many fermented products are made in the same way. First, workers fill large metal containers with water and *nutrients* (nourishing substances). The nutrients commonly include some kind of sugar. Then the microbes are added. Workers adjust the temperature of the containers while the microbes grow. After several days, the microbes have changed the nutrients into different chemicals. The workers then drain the containers. They separate the desired products from the rest of the liquid.

Other articles to read include: **Alcohol.**

Enrico Fermi was the first scientist to split the atom.

Fermi, Enrico

Enrico Fermi *(ehn REE koh FUR mee or FEHR mee)* (1901-1954) was an Italian-born American physicist *(FIHZ uh sihst)*. A physicist is a scientist who studies *matter* (physical substance) and energy. Fermi made many important contributions to modern nuclear physics. He was the first scientist to "split" the *atom*—that is, cause the *nucleus* (core) to break into two pieces. However, he did not realize his success at the time. Fermi won the 1938 Nobel Prize in physics for his discoveries about *radioactive materials*. Radioactive materials release energy as they *decay* (break down). A part of this energy is released as heat.

Fermi worked with a metal called uranium *(yu RAY nee uhm)*. When the nucleus of a uranium atom is split, it releases tiny particles called *neutrons (NOO tronz)* and a tremendous amount of energy. The neutrons hit other atoms and split their *nuclei* (the plural of nucleus) in turn. More energy is released each time another nucleus splits. This process is called a *chain reaction*. Fermi and his team produced the first nuclear chain reaction. This accomplishment led to the development of the first atomic weapon.

Other articles to read include: **Chain reaction; Nuclear energy; Nucleus.**

Fessenden, Reginald Aubrey

Reginald Aubrey Fessenden *(FEHS uhn duhn)* (1866-1932) was a Canadian inventor and physicist *(FIHZ uh sihst)*. A physicist is a scientist who studies *matter* (physical substance) and energy. Fessenden played an important role in the development of radio and wireless communication. He is generally credited with making the first public broadcast of human speech by radio.

Fessenden was one of the chief chemists at the laboratory of the American inventor Thomas Alva Edison. In 1893, Fessenden became a professor at the Western University of Pennsylvania

Reginald Aubrey Fessenden

(now the University of Pittsburgh). He began to experiment with wireless communication systems. On Christmas Eve in 1906, several radio operators picked up a broadcast by Fessenden. They were surprised to hear Christmas music and a Bible reading instead of Morse code. Before this broadcast, radio transmissions generally consisted of only Morse code signals.

Fessenden was born on Oct. 6, 1866, in East Bolton, Quebec. During World War I (1914-1917), Fessenden developed various types of *sonar* equipment. Sonar uses sound waves to detect under-water objects. Fessenden also obtained *patents* for such useful items as an early version of micro-film and insulating electrical tape. A patent is a government document that gives an inventor sole rights to an invention for a limited time. Fessenden received more than 500 patents.

Other articles to read include: **Radio wave.**

Feynman, Richard Phillips

Richard Phillips Feynman *(FYN muhn)* (1918-1988) was an American *physicist*. Physicists study the basic parts and laws of the universe.

Feynman won the 1965 Nobel Prize in physics. He shared the prize with Julian S. Schwinger of the United States and Sin-Itiro Tomonaga of Japan. The three scientists won for improving ideas in *quantum mechanics*. Quantum mechanics is a branch of physics that describes the structure and behavior of tiny *particles* (bits of matter that are smaller than atoms).

Feynman also created a new kind of diagram to show how particles act on one another. Such diagrams are called *Feynman diagrams*.

Feynman was born in Far Rockaway, a suburb of New York City. He earned his Ph.D. degree from Princeton University. Feynman taught at the California Institute of Technology from 1950 until his death in 1988. He wrote about his experiences in *Surely You're Joking, Mr. Feynman!* (1985). Feynman served on the presidential commission that investigated the 1986 accident that destroyed the space shuttle Challenger. He helped explain why the explosion occurred.

Other articles to read include: **Quantum mechanics.**

Firefighters spray water on trees burning in a forest fire.

A blacksmith shapes an iron decoration that has been heated to a red glow by fire in a forge.

Fire

Fire is the light and heat that comes from burning substances. Burning is also called *combustion*. Burning is the result of the rapid union of oxygen with other substances.

Three things must happen before a fire can be made. First, there must be a *fuel*. A fuel is a substance that will burn. Second, the fuel must be heated to a certain temperature. This is the temperature at which combustion can begin and continue. Third, there must be plenty of oxygen, which usually comes from the air.

Substances that burn in air are nearly always composed of two *chemical elements*—carbon and hydrogen, or combinations of these elements. A chemical element is a substance that is made up of only one type of atom. When fuels burn, oxygen from the air unites with the carbon and hydrogen. The uniting of the oxygen with the hydrogen and the carbon produces the heat and flame of the fire. Most of the energy caused by a fire goes into heat. But some of it goes into light.

All substances do not burn in the same manner. Charcoal, for example, gives off heat with a faint glow. But other substances, such as coal, gas, oil, and wood, give off heat with a flame. The color of the flame depends chiefly on the kind of material being burned and on the temperature.

Early people used fire to keep warm. Over time, people learned to use fire in many other ways. They used fire to cook food, to make weapons and tools, and to provide light. Today, we have better ways to make fires than early people did, and we use fire in many more ways. Fire supplies the power to move trains, ships, and planes. Fire is used to make electric energy. It is also used to get rid of waste materials.

Fire can also destroy many things. Fires that burn out of control kill thousands of people and do billions of dollars worth of damage each year.

Other articles to read include: **Ash, Combustion; Fuel.**

Fission

Fission is the splitting of the *nucleus* (center) of an atom. When a nucleus splits, it breaks into two lighter *nuclei* (the plural of nucleus). This process releases a tremendous amount of *radiation* (energy). The word *fission* means *breaking apart*. Fission happens easily in a metal called *uranium* (*yu RAY nee uhm*).

Nuclear power stations use the heat from nuclear fission to generate electric power. But nuclear fission must be carefully controlled. When the nucleus of a uranium atom is split, some of its neutrons *(NOO tronz)* escape. Neutrons are tiny particles found in the nucleus of atoms. These neutrons crash into other uranium atoms, causing them to split, and so on. This ongoing process is called a *chain reaction*. Chain reactions produce the energy in nuclear reactors and atomic bombs.

Other articles to read include: **Chain reaction; Neutron; Nuclear energy; Nucleus; Radiation.**

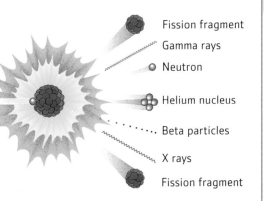

Fission fragment
Gamma rays
Neutron
Helium nucleus
Beta particles
X rays
Fission fragment

Nuclear fission releases several types of radiation, including neutrons, alpha and beta particles, gamma rays, and X rays.

Fluid

A fluid is any substance that flows easily. All liquids are fluids. So are all gases. Water and oil are examples of fluids that are liquids. Air is the best-known fluid that is a gas. A slight pressure or force will change the form of a fluid. But fluids tend to return to their former size when the pressure is removed.

Even though gases and liquids are both fluids, they have differences. A liquid takes the shape of a container into which it is poured and then does not change. A gas behaves differently. A gas easily changes it volume. It expands or contracts to fill any container into which it is placed. A gas that is put into a container must be held on all sides. If a container does not have a top, the gas inside can expand and leave the container.

Gases and liquids have other differences. A gas can also be *compressed* (squeezed) into a smaller space. A liquid can hardly be compressed at all.

Other articles to read include: **Gas; Liquid.**

Liquids and gases are both called fluids because they can flow to fit the shape of any container in which they are put.

Some bottled water contains fluoride.

Fluoridation

Fluoridation is the addition of a chemical called *fluoride* to drinking water. Fluoride helps protect teeth from *cavities* (holes in the teeth). They are caused by tiny germs called *bacteria*.

In the 1930's, researchers discovered that people who grew up where water naturally contained fluoride had many fewer cavities than people living in areas without fluoridated water. Some cities started adding fluoride to drinking water in 1945 as an experiment. By the 1950's, scientists found that the people in those cities had fewer cavities than people elsewhere. Government health experts recommended that all communities add fluoride to drinking water. Today, about half the people in the United States drink fluoridated water. Fluoridation is not as widespread in other countries.

Some health experts question whether fluoridation is safe. They say a small number of people might develop health problems from it. But most scientists think the health risks of fluoridation are very small.

Other articles to read include: **Fluorine.**

Compounds containing fluorine are often added to toothpaste to help prevent cavities.

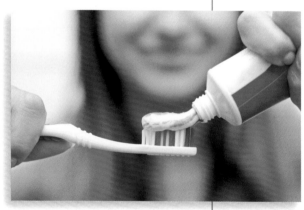

9	F	2 7
Fluorine 18.9984032		

Fluorine atomic symbol

Fluorine

Fluorine *(FLOO uh reen)* is a *chemical element.* A chemical element is a substance that contains only one type of *atom.* An atom is a tiny bit of matter. At ordinary temperatures, pure fluorine is a pale yellow gas. Fluorine combines with other elements more easily than does any other element. Compounds that contain fluorine are called *fluorides.* The chemical symbol for fluorine is F.

Fluorine comes from minerals in the ground. Factories use fluorine in making such metals as steel and aluminum. Some fluorides can help prevent dental cavities. These fluorides are added to toothpaste and, in some places, to drinking water.

Other articles to read include: **Element, Chemical; Fluoridation.**

Force

A force is a push or a pull. Force causes something to change speed or direction.

You experience many forces every day. For example, when you push a cart, you use force to make the cart move. When you squeeze a piece of soft clay, force changes the shape of the clay. If you throw a ball into the air, you are using force to give the ball speed. Then the *force of gravity* (also called *gravitation)* slows the ball and makes it fall back to the ground. When you catch the ball, the ball applies a downward force to your hands. But your hands apply an upward force to the ball to stop it.

Often, more than one force acts on an object at the same time. When you sit in a chair, the force of gravity pulls you toward Earth. But the chair pushes you up, away from Earth. The two forces "cancel" each other out, and you stay still. The same thing may happen during a game of tug-of-war. One team may pull harder on the rope than the opposing team does. In that case, the rope will move toward the first team. But the two teams may pull equally hard. In that case, the rope will not move.

A force acts by overcoming *inertia,* which is a *property* (characteristic) of all matter. Because of inertia, an object that is not moving stays still unless an outside force acts on it. Inertia also makes a moving object keep moving at the same speed and in the same dirction unless an outside force changes that object's motion.

Other articles to read include: **Centrifugal and centripetal forces; Gravitation; Inertia; Magnetism; Motion.**

When you push a cart, you use force to make the cart move.

When you play tug-of-war, you create *tension* (stress) in the rope in both directions. Tension is caused by the action of a pulling force.

Fractal

A fractal *(FRAK tuhl)* is a special shape or pattern that looks similar both close up and far away. The shapes and patterns of a fractal repeat themselves at smaller and smaller scales. The study of fractals involves special mathematics.

Many shapes and patterns found in nature are fractals. A fern plant is one example. Fern leaflets have a similar shape to the branch that holds them. Also, each leaflet is made of smaller leaflets that have the same shape. Fractals also can describe the shapes of coastlines, mountains, and clouds.

The study of these kinds of shapes began in the late 1800's. Interest increased greatly in the late 1960's, especially in the work of Benoit Mandelbrot, a Polish-born French mathematician. Mandelbrot invented the term *fractal* in 1975. One of the most famous fractals is based on a mathematical formula called the Mandelbrot set.

Other articles to read include: **Geometry.**

Fraction

A fraction is a part of something. Fractions come from breaking something into equal parts. For example, you might cut a sheet of paper into two equal pieces. Each of those pieces would be *one-half* of the sheet. If you cut each of those pieces in half, you would have four equal pieces. Each piece would be *one-fourth,* or a *quarter,* of the sheet. When something is broken into three equal parts, each part is called *one-third.*

A unit can be broken into any number of parts. You might break a stick into two pieces. But you cannot have two halves of the stick unless the two broken pieces are the same length.

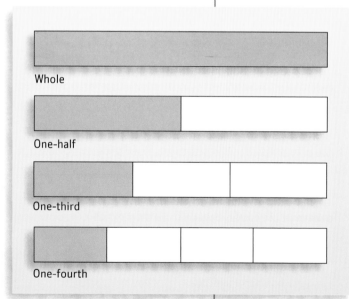

Whole

One-half

One-third

One-fourth

Fractions are parts of something. When something is divided into equal parts, the parts are fractions of the whole.

Continued on the next page

Fractions are written as two numbers separated by a line, for example: 2/5. The fraction 2/5 stands for two parts of something that has been broken into five equal parts. The bottom, or second, number is 5. It is called the *denominator (dih NAH muh NAY tur)*. It shows that something has been divided into five equal parts. The top, or first, number is 2. It is called the *numerator (NOO muh ray tur)*. It represents 2 of the 5 equal parts. The names for most fractions are made by adding *th* to the end of the word that shows the number of equal parts. So the word for 2/5 is *two-fifths*. The word for 3/10 is *three-tenths*.

Other articles to read include: **Decimal system; Number.**

Freezing point

The freezing point is the temperature at which a liquid becomes a solid. For example, the freezing point of water is 32 °F (0 °C). At that temperature, water begins to turn into ice.

A substance's freezing point is almost always the same as its melting point. Ice that is getting warmer starts to melt at 32 °F. Liquid water that is getting cooler starts to freeze at 32 °F. At exactly 32 °F, ice and water can exist in a stable mixture.

A substance's freezing point can change. For example, the freezing point of almost every substance gets higher as air pressure rises. This is because an increase in pressure squeezes a substance, helping it to remain a solid. More heat energy is needed to overcome pressure and melt the solid into a liquid. The opposite is also true. Lowering the pressure generally enables a substance to melt at a lower temperature.

Other articles to read include: **Ice; Melting point; Temperature.**

The freezing point of water is 32 °F (0 °C). Water's freezing point is the same as its melting point.

Frequency

Frequency *(FREE kwuhn see)* is measurement used to describe waves. A wave has *crests* (peaks) and *troughs* (lows). Imagine a wave passing a certain spot. A number of crests or troughs will pass in a given time. This number is the wave's frequency. Frequency depends on the speed of the wave and the distance between neighboring crests or troughs. Frequency is measured in units called *hertz,* or *Hz.*

Sound is a kind of wave. The frequency of sound waves equals the number of *vibrations* made by an object each second. Vibrations are quick, tiny movements back and forth or up and down. An object that vibrates more rapidly will give off higher frequency sound waves than will an object that vibrates more slowly. As the frequency increases, the *wavelength* generally decreases. Wavelength is the distance between neighboring crests of a wave. A pattern of waves that travel slowly and far apart is a low-frequency wavelength. A pattern of waves that travel quickly and close together is a high-frequency wavelength.

The frequency of a sound determines its *pitch*. Pitch is the highness or lowness of a sound as we hear it. High-pitched sounds have higher frequencies than low-pitched sounds.

Scientists also use frequency to measure electromagnetic waves. Electromagnetic waves include all forms of light. The different types of electromagnetic waves have different wavelengths and frequencies. For example, X rays are electromagnetic waves with high frequencies and short wavelengths. Radio waves have low frequencies and long wavelengths.

Most people can hear sounds with frequencies from about 20 to 20,000 Hz. For example, a person's voice can produce frequencies from 85 to 1,100 Hz. Bats, cats, dogs, dolphins, and many other animals can hear sounds with frequencies far above 20,000 Hz.

Other articles to read include: **Electromagnetic spectrum; Hertz; Sound; Vibration; Wavelength.**

The frequency of a sound wave equals the number of vibrations made by an object each second. The more rapidly an object vibrates, the higher the frequency will be. As the frequency increases, the wavelength decreases. The frequency of a sound determines its pitch. High-pitched sounds have higher frequencies than low-pitched sounds.

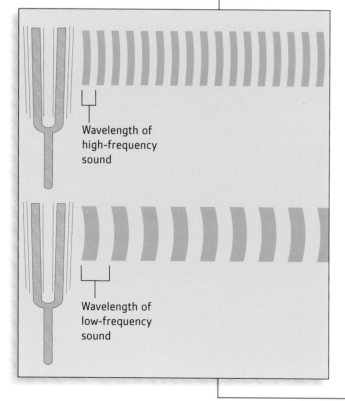

Wavelength of high-frequency sound

Wavelength of low-frequency sound

Friction

Friction is what makes two objects *resist* (act against each other) when when they rub against each other. Friction keeps objects from sliding across each other. For example, the wheels of a train grip the track using friction. Friction also keeps your shoes from sliding on the sidewalk. It is easier to slip on ice because ice provides less friction than a sidewalk.

Friction causes heat. When two substances rub against each other, the *molecules* (small pieces of matter) in each substance move faster. This movement can be felt as heat.

The rubbing and heat can cause objects to wear down. That is why oil and other liquids are used on moving machine parts. These liquids reduce friction. The parts move more easily, and their movement makes less heat.

There are three main kinds of friction: *sliding friction, rolling friction*, and *fluid friction*. Sliding friction is caused when two surfaces slide across each other. An example of sliding friction is when a book moves across the surface of a desk. Rolling friction is the resistance made when a wheel or other round object moves over a surface. The friction between an automobile tire and a street is rolling friction. Fluid friction is friction between a *fluid*—a liquid or gas that flows easily—and a solid. The friction between a swimmer and the water is an example of fluid friction.

Other articles to read include: **Fire; Heat.**

Atmospheric friction—the collision between air and an object—causes a piece of space rock called a meteoroid to glow and appear as a *meteor* (streak of light) in the sky.

A camper tries to start a fire using a firebow. This device makes one piece of wood spin against another. The friction produces enough heat to start a fire in small pieces of wood.

Fuel

Fuel is a material that can be used to produce useful energy. We use fuels to heat and cool buildings. We also use fuels to cook food and make electric power. Fuels are used to run the engines in cars, airplanes, and other machines. Most fuels release energy by combining with oxygen in air. This process is called *burning* or *combustion*.

Some fuels, including coal, petroleum, and natural gas, are called *fossil fuels*. Fossil fuels are found underground. They were formed over millions of years from the remains of ancient living things. Almost all the energy people use today comes from fossil fuels.

Some fuels are made from crops that can be regrown each year. These fuels are called *biofuels*.

There are five kinds of fuels: (1) solid fuels, (2) liquid fuels, (3) gas fuels, (4) chemical fuels, and (5) nuclear fuels.

Solid fuels include coal, peat, and biomass *(BY oh MAS)*. Coal is used mainly to make electric power. It is burned to make heat. The heat turns water into steam. The steam is used to turn special machines called turbines *(TUR bynz)*. The turbines make electric energy.

Peat is made up of partly decayed plants. It is found mostly in swamps called *bogs*.

Biomass is fuel made from plant or animal matter. Wood, garbage, and animal manure are examples of biomass.

Liquid fuels are made mainly from petroleum. Petroleum is also called *crude oil*. Most petroleum is turned into such fuels as gasoline, diesel oil, and kerosene.

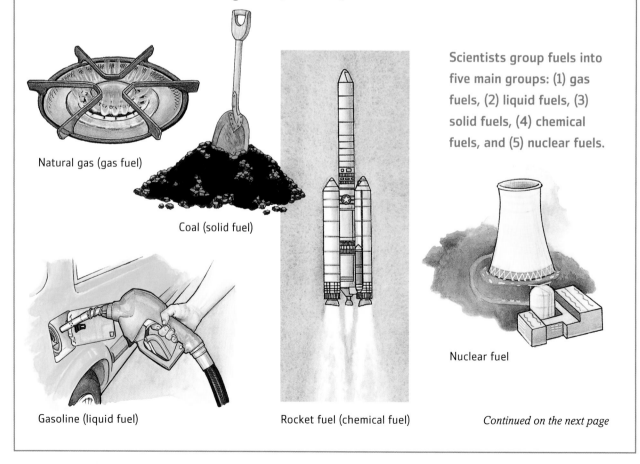

Natural gas (gas fuel)

Coal (solid fuel)

Scientists group fuels into five main groups: (1) gas fuels, (2) liquid fuels, (3) solid fuels, (4) chemical fuels, and (5) nuclear fuels.

Nuclear fuel

Gasoline (liquid fuel)

Rocket fuel (chemical fuel)

Continued on the next page

Synthetic (artificially made) liquid fuels are made from coal, natural gas, and biomass. They are also made from oil shale, a type of rock with petroleum in it. Synthetic fuels may also be made from a special type of sand.

Gas fuels include natural gas and manufactured gases. Natural gas is found underground in various types of rocks. Natural gas is mostly methane, a gas with no color or odor. Manufactured gas is produced mainly from coal or petroleum.

Chemical fuels can be solid or liquid. They can produce great amounts of heat and power. Chemical fuels are used mostly for rocket engines.

Nuclear fuels produce heat from the *splitting* (breaking apart) of the *nuclei* (cores) of *atoms.* Atoms are one of the basic units of matter. Nuclear fuels are used mainly to make electric power.

Other articles to read include: **Combustion; Electricity; Fission; Gasoline; Nuclear energy.**

Fusion

Fusion *(FYOO zhuhn)* is the joining of two lightweight atomic nuclei *(NOO klee eye)* to form the *nucleus* of a heavier atom. A nucleus (plural, nuclei) is the center of an atom. The word *fusion* means *joining.* During nuclear fusion, huge amounts of energy are released. This process gives stars their tremendous energy. Fusion also powers some nuclear weapons.

The sun's energy comes from the nuclear fusion of hydrogen atoms. The hydrogen atoms in the sun continually crash into one another and fuse. They combine to make larger nuclei of helium atoms. Scientists are trying to find a way of using nuclear fusion in power stations. A fusion station would be one of the cleanest ways of producing electric power.

Other articles to read include: **Nuclear energy; Nucleus**

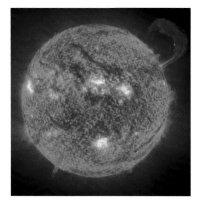

The sun's energy comes from the nuclear fusion of hydrogen atoms.

A hydrogen bomb explodes over the Pacific Ocean. Such bombs, also called fusion weapons, get their power from the *fusion* (joining) of atomic nuclei under intense heat and pressure.

Gas

Gas is one of the three basic forms of matter. The other two forms are *solids* and *liquids.* Air is a mixture of gases.

Gases, like solids and liquids, are made up of tiny particles called atoms and molecules *(MOL uh kyoolz).* Atoms and molecules are always moving and crashing into one another. But gas atoms and molecules move faster than the atoms and molecules of solids or liquids. If a gas is in a container, the moving particles bounce off the container's sides. This bouncing creates a push against the sides called the *pressure* of the gas. If gas in a container is heated, the molecules move faster. They strike the sides harder and more often, and the pressure increases.

Most gases in air have no color or smell. But some gases have a color or a smell, or both. When eggs rot, they give off a gas that smells bad. Ozone, a gas found in Earth's atmosphere, is a pale blue. Gases also have weight. The weight of the air that surrounds Earth pushes against everything on the surface. That weight is called *atmospheric (AT muh SFEHR ihk) pressure.*

Water is an example of a material that can take all three forms of matter. When water is frozen into an ice cube, it becomes a solid. Like all solids, it has a particular size and shape. At room temperature, water is a liquid. Like other liquids, water has no shape of its own but takes on the shape of its container. Water becomes a gas when it is heated. It becomes a vapor. Vapor, like all gases, spreads out to fill whatever container it is in.

Scientists discovered and studied many gases in the 1600's and 1700's. In 1823, the British scientist Michael Faraday figured out that a gas can be changed into a liquid—and even into a solid—by cooling and *compressing* (squeezing) it.

Other articles to read include:
Condensation; Hydraulics; Liquid; Solid; Sublimation.

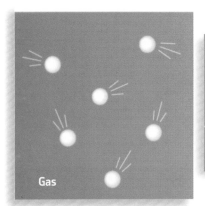

Gas

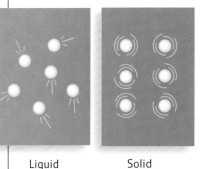

Liquid   Solid

In a gas (above), atoms or molecules fly about in a disorderly way. Their energy of motion is known as *kinetic energy.* The atoms or molecules in a gas have a large amount of kinetic energy. The motion of the atoms and molecules in a liquid (above, center) and a solid (above, right) is more orderly. A gas can be changed into a liquid or a solid by cooling and *compressing* (squeezing) it.

The greater the number of gas molecules in a given volume, the greater the pressure of the gas. Gas under high pressure will always flow toward an area of lower pressure.

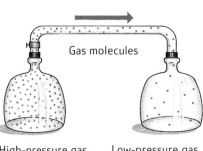

Gas molecules

High-pressure gas   Low-pressure gas

Gases expand and contract

All gases are made up of tiny particles called *atoms*. These atoms are always moving. Groups of atoms are called *molecules*. When a gas is heated, its molecules move about faster, bouncing off one another. As the molecules become scattered, the gas takes up more space. It *expands* (spreads out) and becomes less dense. When a gas cools, it *contracts* (takes up less space). This experiment shows how air contracts when it is cooled.

1. Blow up the balloon and tie the end. Tie a piece of thread around the balloon, just tightly enough so that the thread doesn't move.

2. Put the balloon in a refrigerator or freezer overnight or longer.

3. Take out the balloon. Feel how the balloon is different. Explain what has happened, and why.

   As the air warms up, the balloon changes. How? Explain.

What's going on:

The cool air in the refrigerator slowed down the molecules in the balloon. The slower moving molecules pulled closer together, taking up less space. The balloon shrank and became softer.

What you need:

- a sausage-shaped balloon
- cotton thread
- a refrigerator or freezer

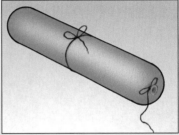

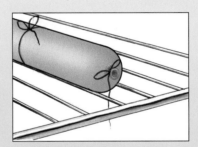

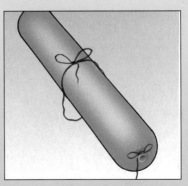

http://bit.ly/UKVUwo

Gasoline

Gasoline is one of the most important fuels used for transportation. Gasoline is most often used in engines that power trucks and cars. It is also used to power boats, airplanes, lawnmowers, and other machines. People in some countries call gasoline *petrol* because it is made from petroleum. Petroleum is an oil that is found underground.

Gasoline is made in a factory called a *refinery*. Oil at a refinery is separated into many useful products, including gasoline and several other fuels. Gasoline is a mixture of hundreds of chemicals called *hydrocarbons*. Hydrocarbons are compounds of the chemical elements hydrogen and carbon. Gasolines are made with different combinations of hydrocarbons. Different engines require different mixtures of gasoline to run smoothly. Each gasoline type

The octane number on a gasoline pump indicates the quality of the fuel, based on how efficiently it burns. The higher the number, the better the quality. Yellow squares on this pump display the octane numbers for three different grades of gasoline. As cars age, they often require higher-octane fuel.

is given a number called an *octane number*. A gasoline's octane number tells how well it will work in an engine. Many sports cars need gasoline with a high octane number.

Gasoline became very important in the early 1900's, when cars began to become popular. Cars made travel easy. They enabled people to live far from work. Gasoline also became important to farmers. They began to use tractors and other machines with gasoline engines. With these machines, farmers were able to grow more crops to feed more people. The use of gasoline has also caused problems. Burning gasoline creates air pollution. The United States and many other countries have passed laws that require fuel producers to develop cleaner-burning gasoline.

Other articles to read include: **Hydrocarbon; Fuel.**

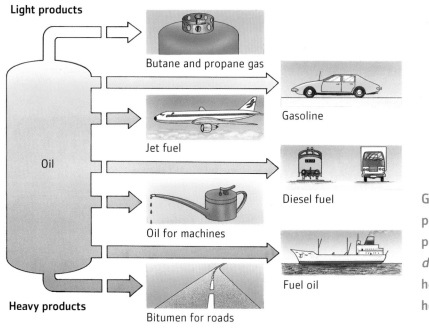

Gasoline is one of many products made from petroleum. The oil is *distilled* (broken up by heating) into lighter and heavier products.

Geometric shapes

Geometric *(JEE uh MEHT rihk)* shapes are figures that are commonly used in science, art, and construction and in many other ways. They have been used for thousands of years.

There are two basic kinds of geometric shapes: *plane* (flat) and solid. Plane shapes are also called two-dimensional shapes. That is because they have just two *dimensions* (ways of being measured) —height and width. Plane shapes include the circle, the square, the triangle, and the rectangle.

Solid shapes are also called *three-dimensional* shapes. These shapes have *depth* (thickness) in addition to height and width. Solid shapes include the sphere, the cube, the cone, the cylinder, and the pyramid.

Many geometric shapes can be seen in nature. Worms, for example, are shaped like cylinders, or tubes. Earth is shaped like a sphere.

Geometry is the branch of mathematics that deals with the form, size, and position of geometric shapes. Geometry is important to many kinds of work, including engineering and physics.

Other articles to read include: **Circle; Geometry; Square; Triangle.**

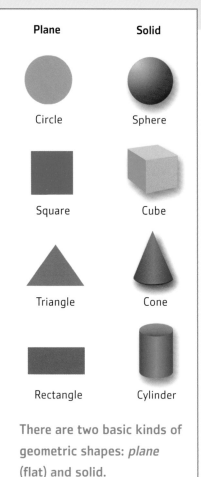

There are two basic kinds of geometric shapes: *plane* (flat) and solid.

Geometry

Geometry *(jee OM uh tree)* is a part of mathematics. It is the study of lines, angles, curves, and shapes. Such shapes can be either *plane* (flat) or *solid* (three-dimensional). Plane shapes include the circle, the square, and the triangle. Solid shapes include the cube, the sphere, and the pyramid.

Many people use geometry. For example, engineers and architects use it to design structures. Geometry is also used in *navigation* (the skill of charting a path from place to place).

Geometry is one of the oldest forms of mathematics. It was used by the ancient Egyptians and Babylonians. An ancient Greek mathematician named Euclid wrote a famous book about geometry called *Elements*. The word *geometry* comes from Greek words meaning *to measure Earth*.

Other articles to read include: **Euclid; Geometric shapes.**

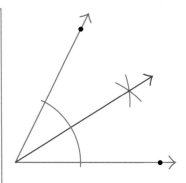

Bisecting an angle (dividing it into two equal parts) is a basic geometric construction.

Googol

Googol *(GOO guhl)* is a very large number. It is written as a 1 followed by 100 zeros.

A googol can also be written as 10^{100}. That means a hundred tens multiplied by one another. It is read as "10 to the one-hundredth power."

A *googolplex* is a related number far larger than the googol. That number is 10 to the googol power, or a googol tens multiplied by one another. A googolplex could be written as a 1 followed by a googol zeros. But that would take a piece of paper longer than the known universe.

The googol was introduced in 1938 by Edward Kasner, an American mathematician.

Other articles to read include: **Number; Zero.**

Graph

A graph *(graf)* is a type of drawing used to compare things. Graphs show whether sizes or numbers get bigger or smaller or stay the same.

There are four main types of graphs. They are line graphs, bar graphs, picture graphs, and circle graphs.

Line graphs are the simplest kind of graph. They are made on *grids*. Grids are networks of lines on a page or electronic screen. Dots are placed on these lines or between them. Each dot stands for a certain size or number. A line connects the dots. This line shows whether the size or number has changed. On most line graphs, a line that goes up shows that the size got bigger. A line that goes down shows that it got smaller. Lines

There are four main kinds of graphs: *line graphs, bar graphs, picture graphs,* and *circle graphs.*

Number of pupils present

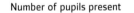
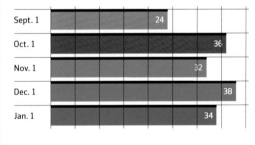

Line graph

Number of pupils present

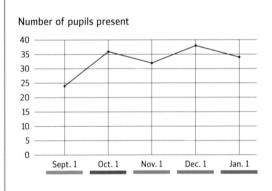

Bar graph

Continued on the next page

that do not go up or down show that there was no change.

Bar graphs use bar-shaped lines of different lengths to show change. Bigger sizes or numbers have longer or taller bars. Smaller sizes or numbers have shorter bars.

Picture graphs use pictures instead of lines or bars. They are often used in magazines and newspapers.

Circle graphs are often called pie charts. They look like pies sliced into pieces of different sizes. Each piece of the pie stands for a different amount.

Other articles to read include: **Number; Statistics.**

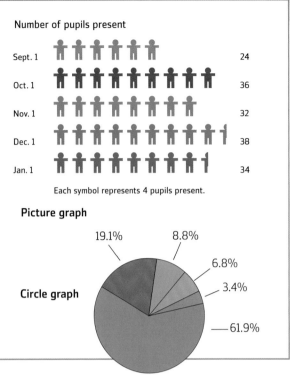

Number of pupils present

Sept. 1	𝕋𝕋𝕋𝕋𝕋𝕋	24
Oct. 1	𝕋𝕋𝕋𝕋𝕋𝕋𝕋𝕋𝕋	36
Nov. 1	𝕋𝕋𝕋𝕋𝕋𝕋𝕋𝕋	32
Dec. 1	𝕋𝕋𝕋𝕋𝕋𝕋𝕋𝕋𝕋𝕀	38
Jan. 1	𝕋𝕋𝕋𝕋𝕋𝕋𝕋𝕋𝕀	34

Each symbol represents 4 pupils present.

Picture graph

Circle graph

19.1% 8.8%
6.8%
3.4%
61.9%

Gravitation

Gravitation is the force that causes objects to be pulled toward one another. Gravitation keeps the planets in orbit around the sun. It also keeps your feet firmly on the ground. Gravitation causes things to fall when they are dropped. Another name for gravitation is the *force of gravity*.

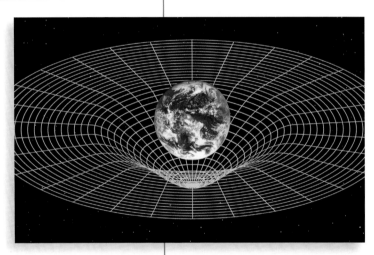

Gravitation acts between objects because of their *mass* (amount of matter). Every object has its own gravitational pull. But objects with a greater mass have a stronger gravitational pull than objects with less mass. Earth's gravitational pull keeps the moon in orbit around Earth. The moon's gravitational pull is not as strong as that of Earth because the moon has less mass. The moon's weaker gravitational pull is why astronauts visiting there can carry equipment that would be too heavy to carry on Earth.

In the late 1600's, the English scientist Sir Isaac Newton developed several important laws of gravitation. He explained that the

Continued on the next page

Einstein calculated that gravitation is an effect of the *distortion* (curvature) of *space-time.* Space-time is a combination of time and the three dimensions of space— length, width, and height. The distortion in the fabric of space causes objects near Earth to be pulled toward us.

Gravitation *Continued from the previous page*

force of gravity between two objects is directly related to their masses. The more mass an object has, the greater its gravitational pull. Newton also explained that the force of gravity gets weaker as objects get farther apart. Newton explained that gravitation caused both objects to fall to the ground and the planets to orbit the sun. However, Newton could not explain what causes gravitation. Even so, scientists accepted Newton's ideas for more than 200 years.

In 1915, the German-born American scientist Albert Einstein developed new ideas about gravitation that added to Newton's work. Einstein's ideas were called the *general theory of relativity*. Before Einstein, people had thought of space as being just emptiness. But Einstein said space is somewhat like a rubber sheet. His theory says that objects in space, such as the sun, actually change the shape of space. They cause space to curve, just as a bowling ball would make a rubber sheet bend downward. The curving of space causes objects to move toward one another. Many experiments have proved Einstein right. Although Einstein's work is widely accepted, the source of gravitation is still unknown.

Other articles to read include: **Einstein, Albert; Mass; Newton, Sir Isaac; Relativity.**

The center of gravity for a seesaw is in the middle of the board when no one is sitting on it. When two people sit on the seesaw, the center of gravity shifts toward the heavier person.

Gravity, Center of

An object's center of gravity is the point in the object where *gravitation* (the force of gravity) seems to act. Gravitation pulls objects together. An object on Earth is pulled downward by Earth's force of gravity.

The center of gravity of a seesaw is at the middle of the board when no one is sitting on it. Both ends of the board are pulled down equally, so the board stays level. But if one person gets on, the center of gravity shifts toward that person. That end of the board then goes down. If a heavier person then sits down on the other end of the seesaw, the center of gravity shifts toward that person. The board then tilts down on that end.

Other articles to read include: **Gravitation.**

Hawking, Stephen William

Stephen William Hawking (1942-   ) is a British *theoretical physicist (THEE uh REHT uh kuhl FIHZ uh sist)*. Theoretical physicists study how the world is put together, and how it changes.

Hawking has made important discoveries about *gravitation,* the force that pulls things together. His work supports the *theory* (scientific belief) that the universe began in a cosmic explosion called *the big bang.* He is also noted for his theories about *black holes,* invisible bodies in space. Their force of gravity is so strong that not even light can escape it. Hawking is the author of the book *A Brief History of Time: From the Big Bang to Black Holes* (1988).

Hawking was born in Oxford, England. Because of a disease of the nervous system, he cannot speak or walk. He uses a wheelchair that has a computer voice machine. This equipment helps him work and travel.

Other articles to read include: **Gravitation.**

Stephen William Hawking

Heat

Heat is one of the most important forms of energy. Heat warms our homes and cooks our food. It gives us hot water and dries our laundry. Heat also runs machines. The heat from burning fuels in engines makes the power to move cars and airplanes. Heat drives machines called generators that produce electric power. Electric power provides lighting. It also furnishes power to run all kinds of equipment, from computers to electric trains. Heat is used in factories to melt, shape, and join metals. Heat is used to make foods, glass, paper, textiles, and many other products.

Heat is closely related to a kind of energy called *thermal energy.* Thermal energy is the energy an object has because of its temperature. Heat is just thermal energy as it moves from a warmer object to a cooler object.

The sun is our most important source of heat. The sun's heat keeps Earth warm and helps humans, plants, and animals to live. Earth also has its own heat deep inside. When a volcano

Continued on the next page

Heat *Continued from the previous page*

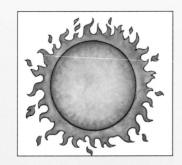

The sun produces heat from nuclear reactions deep inside it. All life on Earth depends on the sun's heat.

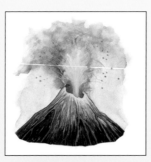

Earth contains much heat deep inside. Some of this heat escapes to the surface when a volcano erupts.

Chemical reactions produce heat by causing a chemical change in a substance. Fire is a chemical reaction in which oxygen rapidly combines with a substance, such as the wood of a match.

Friction—the rubbing of one object against another—produces heat. Campers learn to start a fire with friction by rubbing two sticks together.

erupts, some of this heat comes to the surface.

Chemical reactions can make heat. Fire is an example of a chemical reaction. Fire happens when wood, gas, or another fuel mixes with oxygen in the air. Rubbing one object against another also produces heat. This is called *friction*.

The flow of electricity through metals and most other materials also makes heat. Nuclear energy produces large amounts of heat. Nuclear energy is produced when the *nuclei* (cores) of atoms break apart or join together.

Other articles to read include: Boiling point; Energy; Fire; Melting point.

Sources of heat include the sun, Earth, chemical reactions, and friction. Electric energy and nuclear energy are two other sources of heat.

Helium

2	He	2
	Helium	
	4.002602	

Helium atomic symbol

Helium *(HEE lee uhm)* is a light gas. It is also a *chemical element.* A chemical element is a material with only one kind of atom. Helium weighs less than any other chemical element except hydrogen.

Helium makes up only a small part of Earth. However, it is one of the most common elements in the universe. The sun and other stars are made

Continued on the next page

mostly of helium and hydrogen. The energy of these stars is produced when hydrogen atoms *fuse* (join together) to form helium atoms. This process also gives the hydrogen bomb its energy.

In 1868, two scientists discovered helium in the sun while using an instrument called a *spectroscope*. This device is a telescope that spreads out visible light and displays it for study. The name *helium* comes from the Greek word for *sun*. Scientists first found helium on Earth in 1895.

Scientists use helium to maintain the correct pressure in rockets. People who have trouble breathing must *inhale* (breathe in) a mix of helium and oxygen. Helium is also used in industry in *welding* (permanently joining two pieces of material using heat or pressure).

Other articles to read include: **Element, Chemical; Fusion; Gas; Hydrogen.**

Helium has numerous uses. These divers prepare tanks filled with a mixture of helium and oxygen. Breathing this mixture prevents a certain type of illness caused by the pressure of diving deep in the ocean.

Hertz

The hertz *(hurts)* is a measure of the *frequency* of waves and vibrations. The frequency of a wave or vibration is the number of cycles in a certain time. A cycle is one complete back-and-forth motion. One hertz equals one cycle per second. The symbol for hertz is *Hz*.

Objects that produce waves with cycles include tuning forks, human vocal cords, and radio transmitters. The musical note "A" has a frequency of 440 Hz. In other words, the wave undergoes 440 cycles per second. Radio waves may have frequencies of many million hertz.

Continued on the next page

A tuning fork is a device for tuning musical instruments. It produces a sound of a single frequency, the rate at which the fork vibrates. Frequency is measured in a unit called the hertz.

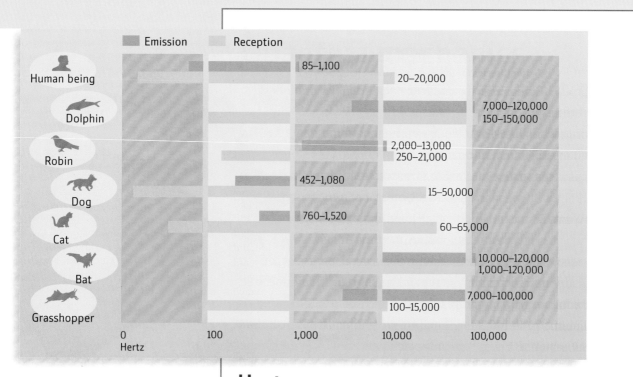

	Emission	Reception

Human being — 85–1,100 / 20–20,000
Dolphin — 7,000–120,000 / 150–150,000
Robin — 2,000–13,000 / 250–21,000
Dog — 452–1,080 / 15–50,000
Cat — 760–1,520 / 60–65,000
Bat — 10,000–120,000 / 1,000–120,000
Grasshopper — 7,000–100,000 / 100–15,000

0 100 1,000 10,000 100,000
Hertz

One hertz equals one *cycle* (vibration) per second. This graph shows the range of frequencies, in hertz, that people and some animals can *emit* (give off) and receive. Many animals hear frequencies far above those heard by people.

Hertz *Continued from the previous page*

The hertz was adopted in 1960 by an international group of scientists at the General Conference on Weights and Measures. It was named for Heinrich R. Hertz, a German scientist.

Other articles to read include: **Frequency; Sound; Vibration; Wavelength.**

Hertz, Heinrich Rudolf

Heinrich Rudolf Hertz (1857–1894) was a German *physicist.* A physicist is a scientist who studies matter and energy. In the 1880's, Hertz proved the existence of *electromagnetic (ih LEHK troh mag NEHT ihk) waves.* An electromagnetic wave is a moving pattern of electric and magnetic influence. Visible light, radio waves, and X rays are kinds of electromagnetic waves. Hertz's discovery allowed later scientists to develop radio, television, and radar. The British scientist James Clerk Maxwell had predicted the existence of electromagnetic waves in 1864.

Hertz was born in Hamburg, Germany. A unit of measure called the *hertz* is named in his honor. The hertz is used to measure the *frequency* (rate of occurrence) of waves and vibrations.

Other articles to read include: **Hertz; Waves.**

Heinrich Rudolf Hertz

Higgs boson

The Higgs boson is an important *subatomic particle* in physics. The word *subatomic* means *smaller than an atom.* Scientists think that the Higgs boson gives other particles their *mass.* Mass is the amount of matter in an object. It accounts for an object's weight. The Higgs boson is named for the British physicist Peter Higgs. He proposed the idea of such a particle in 1964. Scientists did not find evidence that the particle exists until 2012.

Higgs bosons are found everywhere there is matter. They form a "field" around matter, much as a magnet creates a magnetic field. The field, often called the *Higgs field,* acts on matter to give it mass. The Higgs boson has a large mass for a subatomic particle. Estimates range from about 400 to 1,000 times the mass of a *proton,* a positively charged subatomic particle.

In 2012, scientists working at CERN, a major research center in Europe, announced the first evidence for the Higgs boson. They were working with a particle accelerator, a machine that smashes particles together.

Other articles to read include: **Boson; CERN.**

British physicist Peter Higgs stands before the Large Hadron Collider, a particle accelerator at CERN, where scientists in 2012 first found evidence for the particle Higgs proposed in 1964.

Hodgkin, Dorothy Crowfoot

Dorothy Crowfoot Hodgkin (1910–1994) was a British scientist. She won the Nobel Prize in chemistry in 1964 for figuring out the *structure* (makeup) of the vitamin B_{12} *molecule.* A molecule *(MOL uh kyool)* is a tiny piece of *matter.* Her work helped other scientists understand how the human body uses vitamin B_{12} to build red blood cells and to prevent a disease called *pernicious anemia.*

Hodgkin also studied how many other chemical *compounds* are made. A compound is a material made of more than one kind of *atom.* In 1969, she revealed the three-dimensional structure of insulin. Insulin is a protein used to treat people with diabetes.

Hodgkin was born in Cairo, Egypt. She graduated from Oxford University in 1931 and became an Oxford professor in 1934.

Other articles to read include: **Compound.**

Dorothy Crowfoot Hodgkin

Horsepower

Horsepower is a measurement of *power*. Power is the rate or speed of doing work. The work used to move one pound a distance of one foot is called one *foot-pound*. One horsepower equals 550 foot-pounds of work per second.

If an engine lifts a 550-pound object to a height of 1 foot in 1 second, it is working at a rate of one horsepower. A person who is accustomed to hard work can work at a rate of between $\frac{1}{10}$ and $\frac{1}{8}$ horsepower over an 8-hour day.

The Scottish engineer James Watt first used the term *horsepower* in the 1700's. He used the term to compare the power of steam engines with the power of horses. Today, horsepower is used to measure the power of such devices as automobile engines and electric motors.

The *watt* is the measurement of power in the metric system. One horsepower equals 745.700 watts.

Other articles to read include: **Work.**

Christiaan Huygens

Huygens, Christiaan

Christiaan Huygens *(KRIHS tee ahn HY guhnz)* (1629–1695) was a Dutch astronomer, mathematician, and *physicist* (a scientist who studies matter and energy). In 1678, Huygens proposed that light is made up of a series of waves. Another scientist, Sir Isaac Newton, believed that light was made up of particles. Today, we know that light acts as both a particle and a wave.

Huygens also made important advances in other fields. In 1651, he described a new way to measure the area of a circle. He worked with his brother Constantijn to develop more powerful telescopes. He also discovered Saturn's moon Titan. He figured out that what astronomers called "Saturn's arms" was a ring. Huygens was born in The Hague, the Netherlands.

The European Space Agency honored Huygens's discovery of Titan by naming a space probe after him. The Huygens probe landed on Titan in 2005. It was carried and released by the Cassini spacecraft of the United States.

Other articles to read include: **Light.**

Hydraulics

Hydraulics *(hy DRAW lihks)* is the study of the behavior of liquids. In hydraulics, scientists study how liquids flow and how they act when standing still. Some laws of hydraulics apply to gases in certain cases.

Engineers study hydraulics to design and make things. Some engineers study the flow of water in pipes and channels. They design canals and other systems that control floods, water crops, provide water to towns and cities, and carry away sewage.

Other engineers study the flow of liquids under pressure in pipes. They use hydraulics to design devices that use the flow of liquids to do work. Such devices are called hydraulic devices. Hydraulic devices are used in automobile brakes and power-steering systems, controls for airplanes and spacecraft, and construction equipment.

Other articles to read include: **Gas; Liquid.**

Refinery gas for bottled gas

Hydrocarbon

A hydrocarbon *(hy droh KAHR buhn)* is part of an important group of chemicals. Hydrocarbons are made up only of the *chemical elements* hydrogen and carbon. A chemical element is a material made of only one type of atom.

Hydrocarbons are found in *petroleum* (oil) and natural gas. Such products as gasoline, kerosene *(KEHR uh seen),* and airplane fuel are mixtures of hydrocarbons. Some hydrocarbons are found in coal tar and coal gas. Many other hydrocarbons are made artificially from hydrocarbons found in nature.

Some chemical companies use hydrocarbons as starting materials for their products. Some companies use hydrocarbons from some types of oil and gas to make such items as plastics and rubber.

Other articles to read include: **Carbon; Gasoline; Hydrogen.**

Petroleum

Hydrocarbons are a main source of energy, such as the ones shown here.

Gasoline for cars

Hydrogen

Hydrogen
atomic symbol

Hydrogen *(HY droh juhn)* is a gas. It is lighter than air, and it has no taste, odor, or color. It is the most plentiful *chemical element* in the universe. A chemical element is a material that is made up of only one type of atom. About 90 percent of all atoms in the universe are hydrogen. Stars consist mainly of hydrogen.

In stars, the *nuclei* (cores) of hydrogen atoms *fuse* (combine) to form helium nuclei. This process produces tremendous energy. Large amounts of hydrogen also occur in *interstellar clouds,* clouds of gas and dust in the space between stars.

Hydrogen is plentiful on Earth. But most of it is combined with other chemical elements. Hydrogen makes up part of water, petroleum, plants and animals, and plastics. On Earth, pure hydrogen is an extremely flammable gas.

Hydrogen has many uses. Some industries use it in a process that makes metals pure. Hydrogen can also be used as fuel. Some experimental cars use hydrogen fuel. Scientists are trying to find more and better ways to use hydrogen as an energy source.

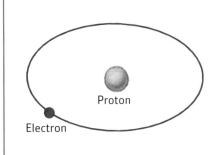

Proton

Electron

The English scientist Henry Cavendish first described hydrogen as an individual substance in 1766. He burned hydrogen in air and showed that the result was pure water. From this, the French chemist Antoine Lavoisier concluded that water is a compound of hydrogen and oxygen. The name *hydrogen* comes from the Greek words meaning *water-forming.*

Other articles to read include: **Element, Chemical; Fuel; Fusion; Helium.**

Hydrogen has the simplest atom of all chemical elements. The basic hydrogen atom consists of a single positive particle called a *proton* linked to a single negative particle called an *electron.*

Hydrogenation

Hydrogenation *(HY druh juh NAY shuhn)* is the chemical process of adding hydrogen to a substance. Food manufacturers often hydrogenate liquid oils to make solid fats. For example, peanut oil is hydrogenated to change it to a solid and to improve its odor and flavor. Hydrogenation can produce a special kind of fat called *trans fat.* People who eat a diet high in trans fats have an increased risk of heart disease. Hydrogenation is also used in making gasoline and in making crude oil from coal.

A substance whose molecules contain some hydrogen atoms but can accept more is said to be *unsaturated.* The molecules of a substance that is *saturated* contain as many hydrogen atoms as they can hold.

Other articles to read include: **Hydrogen.**

Hydrology

Hydrology *(hy DRAHL uh jee)* is the study of the movement and distribution of water. People use billions of gallons of fresh water every day. *Hydrologists,* the scientists who specialize in hydrology, help find supplies of water. They also study the chemical and physical properties of water. In nature, water circulates through a system called the *hydrologic cycle* or *water cycle.*

Some hydrologists try to prevent or reduce water pollution. They also study the effects of water pollution. Hydrologists help plan dams and irrigation projects. Hydrology also provides information that scientists need to predict and control floods.

Hypatia

Hypatia *(hy PAY shee uh)* (A.D. 370?–415) was an Egyptian mathematician and *philosopher (fuh LOS uh fuhr).* A philosopher is a person who studies the truth of knowledge. She was also a leader of a way of thinking based on the ideas of the Greek philosopher Plato.

Hypatia was the first notable female mathematician. She gave public talks on astronomy, mathematics, philosophy, and religion in her home and at lecture halls in Alexandria. People apparently consulted her on governmental matters. Hypatia is believed to have written several works, but they no longer exist. Most of what is known about her life and teaching is based on letters written by one of her students.

Hypatia was born in Alexandria. She learned science and mathematics from her father. Together they wrote commentaries on the works of the Greek astronomer Ptolemy *(TOL uh mee).* Hypatia was murdered by the followers of Cyril of Alexandria, a Christian bishop. Some scholars believe Cyril's followers killed Hypatia because of her scientific views. Others believe she was killed because she supported a political enemy of Cyril.

Hypatia

I i

Ice is unusual in that it expands as it forms. Most liquids *contract* (shrink) when they become a solid.

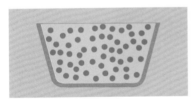

At room temperature, water molecules move about freely.

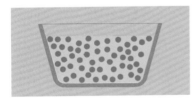

As water gets colder, the molecules slow down and move closer together.

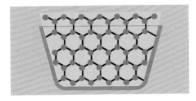

When water freezes, the molecules move apart and form a rigid pattern called a crystal.

Ice

Ice is frozen water. Ice forms on lakes and rivers and on wet streets and sidewalks in cold temperatures. Snow, sleet, frost, hail, and glaciers are kinds of ice. Even in summer, ice may be present in high clouds. Ice is made of *crystals*. A crystal is a solid object made up of *atoms* (tiny bits of matter) that have come together in a well-organized pattern.

Ice is plentiful throughout the universe. It is a main element in comets, which are much like dirty, loosely packed snowballs. Jupiter's moon Europa has a thick layer of surface ice. The planet Mercury and Earth's moon also have water ice within craters that are never fully exposed to sunlight.

Ice has some unusual properties. Most liquids *contract* (shrink) when they become solid. But when water freezes into ice, it *expands* (grows larger). This change in volume can have harmful results. The expansion of freezing water in pipes may cause the pipes to burst. The expansion and contraction of freezing and thawing water in road pavements can cause the pavements to crumble. When water breaks apart roads, rocks, or bricks, the effect is called *weathering*. Solids also usually weigh more than liquids. But ice is lighter than water. Without this property, ice would form on the bottom, rather than on the top, of lakes and rivers.

Pure water freezes into ice at 32 °F (0 °C). Water that contains such other substances as alcohol, salt, or sugar freezes at a lower temperature. For this reason, road crews put salt or other chemicals on icy streets to melt the ice and make roads less slippery.

Ice is slippery because the outermost layer of a crystal is easily changed back into a liquid. Heat from our hands or warm objects quickly causes a slick liquid layer to form on the surface of an ice crystal. Even if the ice touches a cold object, a tiny amount of *friction* (rubbing) will turn the outermost layer into liquid water.

Ice attaches itself strongly to objects on which it forms. This property can be an annoyance when ice sticks to an automobile windshield. It can be a danger when ice sticks to airplane wings.

Not all ice is water ice. The chemicals methane and ammonia are sometimes called ices when they are frozen. The large gas planets—Jupiter, Neptune, Saturn, and Uranus—are thought to contain different types of ice.

Other articles to read include: **Dry ice; Freezing point; Physical change.**

ACTIVITY

Finding out about ice: Under pressure

Have you ever skated on ice? When you skate, all your weight pushes down on the thin blades of the skates. Your weight puts a large amount of pressure on a small, thin area of the ice. This pressure makes the ice melt. As you glide along, the surface instantly melts beneath the blades. You are really skating on a very thin line of water. This water freezes up again as you move on, and the pressure is released.

Here is an experiment you can do to find out about ice under pressure.

What you need:

- a small, strong, plastic bottle
- enough water to fill the bottle
- a freezer
- a saucer
- an ice cube
- a glove
- a spoon

1. Fill the plastic bottle to the top with water. Place it in the freezer overnight. In the morning, the water will be frozen, and the ice will stick out from the top of the bottle. Does water increase in volume when it freezes?

2. Now put the saucer in the freezer overnight. Take the saucer out the next morning. Using a glove to protect your hand, put the ice cube on the cold saucer.

3. Now press down firmly with the spoon on top of the cube. You will see a little water appear under the ice cube. Does pressure make ice melt more quickly?

http://bit.ly/Xsq098

The inch is the smallest whole unit of distance in the inch-pound system of measurement used in the United States. Here, it is divided into 16 parts, measured as fractions of an inch.

Inch

The inch is the smallest unit for measuring distance in the *inch-pound* system. The United States is the only major country that uses the inch-pound system of measurement. An inch is roughly the width of an adult male's thumb.

There are 12 inches in one foot and 36 inches in one yard. Distances smaller than one inch are often measured in fractions, such as one-eighth of an inch or ¾ inch.

Edward II of England set the standard length of an inch in the 1300's. One inch equaled three grains of barley laid end to end. Today, an agency of the United States government keeps exact standards for the inch and other units of measurement.

The metric system is the most widely used system of measurement. This system measures short distances in centimeters or millimeters. One inch equals 2.54 centimeters or 25.4 millimeters.

Other articles to read include: **Metric system; Weights and measures.**

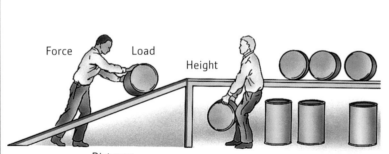

Force   Load   Height

Distance

A kind of inclined plane called a ramp makes it easier to roll a barrel onto a platform than to lift it.

Inclined plane

An inclined plane is a slanted surface, such as a ramp. It is one of the six simple machines.

An inclined plane can be used to raise heavy loads. Pushing a load up an inclined plane takes less force than lifting the load straight up. For example, imagine a box weighing 200 pounds (90 kilograms). An average person could not lift the box 3 feet (90 centimeters) into the back of a truck. But an average person could push the box up a 10-foot- (3-meter-) long ramp and into the truck. The box travels a longer distance with the ramp. But it takes less force to move. As an inclined plane gets longer, the force needed to move a load grows less.

Other articles to read include: **Work.**

Inertia

Inertia *(ihn UR shuh)* is a property of all matter. Because of inertia, an object that is not moving stays still unless an outside force acts on it. Inertia also makes a moving object keep moving at the same speed and in the same direction unless an outside force changes the object's motion. Only an outside force can make a moving object slow down, speed up, turn, or stop.

Another rule of inertia is that the greater an object's *mass* is, the harder it is to move the object or change its motion. Mass is the amount of matter in an object. A car has more mass than a bicycle. For this reason, stopping a car is harder than stopping a bicycle, even if they are moving at the same speed.

The English scientist Sir Isaac Newton first described inertia. He introduced the idea in his first law of motion, which was published in 1687.

Other articles to read include: **Force; Motion.**

Inertia makes an object that is not moving stay still unless an outside force moves it.

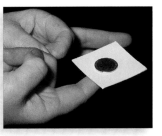  

Balance a coin on a card at the end of your finger.

Now snap the card out from under the coin—without touching the coin.

The card goes flying away, but inertia will keep the coin on your fingertip.

Infinity

Infinity *(ihn FIHN uh tee)* is an amount or distance that is so large you cannot count or measure it.

A collection of objects or ideas is called a *set* in mathematics. A *finite (FY nyt)* set has a definite number of objects. A deck of playing cards, for example, is a set of 52 cards. So the deck is a finite set.

An *infinite* set has an endless number of objects. The numerals you use to count—1, 2, 3, 4, and so on—form an infinite set.

One way to show an infinite set is to list the first few objects and then write three dots. For example, the set of even numbers may be written: {0, 2, 4, 6, ...}. Another way to show infinity is to use the symbol ∞.

Other articles to read include: **Number.**

Infrared rays

An infrared *(IHN fruh REHD)* ray is a form of energy that cannot be seen by human eyes. Infrared rays are also called *heat rays* or *thermal radiation*. A warm object *emits* (gives off) infrared rays because of its heat.

As an object's temperature increases, it emits more infrared rays. If the temperature becomes very high, the object will emit rays of visible light as well as infrared rays.

The British astronomer Sir William Herschel discovered infrared rays in 1800. He split sunlight using a *prism*. A prism is an object that spreads white light into a *spectrum* (rainbow) of colors. Using a thermometer, Herschel measured the temperature at various parts of the spectrum. He noticed that the temperature was high even beyond the red end of the spectrum, where there was no visible light. He realized this heat came from invisible rays.

Other articles to read include: **Electromagnetic spectrum; Heat; Radiation.**

Infrared photography is used to show sources of heat. This infrared photograph shows heat escaping from a house and radiating from its surfaces. Yellow and red areas are the warmest. Green and black areas are the coolest.

Inorganic chemistry

Inorganic *(IHN awr GAN ihk)* chemistry is a branch of chemistry that deals with chemical elements and compounds that are not *organic*. A chemical element is a substance that is made of only one type of atom. A compound is a substance that contains two or more types of atoms. Organic compounds are based on the chemical element carbon. They generally include chains or rings of carbon atoms *bonded* (linked) together. Inorganic chemists study compounds that contain carbon atoms that are not bonded together.

Inorganic chemists also create new compounds and figure out their atomic structures. They study how compounds interact or react with one another. In industry, inorganic chemists work to develop materials that are useful in our lives. These materials include compounds that stop the growth of cancer cells and glass fibers that transmit telephone messages and computer data with light.

Other articles to read include: **Bond, Chemical; Carbon; Chemistry; Compound; Element, Chemical.**

Table salt is a solid *inorganic* compound. Inorganic compounds do not contain the chemical element carbon.

Integer

An integer *(IHN tuh juhr)* is a positive or negative whole number or the number zero. Integers can be odd or even numbers. Such numbers as 1, 8, 31, and 211 are positive integers. Negative integers include –1, –8, –31, and –211. The positive integers are sometimes called the *natural numbers* or *counting numbers.* Zero is sometimes considered a natural number.

The number of integers is infinite. That is, they can never all be counted. But not all numbers are integers. For example, fractions and decimals, such as ½, ¾, 1.75, and 0.999, are not integers.

You can add, subtract, multiply, and divide integers. When you add a positive integer to its like negative integer, the sum is zero. For example, 5 + (–5) = 0.

People use integers every day for street addresses, phone numbers, time, temperature, and calendar dates.

Other articles to read include: **Digit; Number.**

Integers are used to solve many kinds of math problems.

Interference

Interference is a term used in *physics.* Physics is the study of matter and energy. Interference takes place when two waves of the same kind pass through the same space. Interference occurs in all kinds of waves, including sound waves, light waves, radio waves, and water waves. It causes the waves to become stronger in some locations than in others.

Scientists have studied interference to understand the nature of light and the structure of atoms and molecules. Interference also has many other uses. It is used to control the sending and receiving of radio transmissions. The interference of light waves is used to produce three-dimensional images called *holograms.*

Other articles to read include: **Light; Waves.**

A *hologram* (three-dimensional image) of a bicycle was created using the interference of light waves.

Iodine

Iodine
atomic symbol

Iodine is a *chemical element*. A chemical element is a substance made up of only one kind of *atom*. Atoms are tiny bits of matter. Iodine has the chemical symbol *I*.

Usually, iodine is a bluish-black solid. But when it is heated, it becomes a purple *vapor* (gas). Pure iodine is poisonous if swallowed. But tiny amounts of iodine have many different uses. Compounds with iodine are used to make water clean enough to drink and to keep wounds free of germs. They are added to certain kinds of flour to improve the quality of bread. Animals and plants need iodine to grow. Iodine is often added to table salt. The human body makes use of iodine in a tiny organ in the throat called the *thyroid gland*.

Other articles to read include: **Disinfectant; Element, Chemical.**

Iodine is a bluish-black solid at room temperature. It becomes a purple vapor when heated.

Ion

An ion *(EYE uhn)* is an *atom* or molecule *(MOL uh kyool)* that has an electric charge. An atom is a tiny bit of matter. A molecule is a group of atoms bound together. Atoms and molecules become charged if they gain or lose *electrons*. Electrons are subatomic particles with a negative charge.

Each atom has a cloud of electrons that surrounds a small, heavy center called the nucleus *(NOO klee uhs)*. The nucleus contains protons *(PROH tonz)* (particles with positive charges). If the number of electrons equals the number of protons, the atom has no overall charge. Electrons that are removed from an atom may join other atoms or molecules. The addition of the negative electrons causes the atoms or molecules to become negative ions. Atoms or molecules that lose electrons become positive ions because they have more positively charged protons than electrons.

Many common items include ions. For example, table salt has equal numbers of sodium ions, which are positive, and chloride ions, which are negative. Seawater and Earth's air also contain many kinds of ions.

Other articles to read include: **Atom; Electron; Molecule; Proton.**

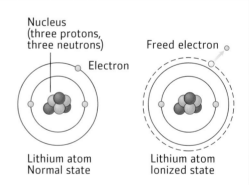

An atom becomes an ion when it gains or loses an electron and so acquires an electric charge. An atom in a normal state (left) has an equal number of positive protons and negative electrons. If it loses an electron (right), it becomes a positively charged ion.

Iron

26	**Fe**	2
	Iron	8
	55.845	14
		2

Iron
atomic symbol

Iron is the most abundant *chemical element* on Earth. A chemical element is a material that has only one kind of atom. Iron is a silvery-white metal in its pure state. But it rarely appears in a pure state in nature. The vast majority of iron on Earth is found in the planet's core.

Iron is one of the most useful metals in the world. It is inexpensive. It can be used by itself or mixed with other metals in alloys. It can be hammered into thin sheets or drawn out into fine wires. Iron is used to make everything from cooking pans to cars. One of the most common products made from iron is steel. Steel is iron that has been *alloyed* (combined with the chemical element carbon and often with other metals).

Most of the iron we use comes from underground rocks or minerals called *ores.* Miners and machines dig out the ore. Then processors crush it. They separate the iron from other materials. Iron-makers melt the iron and then pour it into molds. Inside the molds, the iron hardens into different shapes.

Other articles to read include: **Element, Chemical; Metal.**

Iron and steel are used to construct buildings and make many other things.

Isotope

An isotope *(EYE suh tohp)* is one particular form of a *chemical element.* Chemical elements are materials with only one kind of atom. Different isotopes of a chemical element contain different amounts of matter in the *nuclei* (cores) of their atoms.

The nucleus of an atom is made up of *protons* and often *neutrons.* Protons are positively charged particles. Neutrons have no charge. All of an element's isotopes have the same number of protons. But they have a different number of neutrons. For example, every hydrogen atom has one proton. But different isotopes of hydrogen have zero, one, or two neutrons.

Continued on the next page

Isotope *Continued from the previous page*

Scientists use special symbols to identify isotopes. They often use the name or symbol of the chemical element followed by a number. For example, one isotope of uranium is called uranium 235 or U-235. The *U* is the symbol for uranium. The number is the total number of protons and neutrons in the isotope.

Some chemical elements have many naturally occurring isotopes. Tin, for example, has 10 isotopes. Some chemical elements have only 1 naturally occurring isotope. These elements include fluorine, gold, and phosphorus.

Some isotopes are *radioactive*. Atoms of these isotopes *decay* (break down) over time, giving off energy in the form of waves or tiny particles of matter. Scientists have artificially produced many of these *radioisotopes* in a laboratory. Scientists use radioisotopes to date fossils, examine the human body, and treat disease.

Other articles to read include: **Atom; Element, Chemical; Neutron; Proton.**

James Prescott Joule

Joule, James Prescott

James Prescott Joule *(jool or jowl)* (1818–1889) was a British *physicist*. A physicist is a scientist who studies matter and energy. Joule helped prove the law of conservation of energy. This law says that energy is not created or destroyed. It only changes from one form to another. Joule's experiments showed that energy that seemed to be lost actually changed into heat.

In 1840, Joule discovered that the energy of an electric current was related to the amount of heat made by that current. This relationship is called Joule's law. In 1847, Joule discovered a similar relationship between *mechanical energy* and heat. Mechanical energy is the energy present in a machine or other mechanical system.

A unit of the metric system of measurement is named for Joule. The *joule* is used to measure a unit of work or energy. In the inch-pound system used in the United States, energy is measured in *foot-pounds*. One joule equals about 0.738 foot-pound.

Other articles to read include: **Electricity; Energy; Work.**

Kelvin, Lord

Lord Kelvin (1824-1907) was one of the greatest British scientists of the 1800's. He published 661 scientific papers and patented 70 inventions. Queen Victoria knighted Kelvin in 1866 for his work in helping to lay the first successful telegraph cable across the floor of the Atlantic Ocean.

Kelvin may be most famous for developing a temperature scale that begins at *absolute zero* (−273.15 °C, or −459.67 °F). Absolute zero is the lowest temperature possible. The scale he developed is called the *Kelvin scale.*

Kelvin was born on June 26, 1824, in Belfast, Ireland. His birth name was William Thomson. He studied at the University of Glasgow and Cambridge University. He taught at the University of Glasgow. In 1892, he received the title of Baron Kelvin of Largs. He died on Dec. 17, 1907.

Other articles to read include: **Absolute zero.**

Kepler, Johannes

Johannes *(yoh HAHN uhs)* Kepler (1571–1630) was a German astronomer *(uh STRON uh muhr).* An astronomer is a scientist who studies the planets, stars, and other objects in the sky. Kepler also made important contributions to mathematics. He also showed how our eyes work.

Kepler discovered three laws that explained how the planets move. The English scientist Sir Isaac Newton later used Kepler's three laws to come up with his own laws about *gravitation.* Gravitation is the force of attraction among objects with *mass* (amount of matter). It holds us to the ground and keeps the planets in orbit around the sun.

Johannes Kepler

Kepler was one of the first astronomers to support the ideas of the Polish astronomer Nicolaus Copernicus *(koh PUR nuh kuhs).* Copernicus developed the idea that Earth and other planets orbit the sun. At that time, most astronomers believed that Earth was the center of the universe.

Kepler was born on Dec. 27, 1571, in Weil (near Stuttgart), Germany. He died on Nov. 15, 1630.

Other articles to read include: **Gravitation; Newton, Sir Isaac.**

Kinetic energy

The faster an object moves, the more kinetic energy it has.

Kinetic energy is the energy of motion. Another kind of energy is *potential energy*. Potential energy can be thought of as "stored" energy. All forms of energy are kinetic, potential, or both.

Imagine picking up a ball. By raising it above the ground, you give it potential energy. When you let go of the ball, it falls. The potential energy it gained by being lifted is converted to the kinetic energy of its falling motion. The kinetic energy is in the motion of the falling ball.

An object's kinetic energy depends on two things— speed and *mass*. Mass is the amount of matter in the object. Imagine two objects of the same mass. If one is moving faster than the other, it has more kinetic energy. Now imagine two objects with different masses moving at the same speed. The object with more mass has greater kinetic energy.

Other articles to read include: **Energy; Motion; Potential energy.**

Krypton

36	**Kr**	2 8 18 8
	Krypton	
	83.80	

Krypton
atomic symbol

Krypton *(KRIHP ton)* is a gas without color, odor, or taste. It is a *chemical element.* A chemical element is a material made up of only one kind of atom. Krypton makes up about one-millionth of Earth's *atmosphere* (the gases that surround a planet). Krypton was named for a Greek word that means *the hidden one.* Its chemical symbol is *Kr.*

Krypton is a *noble gas.* The noble gases are a group of chemical elements that do not react readily with other elements. Krypton can be made into a liquid that boils at −152.3 °C and freezes at −156.6 °C.

Many fluorescent lamps contain a mixture of krypton and argon, a chemical element similar to krypton. Krypton also is used to produce a greenish-yellow color in luminous glowing signs, commonly called *neon signs.* The British chemists Sir William Ramsay and Morris W. Travers discovered krypton in 1898.

Other articles to read include: **Element, Chemical; Gas; Noble gas.**

Kinetic energy: A domino effect

An object at rest usually has a kind of stored up energy called *potential energy*. That is, the object has the potential of doing work, such as moving, if its situation changes even slightly. Imagine holding a domino in your hand. That domino has potential energy because of its location several feet above the floor. When you move your hand out from under the domino, the potential energy changes to *kinetic energy*—the energy of motion. Sometimes an object in motion passes its energy to another object. Try this experiment and see how.

What you need:

- dominoes
- tape
- books of different sizes
- cardboard

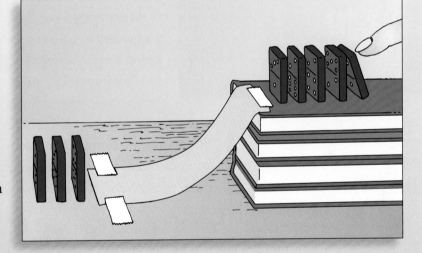

1. Stand three dominoes on end in a line. Inertia keeps each domino upright. But the domino is charged with potential energy that can be released when it falls.

2. Give the first domino a tap. As the domino falls, its potential energy changes to kinetic energy. It hits the second domino and passes along its kinetic energy. This causes the second domino to fall and pass along its kinetic energy.

3. Experiment with the potential and kinetic energy of the dominoes. Make different designs—try using cardboard, books, and tape as shown. Then set off chain reactions with tiny taps.

http://bit.ly/VLrtGl

Laboratory

A laboratory is a place with equipment for people to do scientific experiments. Experiments help scientists investigate many different things and learn from the results. Laboratories also serve as a training ground for scientists and students in many fields. Laboratories may be found in schools, research institutes, industrial organizations, and government departments.

Medical researchers develop new medicines in laboratories. Medical technologists use laboratories to study people's blood and body tissues to figure out why people are sick. Most of these researchers and technologists work in hospitals, public health organizations, and medical research facilities.

Scientists who study Earth can use instruments in a laboratory to figure out what different rocks are made of. Other scientists watch animals and plants as they grow in laboratories. Engineering scientists do laboratory testing of the strengths of materials.

People have discovered many useful products because of work in laboratories. Computers, *superconductors* (materials that conduct electricity freely), various kinds of fabric, and many other things have all been developed in laboratories.

Science students wear protective gear as they conduct an experiment in their high school science laboratory.

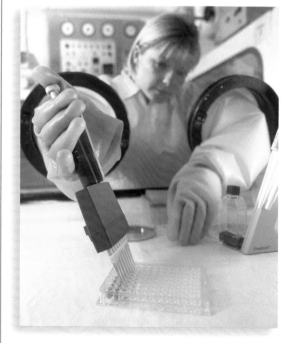

A scientist works with a blood sample in a special laboratory set up with a *glove box.* This safety cabinet protects her from microbes that may be in the sample. It also prevents foreign material from getting into the sample.

Continued on the next page

In 1867, American inventor Thomas Alva Edison created one of the first modern research laboratories. Some scientists and historians regard his development of the research laboratory as his greatest achievement. Edison's lab in West Orange, New Jersey, is now a national historic site.

Other articles to read include: **Chemistry; Physics.**

Lavoisier, Antoine Laurent

Antoine Laurent Lavoisier *(law RAHN lah vwah ZYAY)* (1743-1794) was a French chemist. Many people think of Lavoisier as one of the founders of modern chemistry.

In 1772, Lavoisier began a series of experiments that showed the basic nature of *combustion* (burning). He concluded that combustion results from the rapid chemical combination of a flammable material with a previously unknown gas. He named that gas *oxygen.* Lavoisier also showed that the *mass* (amount of matter) of the materials that remained after combustion equaled the mass of the materials that were burned. This finding became known as the *law of conservation of mass.* It states that mass cannot be created or destroyed; it can only change form. Lavoisier published his findings in what scientists consider the first modern chemistry textbook.

Lavoisier also helped develop a system for naming substances based on their chemical makeup. This system is still in use.

Other articles to read include: **Chemistry; Combustion; Mass.**

Antoine Laurent Lavoisier

82	Pb	2
		8
	Lead	18
	207.2	32
		18
		4

Lead
atomic symbol

Lead

Lead *(lehd)* is a soft, heavy, bluish-gray metal. It is also a *chemical element.*
A chemical element is a material that is made of only one kind of atom.

Lead was one of the first metals that people learned to use. It can be hammered
easily into different shapes. It does not rust and is not harmed by powerful chemicals. For thousands of years, people used lead to make coins, pottery, and weapons. Lead's chemical
symbol is *Pb.* Its name comes from the Latin word *plumbum,* which means *waterworks.* The ancient
Romans used lead to line water pipes.

Today, the main use of lead is in lead-acid storage batteries. Such batteries provide power for the
electrical systems of automobiles, airplanes, and many other vehicles. Lead is also used in insect
poisons, glass, and other products. Lead stops X rays. For this reason, it is used as a shield in rooms
with X-ray machines. Too much contact with lead can be dangerous. Breathing too much lead dust
or fumes, or eating bits of lead, can cause lead poisoning, a serious illness. For this reason, the
amount of lead used in paints and gasoline has been greatly reduced.

People get lead from an *ore,* a mineral or rock containing a valuable element that is mined underground. But much of the lead used today comes from recycling the lead in old batteries.

Other articles to read include: **Element, Chemical; Metal.**

Lead and iron ore

Lepton

The lepton *(LEHP ton)* is a tiny invisible particle. Leptons are
thought to be *elementary particles.* These particles cannot be
divided into smaller particles. Leptons make up one of three major
families of elementary particles. The other families are called
quarks and *bosons.* Together, leptons and quarks are called *fermions.*

Scientists have identified six *flavors* (types) of leptons. These are
electrons, muons, taus, and three kinds of *neutrinos.* Electrons,
muons, and taus all have a negative electric charge. But they have a
different *mass* (amount of matter). A muon has about 207 times the
mass of an electron. A tau has 3,477 times the mass of an electron.

The three flavors of neutrinos are called *electron-neutrinos,*
muon-neutrinos, and *tau-neutrinos.* Neutrinos have no electric
charge. Scientists think a neutrino's mass is extremely small.

Each type of lepton has a related particle called an *antilepton.*
Antileptons have the same mass as leptons, but all their other
properties are opposite.

Other articles to read include: **Boson; Electron; Quark.**

Light

Light is a kind of energy that comes in a range of forms. Human beings can see only a small part of this range. This part is called *visible light*. Some things, including the sun, streetlights, and desk lamps, give off visible light. We see things because visible light bounces off these objects and enters our eyes. This bouncing is called *reflection*. In the eye, light causes chemical and electrical changes that make it possible for us to see.

All forms of light are *electromagnetic energy*. Electromagnetic energy is made of tiny individual packets of energy called *photons*. This energy travels freely through space in patterns of electric and magnetic influence called *electromagnetic waves*. Light waves have *crests* (peaks) and *troughs* (lows), like waves in the sea. The distance between two crests or troughs in a row is called the wave's *wavelength*. In addition to visible light, electromagnetic energy includes radio waves, infrared rays (sometimes called *heat rays*), ultraviolet rays, X rays, and gamma rays. Most scientists consider microwaves to be a form of radio waves.

Different forms of light have different wavelengths. Violet light has the shortest wavelength we can see, and red light has the longest. Ultraviolet rays have wavelengths just a bit too short to be detected by the human eye. Ultraviolet rays cause sunburn and suntan. Infrared rays have wavelengths just a bit too long to be detected by the human eye. Infrared rays cause the warming sensation we feel from sunlight. The shorter the wavelength, the more energy a wave has. Radio waves, which

When sunlight passes through a prism, it separates into all the colors of the rainbow.

A band of colors called the *visible spectrum* forms when white light passes through a prism. The visible spectrum is the light we can see. The prism bends the shortest light waves the most. They appear violet. It bends the longest waves the least. They appear red. All other colors lie in-between. The length of visible light waves is measured in *nanometers*. One nanometer is one-billionth of a meter, or about $1/25{,}000{,}000$ of an inch.

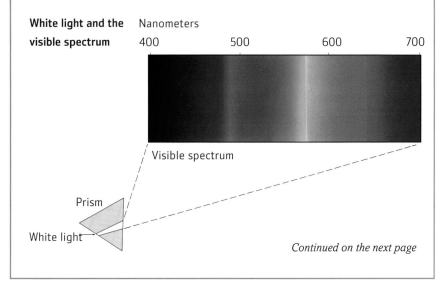

White light and the visible spectrum

Nanometers

400   500   600   700

Visible spectrum

Prism

White light

Continued on the next page

Sunlight is a form of light that comes from nature.

Light that comes from things that people make, such as a flashlight, is known as artificial light.

Light *Continued from the previous page*

have the least energy, are fairly harmless to people. Gamma rays, which have the most energy, can be harmful to people, even in small amounts.

The entire range of wavelengths, from radio waves at the longest end to short gamma rays at the shortest end, is called the *electromagnetic spectrum.* A rainbow is a spectrum of visible light. It can be created using a *prism (PRIHZ uhm).* This device bends and changes the direction of rays of white light passing through it. This bending, called *refraction (rih FRAK shuhn),* produces the colors of the rainbow.

Any object can absorb and *emit* (give off) electromagnetic energy. The spectrum of energy given off by an object depends on its chemical makeup and temperature. By studying the spectrum of an object, such as a star, scientists can determine its makeup and temperature. They search for particular wavelengths of light produced by specific kinds of atoms or molecules. They then compare these wavelengths to the wavelengths given off by the same atoms or molecules on Earth.

Most visible light comes from the action of tiny particles within atoms called *electrons.* Light is produced by electrons that have gained energy from an outside source. They may have absorbed light from another source. They may also have been struck by other particles.

An atom with such an "energized" electron is said to be "excited." Ordinarily, an atom stays excited briefly. It gives off the energy almost as soon as it absorbs it. It can transfer the energy to another atom in a collision. It can also *emit* (give off) a photon of visible light or another kind of electromagnetic energy. The light carries away the extra energy. The energy given off by most artificial lights is provided by electricity.

Calculations by the German-born American scientist Albert Einstein predicted that no object or unit of information can travel faster than light. In empty space, light travels at 186,282 miles (299,792 kilometers) per second.

Other articles to read include: **Color; Electromagnetic spectrum; Light, Speed of; Photon; Rainbow; Wavelength; White light.**

ACTIVITY

Bouncing light

When you stand between a light and a wall, your body blocks the light, and a shadow falls on the wall. This tells you that light travels in a straight line. Hold a mirror and look into it as you turn it slowly from side to side. What do you see? What does that tell you about light? This experiment will give you some clues.

What you need:

- scissors
- a piece of stiff cardboard
- a comb
- tape
- a small mirror
- a table or shelf
- a flashlight
- pen or pencil
- paper

1. Cut a hole in the cardboard, about 1 inch (2.5 centimeters) across. Tape the comb onto the board so the teeth of the comb lie across the hole.

2. In a darkened room or closet, tape the cardboard on a table or shelf, with the teeth of the comb resting on the surface.

3. Stand the mirror on the table or shelf at an angle to the side of the surface.

4. Shine the flashlight through the hole in the cardboard toward the mirror, and look down at the surface. Do you see separate lines of light coming through the teeth of the comb? What direction do the lines take when they hit the mirror? Do they bounce back toward the comb, or go in another direction? Write or draw what you see.

What's going on:

The rays of light bounce off the mirror at the same angle as they struck the mirror, but in the opposite direction.

5. Turn the mirror to several different angles and repeat step 4 each time. What do you notice about the path of the light rays? Write or draw what you see.

http://bit.ly/11VOLNA

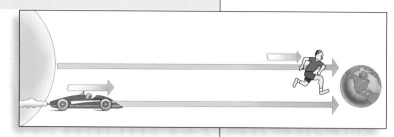

If this boy were a light ray, he could travel from Earth to the sun in eight minutes. A race car traveling at 620 miles (1,000 kilometers) an hour would take 17 years to complete the same journey.

Light, Speed of

The speed of light is how fast light travels. Light seems to travel across the room the instant a lamp is turned on. But the light actually takes some time to move. The speed of light is one of the most important numbers in *physics* (the study of matter and energy).

The speed of light in space is 186,282 miles (299,792 kilometers) per second. At this speed, light could circle Earth's surface over seven times in one second.

It takes eight minutes for light to reach Earth from the sun. When we see the sun, we are really seeing the sun as it was eight minutes earlier. Light reaching our telescopes from a distant galaxy may have been travelling for millions or even billions of years. We see such galaxies as they appeared long ago. They may not even exist anymore.

The speed of light does not depend on the motion of its source. For example, light from a moving flashlight has the same speed as light from a flashlight that is not moving.

Other articles to read include: **Light; Relativity.**

Many farmers spread lime on their fields to reduce potentially harmful levels of acid in the soil. ▼

Lime

Lime is an important chemical used in industry. One type of lime contains only calcium *(KAL see uhm)* and oxygen. Calcium is a common mineral. This kind of lime is sometimes called *quicklime.* Another type of lime is called *slaked lime.* Slaked lime is made by adding water to quicklime.

Slaked lime is used for many purposes. Workers use it to clean copper and other metals. Lime also removes certain minerals from water. Many farmers spread lime on their fields to lower acid levels in the soil. Too much acid in soil interferes with the growth of plants. Lime also strengthens the soil under highways and airport runways. A material called *mortar* is layered between bricks or stones in the walls of buildings. It is composed of lime, sand, and water. Lime is also a key ingredient in plaster and in a kind of cement called *portland cement.*

Other articles to read include: **Calcium.**

Liquid

Liquid is one of the three basic states of matter. The other two states are *gas* and *solid*.

Liquids and gases have no shape of their own. Their *molecules (MAHL uh kyoolz)* can flow past one another. Molecules are tiny particles of matter. Molecules of liquid and gas are not locked in place like the molecules in solids. When liquids and gases are placed into a container, they take the shape of that container. But liquids always have a definite *volume.* Volume is the amount of space something takes up. The molecules in a liquid are in constant contact with the molecules around them.

Gases do not have a definite volume. The molecules in a gas are not in constant contact with the molecules around them. Because a gas has space between its molecules, it can expand or shrink to fill any container into which it flows. Solids always have both a definite shape and a definite volume.

A liquid that is heated beyond a certain temperature changes into gas. Water changes into water *vapor* (gas) if it is heated above its boiling point, 212 °F (100 °C). Liquids that are cooled below a certain temperature change into solids. Water changes into ice when cooled below its freezing point, 32 °F (0 °C). Different liquids have different boiling and freezing points.

Other articles to read include: **Boiling point; Fluid; Freezing point; Surface tension.**

Liquid flows to fit any container.

Molecules in a liquid (below center) are more orderly than those in a gas (below far left). But they are not as orderly than those in a solid (below right). Molecules become more orderly when they lose a certain amount of their *thermal energy* (heat energy), a form of *kinetic energy* (energy of motion). The temperature at which this occurs varies from one substance to another. The molecules in a liquid have less thermal energy than those in a gas. But they have more than those in a solid.

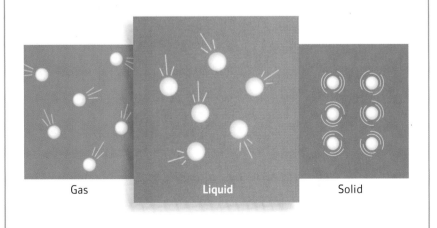

Gas   Liquid   Solid

Mm

Litmus

Litmus *(LIHT muhs)* is a substance used in chemistry to show if something is an *acid* or a *base*. Acids are certain chemicals that tend to have a sour taste. Bases tend to have a bitter taste and slippery feel. Both acids and bases can irritate the skin.

Litmus can be prepared in an acidic form, which is red, and in a basic form, which is blue. Litmus may be added to absorbent paper to make *litmus paper*. The paper is blue or red, depending on which form of litmus is present. A liquid that has a lot of acid will turn blue litmus paper red. But the liquid will not affect red litmus paper. A basic solution will turn red litmus paper blue. But the solution will not affect blue litmus paper. A solution that is *neutral* (neither an acid nor a base) will not change the color of either type of litmus paper.

Scientists obtain litmus from *lichens (LY kuhns)*. Lichens are living things without roots, stems, leaves, or flowers that grow on rocks and trees. Litmus is also used as a stain to make things easier to see under a microscope.

Other articles to read include: **Acid; Base; pH.**

Litmus paper is used to test the strength of acids and bases.

Magnesium

12	**Mg**	2 8 2
Magnesium		
24.3050		

Magnesium atomic symbol

Magnesium *(mag NEE zhee uhm)* is a silver-white metal. It is the lightest metal that is still strong enough to be used in construction. Magnesium and its *alloys* (mixtures) are used for making airplanes, automobiles, and many other products.

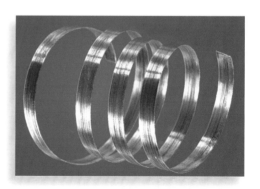

Magnesium is a silver-white metal that is light and strong.

Magnesium is used for many other purposes. For example, pieces of magnesium are placed next to buried steel pipelines and water tanks. The magnesium prevents oxygen and other chemicals in the soil from wearing away the steel. Strips of magnesium are also used to protect the hulls of ships.

Magnesium is a fairly common metal on Earth. But pure magnesium is not found in nature. It is part of various minerals and other substances. Magnesium is often obtained from seawater.

Other articles to read include: **Element, Chemical; Metal.**

Magnetic field

A magnetic field is the area around a magnet where the force of its magnetism can be felt. Magnetism is a force that causes magnets and certain other objects to attract or *repel* (push away) each other.

A magnetic field is invisible. But you can picture the magnetic field of a bar magnet. Place a sheet of paper over the magnet and sprinkle iron shavings on the paper. The shavings will bunch together near the ends of the magnet and form a pattern around it. This pattern will follow the magnet's magnetic field.

A magnetic field can also be thought of as a set of imaginary lines called *magnetic field lines*. We think of these lines going out from the north pole of a magnet, looping around, and returning to the magnet at its south pole. The magnetic field is strongest at the poles, where the lines lie closest to one another.

Earth, the sun, and many other objects in space have a magnetic field. A flow of electricity also creates a magnetic field.

Other articles to read include: **Electricity; Magnetic pole; Magnetism.**

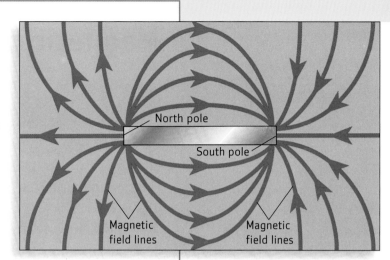

The magnetic field of a bar magnet is strongest near the magnet's poles, where the lines lie closest to each other.

Earth's magnetic poles are not located in the same place as its geographic, or *true,* poles. The geographic poles are the ends of Earth's *axis* (an imaginary line running through Earth's center). The magnetic poles are created by currents in Earth's core.

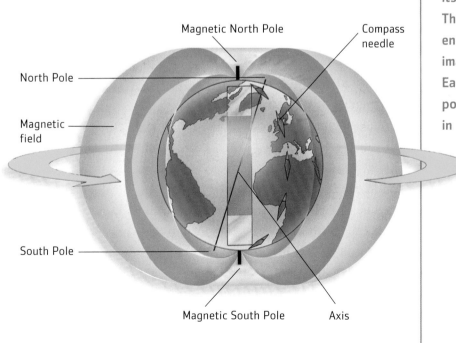

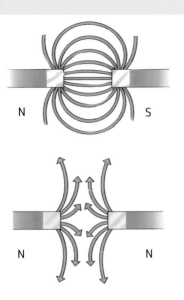

The shape of a magnetic field depends on which poles of a magnet are facing each other. The lines show how the magnets either attract or *repel* (push away) each other.

Magnetic pole

Magnetic poles are the "ends" of a magnet. An ordinary bar magnet has two poles, a *north pole* and a *south pole.*

If a bar magnet is hung from a string, the end that points north is the north pole. The end that points south is the south pole. Earth acts like a giant magnet. A hanging magnet will point north and south because of its attraction to Earth's north and south magnetic poles.

Opposite poles attract each other. For example, the north pole of one magnet will attract the south pole of another magnet. Like poles *repel* (push away) each other. The north pole of one magnet will repel the north pole of another.

Other articles to read include: **Magnetic field; Magnetism.**

Magnetism

Magnetism is an invisible force of nature. Magnetic forces cause certain materials to be *attracted to* (pulled toward) one another. They cause other materials to be *repelled* (pushed away) from one another. Magnets such as a bar magnet have two *poles* (ends). The two poles are called the *north pole* and the *south pole*. If you bring the north pole of one magnet near the south pole of another magnet, a magnetic force will pull them together. If you bring the south pole of a magnet near the south pole of another magnet, a magnetic force will push them apart.

Magnetism attracts these metal paper clips to the poles of this magnet.

Earth is a giant magnet. The point in the Arctic region that we call the North Pole is actually the south pole of Earth's magnetic field. The point in Antarctica that we call the South Pole is actually the north pole of Earth's magnetic field. If you hang a

Continued on the next page

bar magnet by a string tied around its middle, the magnet's north pole will point to the south pole of Earth's magnetic field, in the Arctic.

The magnetic field of Earth is unusual in one interesting way. Unlike other magnets, the magnetic field of Earth switches poles or "flips." The north magnetic pole becomes the south magnetic pole, and the south magnetic pole becomes the north magnetic pole. On average, this event happens about every 2 million years, but it does not happen on a regular basis. Scientists do not know why a flip occurs or exactly when it will happen next.

Some rocks, minerals, and meteorites are natural magnets. Magnetic forces may also be produced by ordinary electric current flowing through a coil of wire, called an *electromagnet*. Electric current is a flow of *electrons* (negatively charged particles) through a material.

Other articles to read include: **Electricity; Magnetic field; Magnetic pole.**

Manganese

25	**Mn**	2 8 13 2
Manganese 54.938049		

Manganese atomic symbol

Manganese *(MANG guh neez)* is a brittle, silvery, metallic *chemical element*. A chemical element is a material that is made up of only one kind of atom. Manganese has many industrial uses, particularly in making steel.

Manganese is plentiful in Earth's crust. But in nature, manganese is found only in *compounds* (mixtures) with other chemical elements. Manganese can also be found in some asteroids. It was first *isolated* (separated) from a mixture by the Swedish chemist Johan Gottlieb Gahn in 1774.

The most widely used compound of manganese is manganese dioxide. It is used in dry cell batteries and paints and dyes. It also gives bricks a red to brown color. Glassmakers have used manganese dioxide for centuries. Manganese sulfate is used in the production of paint and varnish driers. It is also a key substance in certain kinds of fertilizer.

Other articles to read include: **Element, Chemical; Metal.**

Manganese is found on the ocean floor, especially in the Pacific. This manganese is in the form of round masses called *nodules.*

Manhattan Project

The Manhattan Project was a top-secret United States government project created in 1942 to produce the first atomic bomb. In August 1939, the German-born physicist Albert Einstein helped to alert U.S. President Franklin D. Roosevelt to the potential military uses of *nuclear fission*. In fission, the *nuclei* (cores) of atoms are split to release energy. United States scientists feared that Nazi Germany might become the first country to develop an atomic bomb. Nazi Germany became a U.S. enemy in World War II (1939-1945).

Scientists at the University of Chicago under the direction of Italian-born physicist Enrico Fermi worked on the project. They built an atomic reactor beneath the stands of the university's athletic field. On Dec. 2, 1942, this reactor produced the first *chain reaction*. In this process, the splitting of one nucleus leads to the splitting of another, and so on.

Manhattan Project scientists successfully exploded the first atomic bomb on July 16, 1945, near Alamogordo, New Mexico. The American physicist J. Robert Oppenheimer directed the design and building of the bomb.

Other articles to read include: **Chain reaction; Fission; Nuclear energy.**

J. Robert Oppenheimer (left), director of the Los Alamos Atomic Bomb Project, stands near the melted remains of the tower in New Mexico where the first atomic bomb was tested.

Mass

Mass is often described as the amount of *matter* in an object. Nearly all of the objects and substances we see around us are made of matter. Scientists describe mass as a measure of *inertia (ihn UR shuh)*, a property of all matter. Because of inertia, an object that is motionless will remain motionless unless an outside force moves it. For example, a ball lying on the ground will not move on its own. But it will move if a person kicks it. Also because of inertia, a moving object keeps moving at the same speed and in the same direction unless some force acts on it.

Continued on the next page

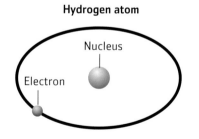

Hydrogen atom

Nucleus

Electron

Atomic mass is the quantity of matter in an atom. The smallest and lightest atom is the hydrogen atom. Its mass is very small.

In everyday use, mass can be substituted for *weight* and vice versa. For example, when you weigh yourself, you are finding out the amount of matter that makes up your body. Mass is often measured in kilograms and pounds. In science and technology, weight refers to the gravitational force on an object.

Other articles to read include: **Inertia; Matter; Motion.**

The sun has 99.8 percent of all the mass in the solar system.

Mass spectrometry

Mass spectrometry *(spehk TROM uh tree)* is a method scientists use to separate and analyze the *atoms* and *molecules* in a substance. Atoms and molecules are tiny bits of matter.

Mass spectrometry has many important uses in *chemistry* and biology. Chemistry is the scientific study of the substances that make up our world and the rest of the universe. Chemists use mass spectrometry to analyze the makeup and structure of molecules. Environmental scientists use mass spectrometry to detect and measure pollutants in water and soil. Biologists and medical researchers use mass spectrometry to analyze proteins and other substances found in bacteria, viruses, and the human body.

In mass spectrometry, scientists convert the atoms and molecules of a substance into electrically charged particles called *ions*. A device called a *mass spectrometer* then separates the various ions according to their *mass* (amount of matter) and electric charge. This information can reveal which atoms and molecules are in the substance and in what combination.

Other articles to read include: **Atom; Ion; Molecule.**

Scientists analyze substances with a mass spectrometer. The device reveals which atoms and molecules are in a substance and in what amounts.

Mathematics

Arithmetic is one *branch* (area) of mathematics. This student is writing an arithmetic problem on the chalkboard.

Mathematics is the study of numbers, measurements, and the relationships among objects or ideas. It is one of the most useful kinds of knowledge. To solve problems in mathematics, people must think carefully and clearly. The word *mathematics* comes from a Greek word meaning *inclined to learn.*

People use mathematics in many ways every day. People tell time and count money with math. Scientists use mathematics to do experiments and to study the results. Engineers use mathematics to design bridges and vehicles. People in business use math to keep records of sales. Some people study mathematics because they enjoy it, just as many people solve puzzles for fun. Mathematical ideas have helped pave the way for many scientific and technological advances. They include engine-powered machines, computers, and space travel.

There are many *branches* (different areas) of mathematics. Different branches are used for different kinds of problems. But the different branches of mathematics use many of the same facts, ideas, and steps to solve problems.

Arithmetic is the study of numbers. People use arithmetic to work with whole numbers, such fractions as ½ and ¼, and such decimals as 0.10 and 0.25. People using arithmetic add, subtract, multiply, and divide numbers. The skills used in arithmetic are used in many other kinds of mathematics.

Algebra is a branch of mathematics that uses numbers as well as letters, such as *x* and *y*, to stand for unknown numbers.

Algebra (AL juh bruh) also works with numbers. But algebra problems also may contain unknown *quantities* (amounts). Letters such as *x* and *y* are used to stand for the unknown quantities. Algebra also uses numbers that are less than zero, called negative numbers.

Geometry (jee AHM uh tree) studies shapes. *Plane geometry* uses squares, circles, triangles, and other flat shapes. *Solid geometry* uses shapes that take up space, including cubes, spheres, and cones.

Other kinds of mathematics include *calculus (KAL kyuh luhs)* and *trigonometry (TRIGH uh NOM uh tree)*. Calculus is the study of changing quantities, such as the changing slope of a curved line. Trigonometry involves

Continued on the next page

People use mathematics to
count money.

We use mathematics to tell time
and make schedules.

measuring angles and distances. Mathematics also includes the study of *probability*. Probability is
figuring out whether something is likely to happen. *Set theory* is a basic branch of mathematics.
It studies the nature and logical relations of *sets* (a collection of numbers, objects, or even ideas).

Early people probably counted with their fingers. Sometimes they used pebbles, made knots
in a cord, or made marks to count things.

By about 5,000 years ago, people in ancient Egypt used *hieroglyphics* (picture writing) to
represent numbers. The Egyptians used mathematics to measure fields and build pyramids.
The ancient Babylonians made important contributions to mathematics. They developed a
counting system based on the number 60. We use this system to count out seconds and minutes.

The ancient Greeks were the first people to study mathematics as a separate subject. They
worked out ways to prove certain ideas were true. The Chinese developed a number system that
used fractions, zero, and numbers less than zero. The Maya of Central America and the Hindus

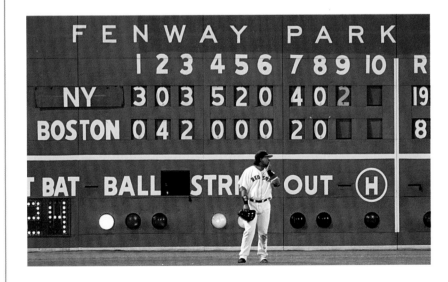

Continued on the next page

Mathematics is used to
keep score in baseball and
other sports.

Mathematics *Continued from the previous page*

of India also developed number systems that used the number zero.

Arabs learned to use zero from the Hindus. The way we write numbers today came from the Arabs. For this reason, it is called the *Arabic numeral system*. The Arabs also saved many ancient Greek works about mathematics. Europeans learned about such mathematical ideas from the Arabs.

During the 1600's, the English scientist Isaac Newton and the German scientist Gottfried Wilhelm Leibniz developed calculus around the same time. Types of mathematics developed in the late 1900's include *fractal geometry* and *chaos theory.*

Other articles to read include: **Addition; Calculus; Division; Geometry; Multiplication; Number; Subtraction.**

The molecules in a solid vibrate in place.

The molecules in a liquid move around freely but still touch each other.

The molecules in a gas move quickly and rarely touch each other.

Matter

Matter is anything that has mass and takes up space. All objects are made of matter. Matter can form huge objects, such as groupings of galaxies so vast that light rays take hundreds of millions of years to cross them. Matter can also form particles so small that scientists describe them as pointlike.

The matter around us takes three common *states* (forms). They are *solid, liquid,* and *gas.* A solid has its own shape and size. A liquid has a particular *volume.* Volume is the amount of space taken up by something. But a liquid does not have its own particular shape. Rather, it takes the shape of the container into which it is poured. A gas does not have a definite volume or its own particular shape. It will *expand* (grow larger) or *contract* (shrink) to fill its container. Matter can change from one form to another. Matter can also be changed into energy, and energy can be changed into matter.

All forms of matter have a property called *inertia.* Because of inertia, an object that is not moving stays still unless an outside force acts on it. Inertia also makes a moving object keep moving at the same speed and in the same direction unless an outside force acts on the object.

Continued on the next page

The force required to change an object's motion depends on the *mass* of the object. Mass is the amount of matter in an object. The greater an object's mass, the harder it is to put the object into motion or to change its direction or speed.

All matter is made up of tiny bits called *atoms*. A material that has only one kind of atom is called a *chemical element*. The atoms of one chemical element are different from the atoms of all other elements. Hydrogen and oxygen are examples of chemical elements. Chemical elements can join together to form *compounds*. Water is a compound of hydrogen and oxygen. Many kinds of matter are compounds.

Other articles to read include: **Gas; Inertia; Liquid; Motion; Solid.**

All matter is made of units called *atoms.* A helium atom (below left) consists of a *nucleus* (core) made of two protons and two neutrons orbited by two electrons. Atoms join together to form *molecules.* A water molecule (below) consists of two hydrogen atoms and one oxygen atom.

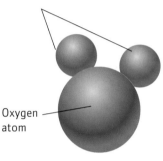

Hydrogen atoms

Oxygen atom

Water molecule

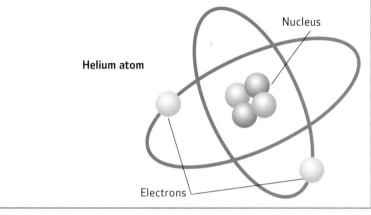

Helium atom

Nucleus

Electrons

Maxwell, James Clerk

James Clerk Maxwell (1831–1879) was a scientist from Scotland. He was one of the greatest mathematicians and *physicists (FIHZ uh sihsts)* of the 1800's. A physicist studies matter and energy.

Maxwell is best known for his research on electricity and magnetism. He is also known for an idea that explains how gas *molecules (MOL uh kyoolz)* behave. Molecules are basic units that make up chemicals. Maxwell also studied color vision, *elasticity (ih LAS TIHS uh tee),* and Saturn's rings. Elasticity is the ability of an object to return to its shape after it has been stretched. In addition, Maxwell studied *thermodynamics (THUR moh dy NAM ihks).* This branch of physics deals with forms of energy, including heat and motion.

Other articles to read include: **Gas; Molecule.**

James Clerk Maxwell

Mechanics

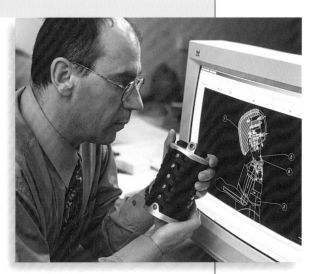

An engineer uses mechanics to design a crash-test dummy that will help make cars safer for people. He is holding the dummy's neck in his hand as he checks its movement against an image of the dummy on a computer.

Mechanics *(muh KAN ihks)* is a science that studies how different forces can change solids, liquids, and gases. Engineers use mechanics to study such machine parts as gears and such structures as support columns in buildings. They use mechanics to design things as small as computer parts and as large as dams. Astronomers use mechanics to study how stars and planets move. Physicists use mechanics to study the movement of *atoms.* Atoms are tiny bits of matter.

There are two main areas of mechanics. *Statics (STAT ihks)* is the study of objects that are at rest or moving at a steady speed and in a steady direction. *Dynamics (dy NAM ihks)* is the study of objects that change their speed or direction, or both, when forces act upon them.

Other articles to read include: **Force; Motion; Quantum mechanics.**

Melting point

The melting point of a pure substance is the same as the temperature at which that substance freezes. The melting point—and freezing point—of pure ice is 32 °F (0 °C).

The melting point is the temperature at which a substance changes from a solid to a liquid. Different substances have different melting points. The metal *tungsten (TUHNG stuhn)* has the high melting point of 6710 °F (3410 °C). Solid hydrogen melts at the low temperature of −434.2 °F (−259 °C).

The melting point of a material partly depends on whether the material is a *pure substance* or a *mixture.* A pure substance may be a pure *chemical element.* A chemical element, such as iron, is a material that has only one kind of atom. A pure substance may also be a simple *compound,* such as a pure alcohol. Compounds are substances with more than one kind of atom that are chemically combined. A mixture consists of two or more substances that are not chemically combined.

Continued on the next page

A pure substance melts at a particular temperature. Mixtures melt at different temperatures depending on the amount and type of each substance in the mixture. Steel, a simple mixture, melts over several temperatures. The melting point depends on how much of each substance, such as iron or nickel, is in the mixture.

Other articles to read include: **Heat; Liquid; Solid; Temperature.**

80	**Hg**	2
		8
	Mercury	18
		32
	200.59	18
		2

Mercury atomic symbol

Mercury

Mercury is a silver-colored metal. It is also a *chemical element.* A chemical element is a material made up of only one kind of *atom.* An atom is a tiny bit of matter.

Mercury is an unusual metal because it is a liquid at room temperature. People sometimes call mercury *quicksilver* because it is shiny like silver and it flows easily and rapidly. Mercury has many useful properties. For example, it *expands* (grows) and *contracts* (shrinks) evenly when heated or cooled. It also remains liquid over a wide range of temperatures and does not stick to glass. Mercury conducts electric current. It is used in electric switches and relays that operate silently and efficiently. Mercury *vapor* (gas) is used in certain kinds of lamps, called *fluorescent (FLOO uh REHS uhnt) lamps.*

Mercury acts as a poison in the body. But liquid mercury is not easily absorbed through the skin or digestive system. Mercury mixed with certain other chemicals can more easily enter the body, however.

Mercury was once widely used in industry. Today, many countries limit the industrial use of mercury compounds and have banned the dumping of wastes that contain mercury. However, mercury still remains in the environment.

Other articles to read include: **Element, Chemical; Metal.**

Mercury is a silver-colored liquid at room temperature (right in photograph above). Most mercury comes from the ore cinnabar *(SIHN uh bahr),* (upper left in photograph).

Metal

Iron is one of the world's cheapest and most useful metals. Most of the world's iron ore comes from open-pit mines.

Metals are the most plentiful material found throughout Earth. They include copper, iron, lead, silver, tin, and many other *chemical elements* that share certain characteristics. A chemical element is a material made up of only one kind of atom. Nearly 80 percent of all known chemical elements are metals.

Metals are important in building and making many products. Factories use metals and *alloys* (mixtures of metals) to make cars, tools, utensils, jewelry, and a wide variety of machines. Metals are also used in making medicines, batteries, and many other products.

Metals are different from other materials in a number of important ways. Metals often are shiny. They *reflect* (send back) light well. Metals are also good *conductors* (carriers) of electricity and heat. Most metals can be hammered into thin sheets or stretched out into wires.

Metals often combine with other chemical elements to form *chemical compounds.* The *properties* (characteristics) of these compounds differ from the properties of the individual elements. For example, table salt (sodium chloride) is a colorless, brittle solid that forms when sodium, a soft, silvery metal, is combined with chlorine gas. Rust forms when iron or steel reacts with the oxygen in air.

Geologists think Earth's core consists mainly of pure *molten* (melted) iron. Aluminum, another metal, makes up about 8 percent of the crust. Nearly all of the metal in Earth's crust, however, occurs in compounds.

The universe contains relatively small amounts of metal. The most abundant metals are, in order, magnesium, iron, aluminum, calcium, and sodium. The nonmetallic chemical elements hydrogen and helium make up more than 99.9 percent of all visible matter. Many scientists believe that the planet Jupiter is composed mostly of hot, metallic liquid hydrogen. On Earth, hydrogen occurs as a gas. But under high pressure, hydrogen can behave like a metal.

Ancient people used copper, gold, and silver to make ornaments, plates, jewelry, and utensils. The production of bronze, an alloy of copper and tin,

Workers make molded metal products called *castings* in a *foundry* (plant). Products made in foundries range from machine parts to toy soldiers.

Continued on the next page

led to the Bronze Age. At that time, bronze replaced stone as the chief tool-making material. In around 1,000 B.C., iron became the chief tool-making material. This period is known as the Iron Age. Iron and *steel* are still widely used in construction and manufactured products today. Steel is made of mostly iron mixed with other metals and nonmetals. Aluminum became an important metal in the 1800's. In the 1900's, engineers developed electric generators and weapons that used uranium and other radioactive metals as fuel. *Radioactive* elements give off energy and small particles.

Metals are used to make automobiles as well as the machines used to build the automobiles.

Other articles to read include: **Alloy; Aluminum; Copper; Iron; Lead; Rust; Silver; Zinc.**

Meter

The meter is the main unit of length in the *metric system*. The metric system is used in most countries to measure distance, weight, and volume. In the United States and a few other countries, people often use the *inch-pound system* instead.

The symbol for the meter is *m*. A meter equals 39.370 inches. When the metric system was adopted in 1795, a meter was defined as the distance from the North Pole to the equator divided by 10 million. In 1960, the meter was defined in terms of the wavelength of light. Scientists now define the meter as the distance traveled by light in a vacuum for $\frac{1}{299,792,458}$ of a second.

People use the meter to measure such dimensions as the length of an athletic field or the height of a tree. To measure longer distances, such as the distance between cities, people use the *kilometer (kuh LOM uh tuhr)*. One kilometer equals 1,000 meters, or 0.62 mile. The *centimeter (SEHN tuh MEE tuhr)* is used to measure shorter distances, such as the length of a pencil or a person's height. One hundred centimeters equal one meter. One inch equals 2.54 centimeters.

Other articles to read include: **Metric system; Weights and measures.**

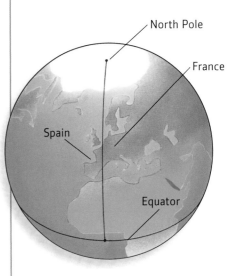

The meter was first used in 1795. A group of French scientists calculated the distance from the North Pole to the equator, passing through Dunkerque, France, and Barcelona, Spain. They decided to divide this distance into 10 million equal lengths and called each length a meter.

Methane

A methane breather pipe allows the gas from a landfill site to be collected. The gas may also be burned off.

Methane *(MEHTH ayn)* is a colorless, odorless (scent-free) gas. It forms when plants *decay* (rot) where there is very little air. It can sometimes be found in areas around swamps. For this reason, it is often called *swamp gas.* Methane is also the chief substance in *fire damp,* a gas that causes serious explosions in mines.

Methane is a major part of natural gas. Energy companies collect natural gas. People use natural gas to heat homes, provide electric energy, and cook food. The chemical industry uses methane as a starting material for many other chemicals.

Methane is extremely *flammable* (easily set on fire) and highly dangerous. Areas with rotting material can produce much methane. One such area is a landfill filled with buried garbage. People who run landfills must be careful to avoid a dangerous buildup of methane.

Other articles to read include: **Gas.**

Metric system

The metric system is a group of units for measuring length, area, volume, weight, and temperature. The United States is the only major country in the world that does not use the metric system for most commercial and everyday measurements. Instead, the United States uses the inch-pound system. However, scientists and many engineers in the United States use the metric system.

In the metric system, the meter is the main unit for measuring length and area. One meter equals 39.370 inches. Millimeters and centimeters are used to measure lengths smaller than one meter. Kilometers measure longer distances. The metric system uses liters and milliliters to measure volume. One liter equals

Metric conversion table

What you know	Multiply by	To find
Length and distance		
inches (in)	2.54	centimeters
feet (ft)	30.48	centimeters
yards	0.9144	meters
miles (mi)	1.609	kilometers
Volume (liquid)		
fluid ounces	29.57	milliliters
pints (U.S.)	0.4732	liters
Weight and mass		
ounces (oz)	28.350	grams
pounds (lb)	0.4536	kilograms
Temperatures		
°Fahrenheit (°F)	5/9 (after subtracting 32)	°Celsius (°C)

Common measurements in the inch-pound system can be converted into metric units. Look up the unit in the left-hand column and multiply the measurement by the number in the center column. Your answer will be approximately the number of metric units shown in the right-hand column.

Continued on the next page

.057 quarts. Weight is measured in grams and kilograms. One kilogram equals 2.205 pounds. Temperature is measured in degrees *Celsius (SEHL see uhs)*. A temperature of 0 degrees Celsius equals 32 degrees *Fahrenheit (FAR uhn hyt)*.

A group of French scientists created the metric system in the 1790's. Since then, the system has been changed many times. The name of the system as it is used today is the *Système International d'Unités*, which means *International System of Units*. It is usually known simply as *SI*.

Other articles to read include: **Celsius scale; Meter; Temperature; Weights and measures.**

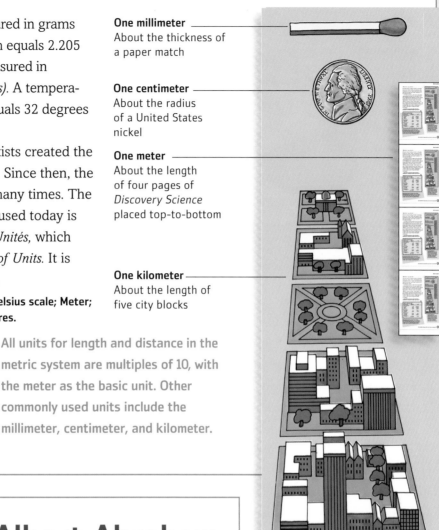

One millimeter
About the thickness of a paper match

One centimeter
About the radius of a United States nickel

One meter
About the length of four pages of *Discovery Science* placed top-to-bottom

One kilometer
About the length of five city blocks

All units for length and distance in the metric system are multiples of 10, with the meter as the basic unit. Other commonly used units include the millimeter, centimeter, and kilometer.

Michelson, Albert Abraham

Albert Abraham Michelson *(MY kuhl suhn)* (1852–1951) was the first United States citizen to win a Nobel *(noh BEHL)* Prize in the sciences. Nobel Prizes are given each year to people who have done something important and new in such areas as chemistry or medicine. Michelson won in 1907 for his work in *physics (FIHZ ihks)*, the science of matter and energy.

Michelson invented an instrument that helped disprove an idea called the *ether theory*. Scientists had thought that light traveled through a space in an invisible substance called *ether (EE thuhr)*. Michelson's instrument helped prove that light does not need ether to travel.

Michelson was born in Poland. His family moved to the United States when he was 2 years old.

Other articles to read include: **Light.**

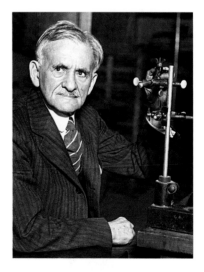

Albert Abraham Michelson

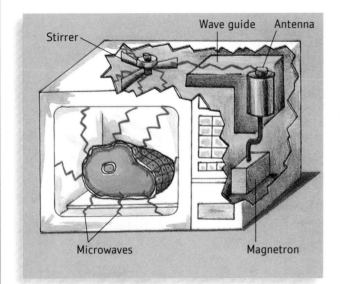

Stirrer

Wave guide   Antenna

Microwaves   Magnetron

Microwave

A microwave is a short radio wave. Microwaves are invisible. They range in length from 1/25 inch to 12 inches (1 millimeter to 300 millimeters). Like visible light (light waves people can see), microwaves can be reflected. They can also be combined to make them stronger. Unlike visible light waves, microwaves can pass through rain, smoke, and fog.

Microwaves are good for communication over long distances and into space. Microwaves can pass through the *ionosphere (eye ON uh sfihr),* a part of Earth's atmosphere. The ionosphere reflects most other radio waves back to Earth. Many satellite communications systems use microwaves. Television programs can be sent all over the world using microwaves. The waves are sent to satellites in space and then relayed back to a distant part of Earth.

Microwaves were first widely used during World War II (1939–1945) in *radar.* Radar is a device for detecting objects. Microwaves cook food in microwave ovens. The waves are also used in cell phones and telephones.

Other articles to read include: **Electromagnetic spectrum; Radio wave.**

The energy used to cook food in a microwave oven consists of high-frequency radio waves. Microwaves cook fast because they produce heat directly inside the food. Microwaves are generated by an electric current and magnetic fields in a *magnetron,* an electronic device. A tiny *antenna* sends the microwaves to a *wave guide,* a hollow metal tube. Before entering the oven, the microwaves pass through the rapidly turning metal blades of a *stirrer,* which spreads the microwaves evenly throughout the oven.

Microwaves

Water molecules

Other molecules

The microwaves used in microwave ovens go about 1 1/2 inches (4 centimeters) into food. They create heat energy by causing water molecules to vibrate. The water molecules strike other kinds of molecules, causing them to vibrate. This heat is transferred deep into the food.

Mirage

A mirage *(muh RAHZH)* is a vision of objects that are not what they seem to be. A mirage is a type of *optical illusion*—that is, a trick of the eyes. For example, a mirage may appear when a person is driving. The driver may see what seems to be a pool of water lying on a hot, paved road ahead. But when the driver reaches that spot, the water has disappeared. Mirages may include faraway objects that appear to be closer than they really are. Other objects, such as a mountain or a ship, may seem to float in the sky.

A vision known as a *Fata Morgana* is a beautiful type of mirage. A Fata Morgana occurs when a layer of hot air traps rays of light coming from distant objects. Objects such as rocks or chunks of ice look like the towers of a fairy-tale castle.

Other articles to read include: **Light; Refraction.**

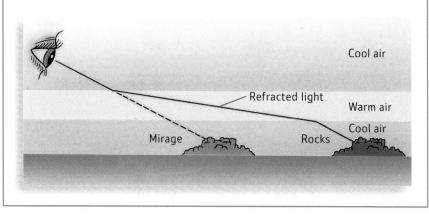

A mirage can be caused by light rays *refracting* (bending) when they pass through substances of different densities. In this drawing, light rays from distant rocks refract as they pass from the cool, heavy air near the surface to the warm, light air above. This produces a mirage that makes the rocks appear closer than they are.

Molecule

A molecule *(MOL uh kyool)* is one of the basic units of *matter.* All objects are made of matter. Molecules are so small that one drop of water contains billions of water molecules.

Molecules are made up of even tinier units called *atoms.* There are over 100 kinds of atoms. They include gold, hydrogen, iron, and oxygen atoms. When atoms join together in a certain way, they form molecules. A molecule's size and shape depend on the size and number of its atoms. The atoms in molecules are linked

Continued on the next page

Water molecule

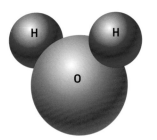

A molecule of water forms when two atoms of hydrogen and one of oxygen join together in sharing their electrons.

Molecule *Continued from the previous page*

together through strong forces of attraction called *chemical bonds*.

A molecule is the smallest unit into which a substance can be divided and still be that substance. For example, a molecule of water is made up of two hydrogen atoms bonded to one oxygen atom. A molecule of water is the smallest amount of water there can be. If you divided a molecule of water, you would no longer have water. Instead, you would have two hydrogen atoms and one oxygen atom.

Other articles to read include: **Atom; Bond, Chemical.**

A carbon dioxide molecule (right) has two oxygen atoms and a carbon atom. An ammonia molecule (right below) has three hydrogen atoms and a nitrogen atom. A butane molecule (far right) is a chain of carbon atoms bonded to hydrogen atoms.

Carbon dioxide molecule

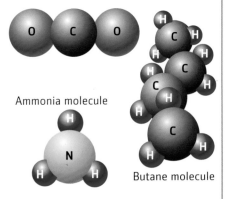

Ammonia molecule

Butane molecule

42	**Mo**	2
		8
Molybdenum		18
95.94		13
		1

Molybdenum atomic symbol

Molybdenum

Molybdenum *(muh LIHB duh nuhm)* is a hard, silvery-white metal. It is also a *chemical element*. A chemical element is material made up of only one kind of atom. Molybdenum melts at a higher temperature than most other metals, about 2623 °C. Manufacturers add molybdenum to steel and to nickel to make strong, heat-resistant *alloys* (combinations of two or more metals). Molybdenum is widely used in aircraft and missile parts.

Molybdenum's name comes from the Greek word *molybdos,* meaning *lead.* People once mistook the metal for lead. In 1778, the Swedish chemist Carl Wilhelm Scheele determined that molybdenum was a separate chemical element. Chile, China, and the United States produce most of the world's molybdenum.

Other articles to read include: **Element, Chemical; Metal.**

Momentum

Momentum *(moh MEHN tuhm)* is a measure of an object's motion. The momentum of an object depends on its *mass* and its *velocity*. Mass is the amount of matter in an object. It is usually measured in kilograms, but it can also be measured in pounds. Velocity is speed in a particular direction. It is sometimes measured in feet per second or miles per hour. In the metric system, it is measured in meters per second or kilometers per hour. To find an object's momentum, you multiply its mass by its velocity.

Consider, for example, an automobile with a mass of 1,000 kilograms (2,200 pounds). Suppose the car is moving in a straight line at 100 kilometers per hour (about 62 miles per hour). The automobile's momentum will be 1,000 x 100, or 100,000 kilometers per hour in the direction it is moving.

It is harder to stop a train than it is to stop a car, even if they are moving at the same speed. This is because the train has more mass, and so it has more momentum. It is also harder to stop a car traveling at 60 miles (96 kilometers) per hour than it is to stop an identical car traveling at 20 miles (32 kilometers) per hour. The first car has more momentum because it is moving faster.

Other articles to read include: **Force; Mass; Motion.**

Before the diver plunges into the water, the total momentum of the diver and boat is zero because neither is moving. As the diver leaps from the boat, he and the boat move in opposite directions. But the total momentum remains zero because the motions of the diver and boat cancel each other out.

Motion

Motion is when an object changes its position. Everything in the universe is in motion. Even if you seem to be sitting still, you are moving because Earth is rotating on its *axis* (imaginary line through the center of Earth). Even vast systems of stars and planets, such as our Milky Way Galaxy, are speeding through space.

The motion of an object can only be described in relation to another object. For example, you may ride in a car past a person standing on a corner. That person will see you in motion. But the same moving object may appear at rest compared to a third object. You would not appear to be moving

Continued on the next page

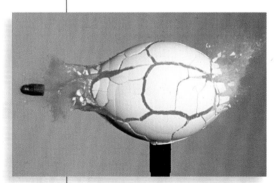

All motion is relative—that is, an object can only be described as moving or *stationary* (at rest) in relation to another object. In this picture, the bullet is in motion; the egg is stationary relative to the surroundings.

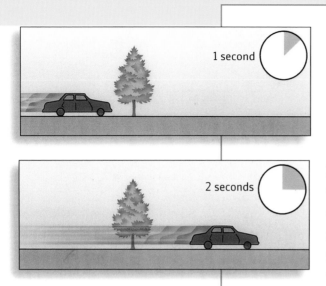

Motion can be described in terms of speed, which measures how far an object travels in a certain length of time. If a car travels 50 feet (15 meters) in one second (top) and 50 feet in another second (bottom), it is traveling at the speed of 50 feet per second.

Motion *Continued from the previous page*

in relation to a person sitting next to you in the moving car.

The English scientist Sir Isaac Newton developed three laws rules to describe motion. His first law states that an object moving in a straight line will continue to move in a straight line unless acted on by a force. It also states that an object at rest will remain at rest unless acted on by a force. Newton's first law is known as the *principle of inertia.* Inertia is the tendency of an object to continue moving if it is moving and to remain motionless if it is at rest.

The second law deals with a change in the speed of an object, *acceleration.* Acceleration is caused by a force. This law says that the amount of acceleration is related to the object's *mass* (amount of matter). For example, an object with a mass of 1 kilogram (2.2 pounds) will accelerate twice as much as an object with a mass of 2 kilograms when an equal force is applied to both.

The third law states that for each action, there is an equal and opposite reaction. For example, rockets take off by shooting hot gases out of their engines. The force that pushes the gases downward is equal to the force that pushes the rocket upward.

Other articles to read include: **Acceleration; Falling bodies, Law of; Force; Kinetic energy; Momentum.**

Erwin W. Müller

Müller, Erwin W.

Erwin W. Müller (1911–1977) was a *physicist (FIHZ uh sihst).* A physicist is a scientist who studies matter and energy. Müller invented the *ion microscope* in 1951. It can be used to see *atoms* (tiny particles of matter).

With his new microscope, Müller took the first picture of the atoms on a metal's surface. In 1954, he improved his design. His new microscope could be used to analyze a single atom.

Müller was born in Berlin, Germany. He became a United States citizen in 1962.

Other articles to read include: **Atom.**

Multiplication

Multiplication *(muhl tip luh KAY shuhn)* is a fast way of counting numbers that are *equal* (the same). It is one of the four basic steps of arithmetic. The other steps are *addition, subtraction,* and *division*.

The symbol of multiplication is X. The statement 6 X 5 = 30 means "six 5's equal 30." (= stands for *equals*.) People can also say, "5 multiplied by 6 equals 30," or they can say "6 times 5 equals 30."

Before people learned to multiply, they had to add numbers together to get a total. Adding numbers was easy when there were only a few things to count, such as the number of sheep in a flock. But adding became hard when people had to add many, many numbers, such as the number of bricks in a wall. They had to count the number of bricks in a row and then add all the rows together, like this:

5 + 5 + 5 + 5.

At some point, people realized that 4 groups of 5 always add up to 20. They wrote out a *multiplication table,* or chart. The table showed the *product* (answer) of any number from 1 to 10 multiplied by any other number from 1 to 10. Today, we memorize the multiplication table in school so that we do not have to add numbers every time.

Other articles to read include: **Addition; Division; Subtraction.**

An important rule in multiplication is shown in the pictures below. Each box contains 12 eggs. You can look at the box on the left in two ways. You could say that there are six rows of eggs with two eggs in each column. Or you could say that there are two rows of eggs with six eggs in each column. You can also look at the box of eggs at the right in two ways. You might say that there are four rows of eggs with three eggs in each column. Or you could say that there are three rows of eggs with four eggs in each column.

6 X 2 = 12
2 X 6 = 12

4 X 3 = 12
3 X 4= 12

Nn

Natural gas liquids

Natural gas liquids are certain chemical compounds that can be obtained in liquid form from natural gas. These compounds rank among the world's most valuable energy resources. Natural gas liquids, also called *NGL's,* are widely used as fuel. They are also used in manufacturing industrial chemicals and other products.

There are several important NGL compounds. From lightest to heaviest, they include ethane, propane, butane, pentane, hexane, and heptane. Chemical manufacturers use ethane in making *ethylene,* an important industrial chemical. Butane and propane, and mixtures of the two, are classified as *LPG* (liquefied petroleum gas). LPG is used chiefly as a heating fuel in industry and homes. Pentane, hexane, and heptane are called *natural gasoline* or *condensate.* These substances are blended with other kinds of gasoline used for transportation.

Other articles to read include: **Ethylene; Fuel.**

Neon is used to make colorful signs.

Neon

10	Ne	2 8
	Neon	
	20.1797	

Neon atomic symbol

Neon is a colorless, *odorless* (scent-free) gas. It is one of the gases that make up the protective layer of air around Earth called the *atmosphere.* Neon is also a *chemical element.* A chemical element is a material that is made of only one kind of atom.

Neon was discovered in 1898 by the British chemists Sir William Ramsay and Morris W. Travers. They named the gas for the Greek word that means *new.*

Neon is mainly used in certain kinds of lamps and in tubes to make colorful signs. Neon light can be seen even in fog. That is why neon lamps are used as beacons to guide airplanes at many airports.

Neon signs are made by filling glass tubes with neon gas. Electric current makes the tubes glow. The tubes can be made of colored glass or coated with different colors of powder to make signs of various colors.

Other articles to read include: **Element, Chemical; Gas.**

Neutralization

Neutralization *(NOO truh luh ZAY shuhn)* is when an *acid* and a *base* combine to form a salt. An acid is a chemical that has a sour taste and can burn the skin if it is strong enough. A base feels slippery and tastes bitter. Strong bases can also harm the skin. Baking soda is one type of base.

In water, acids and bases break down, forming positive and negative particles. These particles come together in a different combination to form a salt. The salt usually appears as crystals once the water has dried up. If the neutralization reaction is complete, the final salt is usually *neutral*. Being neutral means that it is neither an acid nor a base. Neutralization is important in many branches of industry. It is also important in the human body.

Other articles to read include: **Acid; Base; pH.**

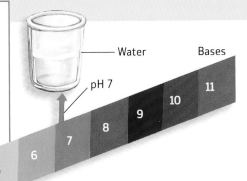

To test the strength of an acid or base, scientists may use an indicator called pH paper. The *pH (potential of hydrogen) number* shows the concentration of hydrogen ions in a solution. When the paper is dipped into a solution, the color changes. The color can then be checked against a color chart to determine the pH of the solution. Neutral substances, such as water, have a pH of 7.

Neutron

A neutron *(NOO tron)* is a part of an *atom.* Atoms are tiny bits of matter. Neutrons, along with particles called *protons,* form the *nucleus* (center) of nearly all of the various kinds of atoms. A neutron has no electric charge. Protons have a positive charge.

Only the atoms of hydrogen, the most common *chemical element,* contain no neutrons. A chemical element is a material with only one kind of atom. Neutrons and protons make up almost all of an atom's *mass* (amount of matter). A cloud of negatively charged particles called *electrons,* which orbit the nucleus, makes up the rest.

A neutron is about one-millionth of a *nanometer (NAN oh MEE tuhr)* wide. A nanometer is approximately $\frac{1}{100,000}$ the width of a human hair. Neutrons are made up of even tinier particles called *quarks.* Scientists use neutrons to make chemical elements *radioactive.* Scientists shower an element with neutrons. After the elements absorb the neutrons, they give off *radiation* (energy or tiny particles of matter).

Other articles to read include: **Atom; Electron; Proton; Radiation.**

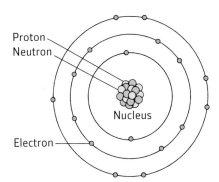

Neutrons and protons form the *nucleus* (center) of atoms and make up almost all of an atom's *mass* (amount of matter). They are held together by an extremely powerful force.

Newton, Sir Isaac

Sir Isaac Newton

Sir Isaac Newton (1642–1727) was an English scientist. He is sometimes described as "one of the greatest names in the history of human thought " because of his significant contributions to astronomy, mathematics, and *physics*. Physics is the study of energy and matter.

Newton showed that all the objects in the universe are attracted to one another by an invisible force. He realized that the force that makes a pebble fall to the ground is the same force that keeps the moon traveling around the sun. This force is called *gravitation*. It also keeps planets in orbit around the sun.

Newton later discovered that sunlight is a mixture of all the colors of light. He passed a beam of sunlight through a glass *prism,* which separated it into colors. He was able to show that objects have color because they reflect light. For example, grass looks green because it reflects green light.

Newton's study of light led him to make a new kind of telescope with a reflecting mirror instead of lenses. Through it he observed the moons of Jupiter. Newton's telescope proved to be much better than any previous telescope. Many modern telescopes use a similar design.

Newton invented a new kind of mathematics, called *calculus (KAL kyuh luhs)*. Calculus was also invented independently by the German mathematician Gottfried Leibniz. Calculus is the study of changing quantities, such as the changing slope of a curved line. Calculus is often used by engineers, physicists, and other scientists to solve practical problems about objects in motion, such as airlines in flight.

Newton also made important discoveries about motion. His book explaining his discoveries, usually called *Principia* or *Principia mathematica,* was published in 1687. This book is thought to be one of the greatest single works in the history of science. Later scientists, such as the German-born physicist Albert Einstein, challenged and changed Newton's work. But Einstein admitted that his own work would have been impossible without Newton's discoveries.

Other articles to read include: **Calculus; Color; Gravitation; Light; Motion.**

Nickel

Nickel atomic symbol

Nickel is a white metal. It is magnetic, polishes easily, and does not rust. It can be hammered into thin sheets or drawn out into wires. Nickel is also a *chemical element*. A chemical element is a material with only one kind of atom.

Most nickel is added to other metals. This creates a mixture called an *alloy*. Nickel makes iron easier to shape. It makes steel stronger for use in machine parts.

Nickel is dug out of the ground in such *ores* (minerals or rocks containing a valuable element) as *pentlandite, millerite,* and *niccolite*. Canada and Russia are the leading producers of nickel. Australia, Indonesia, and New Caledonia are also important nickel-producing areas.

Other articles to read include: **Element, Chemical; Metal.**

Nickel is dug out of the ground in rocks called ores.

Nitrate

A nitrate *(NY trayt)* is any chemical that includes the nitrate *ion*. An ion is an electrically charged atom or group of atoms. The nitrate ion is a group of atoms that includes one nitrogen atom and three oxygen atoms. Nitrates are found in nature and are also produced artificially.

When living things die, they *decompose* (rot). During this process, bacteria and fungi turn the nitrogen in the dead organisms into *ammonia (uh MOHN yuh or uh MOH nee uh)*. Some of the ammonia makes it into the soil. This ammonia may be used directly by plants. Some of it may be taken up by bacteria called *nitrifying bacteria*. This type of bacteria eventually changes some of the ammonia into nitrates. One type of nitrifying bacteria changes the ammonia into *nitrites*. Nitrites have the nitrite ion. Unlike the nitrate ion, the nitrite ion has only two oxygen atoms. Another type of nitrifying bacteria changes the nitrites into nitrates. Plants absorb nitrates. They use them like they would use ammonia.

Nitrates have many uses. For example, some can be used to make explosives. Some nitrates are used in fertilizer.

Other articles to read include: **Ammonia; Ion; Nitrogen.**

The Atacama Desert in Chile, a country in South America, is the world's only source of natural sodium nitrate, which is used in making fertilizers and gunpowder. Sodium nitrate can also be produced in laboratories.

Nitrogen

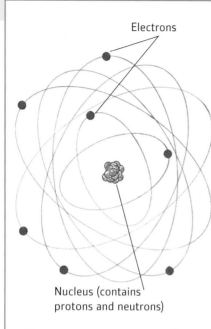

Electrons

Nucleus (contains protons and neutrons)

The most common atom of nitrogen has seven protons, seven neutrons, and seven electrons.

Nitrogen makes up nearly four-fifths of the *troposphere* (the layer of the atmosphere closest to Earth's surface). About one-fifth is oxygen, and the rest is made up of argon, carbon dioxide, and other gases.

7	N	2 5
Nitrogen 14.0067		

Nitrogen atomic symbol

Nitrogen is a type of gas. It has no taste, smell, or color. It makes up most of the *atmosphere,* the blanket of air that surrounds Earth. Nitrogen is also a *chemical element.* A chemical element is a material with only one kind of atom. A Scottish physician named Daniel Rutherford discovered nitrogen in 1772.

Nitrogen is important for all living things. It is part of many kinds of chemicals needed by plants, animals, and other organisms. One such group of chemicals are the *amino acids,* the building blocks of *proteins.* Proteins are important in building, maintaining, and repairing cells and tissues in all living things. Plants get nitrogen from the soil. They make all the amino acids they need. Animals produce only some of these compounds.

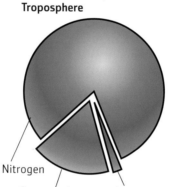

Troposphere

Nitrogen

Oxygen   Argon, carbon dioxide, other gases

They must get the rest by eating other animals and plants.

Nitrogen is used chiefly in the production of the gas ammonia. Ammonia is used in the production of fertilizers and as a cooling chemical in air conditioners and refrigerators. In addition, nitrogen is used to make nitric acid, which is also used to make fertilizer.

Other articles to read include: **Ammonia; Element, Chemical; Gas.**

Nobel, Alfred Bernhard

Alfred Bernhard Nobel *(noh BEHL)* (1833-1896) was a Swedish chemist and inventor. He developed an explosive called *dynamite.* Nobel also established the Nobel Prizes. These prizes honor people who have made human life better. They include awards in the sciences and literature and for promoting international peace.

Nobel was born in Stockholm, Sweden. His family moved to St. Petersburg, Russia, when he was still a child. His father owned

Continued on the next page

a factory in St. Petersburg that made equipment for the Russian army. There, Nobel began to experiment with explosives.

Nobel worked with a liquid explosive called *nitroglycerin (ny truh GLIHS uhr ihn)*. Nitroglycerin was dangerous because it exploded easily. Nobel wanted to make it safe so that it could be used for such work as building tunnels and mining. After many tries, Nobel combined nitroglycerin with a powder that made the explosive much safer. He named it *dynamite*. In 1867, he received a *patent* for dynamite. A patent is a government document that gives an inventor the sole rights to an invention for a limited time. Nobel set up factories around the world, and sales of dynamite and other explosives brought him great wealth.

In his will, Nobel set up a fund. The interest from the money was to be used to award annual prizes to people who have made valuable contributions for the "good of humanity." The Nobel Prizes were first awarded in 1901. They remain among the most honored prizes in the world.

Other articles to read include: **Explosion; Nobel Prizes.**

Alfred Bernhard Nobel

Nobel Prizes

Nobel *(noh BEHL)* Prizes are six prizes given each year to people whose work has made human life better. Five of the prizes were started by the Swedish chemist Alfred B. Nobel, who invented dynamite. He used profits from the manufacture of chemical explosives to provide funds for the prizes. The first prizes were given in 1901.

Science prizes are given in *physics, chemistry,* and *physiology (FIHZ ee OL uh jee)* or medicine. Physics is the study of matter and energy. Physiology is the study of how living things function. Other prizes are awarded for literature and peace. A sixth prize, for important work in the field of economics, was established in 1969 by the Bank of Sweden. Economics is the study of how countries make and use money.

The front side of each Nobel Prize medal has a bust of Alfred Nobel, who established all but one of the prizes in the late 1800's.

Continued on the next page

Nobel Prizes *Continued from the previous page*

The Royal Swedish Academy of Sciences in Stockholm, Sweden, chooses the winners in the sciences and in economics. The Swedish Academy chooses the winner for literature. The Norwegian Nobel Committee chooses the winner of the peace prize. Two or three people may share a prize. Sometimes, prizes are not awarded or are awarded in a later year.

Other articles to read include: **Nobel, Alfred Bernhard.**

King Carl Gustaf of Sweden (right in photo) presents the 2004 Nobel Prize in physiology or medicine to American Richard Axel, who was honored for his research on the sense of smell.

Noble gas

A noble gas is any of a group of six chemical elements. A chemical element is a material that is made up of only one type of atom. The known noble gases are *argon (AHR gon), helium (HEE lee uhm), krypton (KRIHP ton), neon (NEE on), radon (RAY don),* and *xenon (ZEE non)*. They occur naturally in the atmosphere. The atmosphere is the mass of gases surrounding Earth. The British scientists Lord Rayleigh *(RAY lee)* and William Ramsay discovered the noble gases during the late 1890's.

Many gases occur as molecules of two or more atoms. However, the noble gases occur as single atoms. They are called "noble" because they do not usually mix with other elements. But most of the noble gases will form certain *compounds* (mixtures) under certain conditions.

The noble gases have various uses. For example, all except radon are used in certain kinds of lamps. Helium is used to fill balloons that carry scientific instruments high into the atmosphere

The known noble gases are *helium, neon, argon, krypton, xenon,* and *radon.*

Other articles to read include: **Argon; Element, Chemical; Gas; Helium; Krypton; Neon; Radon.**

2	**He**	2
	Helium	
	4.002602	

10	**Ne**	2 8
	Neon	
	20.1797	

18	**Ar**	2 8 8
	Argon	
	39.948	

36	**Kr**	2 8 18 8
	Krypton	
	83.80	

54	**Xe**	2 8 18 18 8
	Xenon	
	131.293	

86	**Rn**	2 8 18 32 18 8
	Radon	
	[222]	

Nuclear energy

Nuclear *(NOO klee uhr)* energy is the plentiful energy released by changes in the *nucleus (NOO klee uhs)* (core) of an *atom.* Atoms are tiny bits of matter.

Changes in the nucleus of an atom are called *nuclear reactions.* A nuclear reaction may split an atom's nucleus. This type of reaction is called *fission.* In a *fusion* reaction, two *nuclei* (plural of nucleus) are combined. Nuclear reactions release tremendous energy. The heat and light from the sun result from nuclear reactions.

Scientists first released nuclear energy on a large scale at the University of Chicago in 1942, three years after World War II (1939-1945) began. This achievement led to the development of the atomic bomb. The United States dropped two nuclear bombs on Japan during the war, on Hiroshima and Nagasaki. The bombs killed many thousands of people.

After the war, scientists began developing peaceful uses of nuclear energy. One important use was the production of electric power. Many countries built nuclear power plants. Like many other power plants, nuclear power plants generate electric power from heat. But instead of burning such fuels as coal or oil, nuclear power plants generate heat in large machines called *nuclear reactors.* Nuclear reactors create *fission reactions.* They split apart the nuclei of special *uranium (yoo RAY nee uhm)* and *plutonium (ploo TOH nee uhm)* atoms.

Fission reactions in a nuclear reactor create more than just heat. They also produce *radioactive* atoms. Radioactive atoms *decay* (break down), releasing invisible energy and particles. This release is called *nuclear radiation.* Large amounts of nuclear radiation can harm or kill living things. Uranium and plutonium are radioactive. So are many of the atoms that result from splitting uranium and plutonium.

Nuclear reactors are kept inside sealed buildings so that the radiation will not get out. Nuclear fission reactions release huge amounts of heat. If too much heat builds up, parts of the reactor can melt or even blow up, causing great harm. Nuclear reactors have special devices called *control rods* that can quickly

Continued on the next page

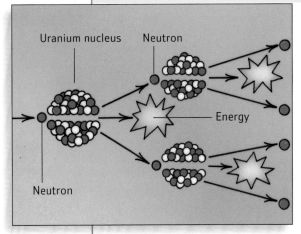

In a nuclear fission reaction, a neutron strikes the nucleus of a heavy element, such as uranium, splitting it into two different parts. In the reaction, energy and more neutrons are given off. These neutrons then can strike and split other uranium nuclei, resulting in a *chain reaction.*

Nuclear energy *Continued from the previous page*

Nuclear fission chain reactions in a nuclear power plant take place in a device called the *reactor vessel.* The reactions heat water that moves through the *reactor core* under high pressure. The hot water flows through pipes to a *steam generator,* where the water becomes steam. The steam spins a *turbine,* which powers a *generator.* This produces electric energy. Finally, the steam goes to a *condenser,* where it is cooled and becomes liquid. The water is then reused.

stop fission reactions. But even if fission stops, the reactor still contains radioactive material. Radiation from this material also makes great amounts of heat, long after a reactor shuts down. Reactors must be constantly cooled with flowing water to prevent them from overheating.

A serious accident took place in 1979 at the Three Mile Island nuclear power plant in Pennsylvania. In 1986, a worse nuclear accident happened at the Chernobyl nuclear power plant in Ukraine. Ukraine was part of the Soviet Union at that time. An explosion and fire at Chernobyl's reactor widely spread radioactive material, making many people sick. Soviet leaders reported that 31 people died as a result of the accident. Thousands of additional deaths were later linked to radioactive materials leaked to the surrounding area.

On March 11, 2011, Japan suffered a nuclear crisis at the Fukushima Daiichi Nuclear Power Station. The crisis was caused by a tremendous earthquake that struck off the east coast of Japan. The earthquake created a massive *tsunami* (series of ocean waves) that flooded the power plant. The plant's cooling rods stopped fission reactions. But the tsunami crippled the plant's cooling system. Heat from nuclear radiation caused several explosions, widely spreading radioactive material.

Continued on the next page

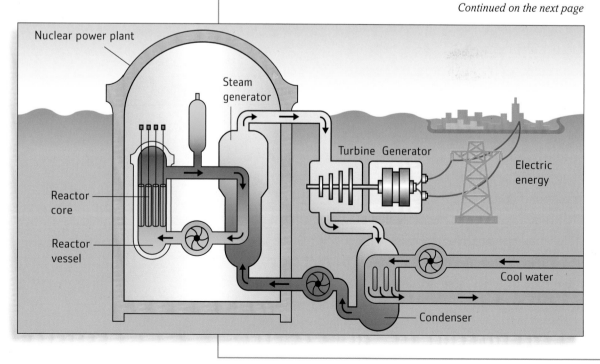

Nuclear power plant

Steam generator

Turbine Generator

Electric energy

Reactor core

Reactor vessel

Cool water

Condenser

Before the late 1800's, scientists knew nothing about nuclear energy. Then in 1896, the French scientist Antoine Henri Becquerel found that uranium is radioactive. Scientists began to study this mysterious source of energy.

In the early 1900's, the British scientist Ernest Rutherford discovered the atom's nucleus. Soon, other scientists began doing experiments to see what happens when parts of the nucleus crash into one another. Uranium was used in some of these experiments. When the uranium nucleus was split, it created energy.

In 1952, scientists created the first fusion reaction in a nuclear weapons test. But only fission reactions are used to produce electric power. Scientists have not yet figured out how to control the more powerful fusion reactions in a power plant.

Other articles to read include: **Atom; Chain reaction; Fission; Fusion; Nucleus; Radiation.**

A nuclear power plant uses the heat of a controlled nuclear reaction to produce steam, which is then used to generate electric energy.

Nuclear physics

Nuclear physics *(NOO klee uhr FIHZ ihks)* is the study of the *nucleus* (core) of the atom. Nuclear physics began in about 1900 as the study of such *radioactive (RAY dee oh AK tihv)* materials as radium and uranium. Radioactive materials give off invisible rays of light, heat, or other energy when their atoms *decay* (break up). Scientists who study nuclear physics are called *nuclear physicists.*

Nuclear physicists study three major nuclear reactions. They are radioactive decay, *fission (FIHSH uhn),* and *fusion (FYOO zhuhn).* Fission is the breakdown of a nucleus to form two smaller

Continued on the next page

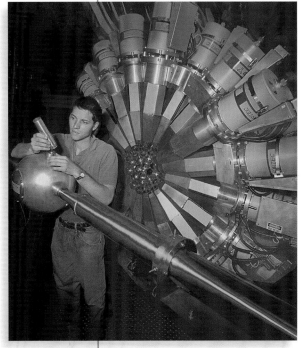

The cyclotron is a machine that *accelerates* (speeds up) electrically charged atomic particles to high energies for study.

Nuclear physics *Continued from the previous page*

nuclei (the plural of nucleus). Fusion is the joining of two nuclei to make a larger nucleus. Both fusion and fission release much more energy than does radioactive decay.

Nuclear physics helps people in different ways. Some physicians use *radioisotopes* (radioactive forms of chemical elements) to check for heart problems. They put a radioactive material into a patient's blood. They can trace the material as it moves through the patient's heart. Other physicians use radiation to treat cancer.

Nuclear fission can be used to generate electric power. For many years, scientists have been trying to discover a way to use fusion to safely generate power. The sun's energy comes from nuclear fusion. Nuclear weapons get their energy through both fission and fusion reactions.

Some scientists use nuclear physics in *radiocarbon dating.* This process helps determine the age of fossils and other once-living remains.

Other articles to read include: **Atom; Fission; Fusion; Nuclear energy; Nucleus; Physics; Radiation.**

Nucleus

The nucleus is a tiny region near the center of the atom. Protons and neutrons are clustered in the nucleus. The electrons whirl at fantastic speeds through the empty space around the atom's nucleus.

A nucleus *(NOO klee uhs)* is the core of an *atom.* Atoms are tiny building blocks of *matter.* Nearly all of the objects and substances we see around us are made of matter.

Atoms are very small, and their *nuclei* (the plural of nucleus) are even smaller. If a hydrogen atom were about 4 miles (6.4 kilometers) wide, its nucleus would be no bigger than a tennis ball. The rest of the atom would mostly be empty space.

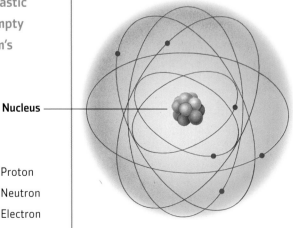

Nucleus

Proton
Neutron
Electron

Continued on the next page

The nucleus contains the *protons* and *neutrons* of an atom. Protons are particles with a positive electrical charge. Neutrons are particles with no electrical charge. A nucleus contains at least one proton. As a result, the nucleus is positively charged.

Electrons orbit the nucleus. Electrons are particles with a negative charge. They are attracted by the positive charge of the nucleus.

The nucleus takes up almost all of the *mass* of an atom. The mass is the amount of matter in an atom. A single proton or neutron has more mass than 1,800 electrons.

Other articles to read include: **Atom; Electron; Neutron; Proton.**

Number

Numbers are what we use to talk about the amounts of things. Numbers tell us "how many" or "how much." Numbers can also tell us the order of things. We can express numbers with words, gestures, or symbols. A number symbol is called a *numeral (NOO muhr uhl)*. When we want to write down a number, we can write either the numeral or the word.

Arabic (AIR uh bihk) numerals are the most common symbols used for numbers. Every number can be shown in Arabic numerals using 10 symbols. The symbols are called digits *(DIHJ ihts)*. They are *0, 1, 2, 3, 4, 5, 6, 7, 8,* and *9.* In an Arabic numeral, the position of a digit tells us its value. For example, the Arabic numeral for the number two hundred and thirty-seven is *237.* The number means 2 hundreds plus 3 tens plus 7 ones.

There are several kinds of numbers. *Natural numbers* are the counting numbers: 1, 2, 3 and so on. They go on to infinity. *Integers* include all the natural numbers as well as the number zero and negative whole numbers: –1, –2, –3 and so on. There are infinitely many integers, too. Even so, other numbers are not integers. *Rational numbers* include fractions—that is, amounts that are between integers, such as ½ and ⁻⅔. Still other numbers are not integers or fractions. These numbers are important in higher mathematics.

Other articles to read include: **Addition; Decimal system; Division; Fraction; Googol; Infinity; Mathematics; Multiplication; Subtraction.**

Arabic numerals (below) are the most common symbols used for numbers. The Egyptian (middle) and Roman (bottom) numeral systems had no zero. To write a number such as *105,* people used the symbols for *100* and *5.*

105
Arabic

Egyptian

CV
Roman

Oo

Oersted, Hans Christian

Hans Christian Oersted *(UR stehd)* (1777-1851) was a Danish chemist and *physicist*. A physicist is a scientist who studies energy and matter. Oersted laid the foundation for the science of *electromagnetism*. Electromagnetism is the *branch* (area) of physics that studies the relationship between electricity and magnetism. Oersted's work led to the development of such devices as the telegraph, the electric bell and, the *electric generator*. Electric generators produce electric power.

Oersted discovered that an *electric current* creates a *magnetic field*. An electric current is a flow of electricity. A magnetic field is the influence of a magnet. In 1820, Oersted put a magnetic needle next to a wire. The wire was carrying an electric current. The needle moved away from the electric current. He realized that the electric current must have a magnetic field. This field pushed away the needle.

Other articles to read include: **Electricity; Magnetic field.**

Hans Christian Oersted

Oppenheimer, J. Robert

J. Robert Oppenheimer *(OP uhn HY muhr)* (1904-1967) was an American *physicist* (a scientist who studies matter and energy). Oppenheimer is sometimes called the father of the atomic bomb. From 1942 to 1945, he directed the Manhattan Project. This project was created by the United States government during World War II (1939-1945) to build the first atomic bomb.

Oppenheimer was born in New York City. He graduated from Harvard University in 1925. In 1927, he received his Ph.D. degree from the University of Göttingen in Germany. From 1929 to 1947, he taught at the University of California at Berkeley and at the California Institute of Technology. He directed the Institute for Advanced Study in Princeton, New Jersey, from 1947 to 1966.

J. Robert Oppenheimer

In 1953, some people questioned Oppenheimer's loyalty to the U.S. government. An investigation by the Atomic Energy Commission (AEC) cleared him of these charges, but he was denied further access to secret information. In 1963, the AEC awarded Oppenheimer its highest honor for his contributions to physics. Many people viewed this as the government's effort to correct a tragic mistake.

Other articles to read include: **Fission; Manhattan Project.**

Optics

Optics *(OP tihks)* is the study of light. In some ways, light acts like a wave. In other ways, it acts like very small particles moving in a straight line. In optics, scientists study how light is made and *transmitted* (sent). They also study how light can be detected, measured, and used.

Optics includes the study of *visible light*. Visible light can be seen by the human eye. Optics also includes the study of the many other kinds of light. These kinds of light are invisible to people.

Mirrors and lenses work by the principles of optics. They are used in such optical devices as binoculars, cameras, and telescopes.

Optics is divided into three main branches. *Physical optics* is the study of light as a wave. *Quantum optics* is the study of light as individual particles. *Geometrical optics* involves the study of optical instruments.

Continued on the next page

Optics describes how light behaves. Two of the most important of these principles are *reflection* and *refraction.*

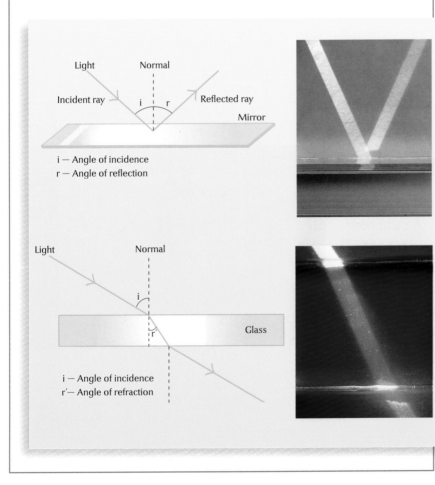

i — Angle of incidence
r — Angle of reflection

i — Angle of incidence
r′— Angle of refraction

Reflection
A beam of light will be reflected by a smooth surface. The beam coming toward the surface is called the *incident ray*. After the beam has been reflected, it is called the *reflected ray*. The incident ray makes an angle with an imaginary line called the *normal*. This angle equals the angle made by the reflected ray.

Refraction causes a beam to bend as it passes from one substance into another. The beam bends toward the normal if it slows down when entering a substance. The *angle of refraction* then is less than the *angle of incidence*. If light travels faster in the substance, the ray bends away from the normal.

Optics *Continued from the previous page*

The Arab scientist Alhazen is sometimes called the founder of optics. In the 1000's, he wrote *Kitab al Manazir* (Book of Optics), an important book on the theory of light and its role in vision. Modern optics began in the 1600's. The Italian scientist Galileo built telescopes. With them, he observed planets and stars.

Sir Isaac Newton, an English scientist, studied lenses and *prisms,* clear pieces of material used to *refract* (bend) light. Newton also proposed that light was made of tiny particles. In Holland, the physicist Christiaan Huygens proposed a wave theory of light. Scientists at the time believed that light could not be both a wave and a particle. During the early 1800's, other physicists proved Huygens's theory to be correct. It was not until the 1900's that scientists proved that Newton's particle theory was also correct. The light particle would eventually be called a *photon.*

Since then, scientists have developed more ways of transmitting light. One of these ways is called *fiber optics.* It sends light through tiny strands of fiber.

Other articles to read include: **Electromagnetic spectrum; Light; Reflection; Refraction.**

Scientists use an instrument called a *spectroscope* to analyze a light spectrum.

Organic chemistry

Organic chemistry is the study of certain *compounds* that contain carbon. A compound is a chemical with more than one kind of *chemical element.* A chemical element is a material made up of only one kind of atom. Carbon atoms can *bond* (join) with other atoms in an unusual variety of ways. As a result, carbon atoms can form a wide range of compounds, called *organic compounds.* Scientists have identified several million organic compounds.

Most of the different molecules in plants and other living things contain carbon.

Continued on the next page

Many organic compounds come from living things. For example, petroleum and natural gas contain many *hydrocarbons*. These organic compounds are made of the chemical elements carbon and hydrogen. The hydrocarbons come from the remains of living things that died millions of years ago. Ethanol is another organic compound. It is a kind of alcohol made from fruits, grains, or vegetables. Other organic compounds in living things include *amino acids, sugars,* and *lipids* (fats). Amino acids are the building blocks of proteins.

Scientists once believed that organic compounds could only be made by living things. However, in 1828, the German chemist Friedrich Wöhler made the organic compound urea in his laboratory. Since then, scientists have found many ways of making organic compounds. These compounds include medicines, insecticides, and chainlike compounds called *polymers*. One such polymer is made from *ethylene,* an organic compound that contains two carbon atoms and two hydrogen atoms. Millions of ethylene molecules bonded together in long chains are called *polyethylene,* a common plastic.

Other articles to read include: **Carbon; Chemistry; Ethylene; Hydrocarbon.**

Osmosis

Osmosis *(oz MOH sihs* or *os MOH sihs)* is the process by which liquid moves from one *solution* to another through a membrane *(MEHM brayn).* A solution is a mixture of two or more substances in which one or more substances *dissolve* (break up) into another. A membrane is a thin, skinlike material through which some substances can pass, but others cannot.

A liquid solution is made up of a liquid, called a *solvent,* and another substance, called a *solute,* that has dissolved in the liquid. During osmosis, solvent from the solution with more of the solute moves through tiny holes in a membrane into the solution with less of the solute. The solute cannot pass through the membrane because its *molecules* are bigger than the holes. Molecules are groups of atoms. Eventually, both solutions will contain equal levels of the solute.

Osmosis is an essential process for living things. Plants absorb most of their water by osmosis. In animals, osmosis helps bring water and nutrients into body fluids and cells.

Other articles to read include: **Absorption and adsorption; Liquid; Solution.**

During osmosis, water containing nutrients moves from the soil, through membranes covering the root hairs, and into the roots of plants.

Ounce

Ounce *(owns)* is the name of two different units of measure used mainly in the United States. The first ounce is a unit of *volume*. The second ounce is a unit of *weight*. Volume is the amount of the space something takes up. As a unit of volume, the ounce is used chiefly to measure liquids. This ounce is often called the *fluid ounce*. There are 32 fluid ounces in a liquid quart. In most other countries, people measure volume in liters or *milliliters* (thousandths of a liter). One fluid ounce equals 29.57 milliliters.

The other ounce measures weight. In everyday situations, weight is used to mean much the same thing as *mass*. Mass is the amount of matter in something. There are 16 ounces in 1 pound. In most other countries, people use *grams* to measure weight or mass. One ounce of weight equals 28.35 grams.

Other articles to read include: **Mass; Volume; Weights and measures.**

Ounces and milliliters are labeled on this liquid measuring cup.

Oxidation

Oxidation *(OK suh DAY shuhn)* is a type of *chemical reaction*. A chemical reaction takes place when one or more chemicals change into one or more other chemicals. Chemical reactions involve *atoms* and *molecules (MOL uh kyoolz)*. Atoms are tiny bits of matter. Molecules are groups of atoms *bonded* (linked) together.

In oxidation, a substance's atoms lose tiny particles called *electrons*. Electrons are negatively charged particles that orbit the *nucleus* (core) of an atom. The electrons lost from one substance in oxidation must be captured by another substance. Thus, oxidation is always accompanied by another reaction called *reduction*. In reduction, a substance gains electrons.

Rust is an example of oxidation. The iron in the key has combined with oxygen in the air in the presence of moisture.

The rusting of iron is a common example of oxidation. Iron combines with oxygen in the presence of moisture to form rust. The process begins with iron atoms losing electrons.

The term *oxidation* originally meant any chemical process in which a substance combines with oxygen. This definition changed when chemists discovered that some oxidation reactions occur without oxygen.

Other articles to read include: **Chemical reaction; Oxygen; Rust.**

Oxygen

| 8 | O | 2 6 |

Oxygen
15.9994

Oxygen atomic symbol

Oxygen is a kind of gas. It is found in Earth's air, soil, and water. Nearly all living things need oxygen to stay alive. Oxygen combines with other chemicals in the cells of plants and animals to produce the energy needed for growth and other purposes.

Oxygen is a *chemical element*. A chemical element is a material made up of only one kind of atom.

Ordinary oxygen makes up about one-fifth of the volume of Earth's *atmosphere* (the mass of gases around Earth). This pure oxygen has no color, taste, or smell. Nitrogen makes up most of the other four-fifths. Oxygen is also found in Earth's crust and water. This oxygen is not pure. It is combined with other chemical elements. On average, 100 pounds (45 kilograms) of Earth's crust contains about 47 pounds (21 kilograms) of oxygen. Every 100 pounds of water contains about 89 pounds (40 kilograms) of oxygen.

Another form of oxygen, called *ozone,* is found in the atmosphere in small amounts. Ozone high up in the atmosphere is very important to life on Earth. A layer of ozone high in the atmosphere protects Earth from some dangerous rays of the sun.

Oxygen has many uses in industry. Oxygen is needed to make most fuels burn. Heat is released during the burning process. Oxygen is used to make steel. It is also sometimes used in explosives.

Oxygen was discovered in the late 1700's by two chemists working independently. They were Carl Scheele of Sweden and Joseph Priestley of England. Scheele called oxygen *fire air.* Priestley called it *dephlogisticated air.* In 1779, the French chemist Antoine Lavoisier named the gas *oxygen.*

Other articles to read include: **Element, Chemical; Gas; Oxidation; Rust.**

Air is made up mainly of nitrogen and oxygen. These gases make up about 99 percent of *dry air*—air from which all water *vapor* (gas) has been removed. Argon and other gases account for about 1 percent.

When plants are in sunlight, they give off oxygen that people and animals can breathe in. To make food, plants use the carbon dioxide that people and animals breathe out.

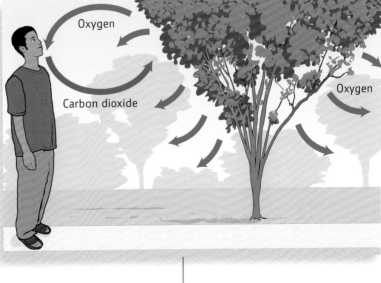

Pp

Palladium

Palladium is often used to make jewelry, such as this ring, which is being polished by a jeweler.

46	**Pd**	2
		8
	Palladium	18
	106.42	18
		0

Palladium atomic symbol

Palladium *(puh LAY dee uhm)* is a soft, shiny, silvery metal. It is sometimes mixed with gold to make "white gold" for jewelry. Palladium is a *chemical element*. A chemical element is a material made up of only one kind of atom.

Palladium has many uses. It is often used as a substitute for the metal platinum. Palladium is harder and lighter than platinum. Palladium can be made into thin sheets or wire. It is also used to make surgical instruments.

A special kind of palladium called *palladium black* is used as a *catalyst (KAT uh lihst)*. A catalyst is a substance that helps start or speed up a chemical reaction. Palladium black is an important catalyst for a process called *hydrogenation*. This process is used in making gasoline and some foods. Automobile manufacturers use palladium in *catalytic converters*. These devices reduce fumes given off by car engines.

William Wollaston, an English chemist, discovered palladium in 1803.

Other articles to read include: **Element, Chemical; Metal; Platinum.**

Pascal, Blaise

Blaise Pascal *(blehz pas KAL* or *PAS kuhl)* (1623-1662) was a French scientist and thinker. He became known for his experiments with *fluids* and for his work on *probability*. A fluid is any substance that flows easily under pressure. Probability is the mathematical study of chance.

In the 1650's, Pascal developed a scientific rule called *Pascal's law*. This rule deals with fluids in containers. According to the law, putting pressure on such a fluid causes the fluid to push out equally in all directions. Pascal's work helped prove that air has weight and that air pressure can produce a *vacuum* (space that contains little matter). At that time, many scientists doubted that a vacuum could exist.

Blaise Pascal

Pascal was born in Clermont-Ferrand, France. In addition to his research, he became a noted writer. In 1656 and 1657, Pascal published a hugely popular series of letters called *Provincial Letters*. These letters defended a religious community to which he belonged.

Other articles to read include: **Fluid; Pressure; Probability.**

Pauli, Wolfgang

Wolfgang Pauli *(PAW lee)* (1900-1958) was an Austrian scientist. Pauli won the 1945 Nobel Prize in physics for his work on *electrons*. Electrons are tiny, negatively charged particles that orbit the *nucleus* (core) of an atom.

Pauli described a rule that became known as the *Pauli exclusion principle*. This rule states that no two electrons in the same atom can have the exact same *orbit* and *spin*. An electron's orbit is the area it occupies as it travels around an atom's *nucleus* (core). Spin is the angle at which it rotates on an *axis* (imaginary line through its center). Pauli's rule helped scientists understand how different substances will react when combined. The rule also helped explain the different qualities of *chemical elements*. Chemical elements are materials that are made up of only one kind of atom.

Pauli also predicted the existence of a tiny, invisible particle called the *neutrino*. Although these particles were first detected in 1956, scientists know little about them.

Other articles to read include: **Electron; Element, Chemical.**

Wolfgang Pauli

Pauling, Linus Carl

Linus Carl Pauling (1901-1994) was an American scientist who won two Nobel Prizes. He won the Nobel Prize in chemistry in 1954 for his work on the way *atoms* are linked together in molecules *(MOL uh kyoolz)*. Pauling's work helped explain the structure of complex molecules called *amino acids* and *proteins*. He explained how the different amino acids combine to produce the much larger protein molecules. His work also led to a better understanding of the blood disease *sickle cell anemia*. Pauling later gained attention for his experimental use of vitamin C in treating cancer and the common cold.

Pauling also won the Nobel Peace Prize in 1962 for trying to get nations to ban *nuclear weapons (NOO klee uhr WEHP uhnz)* and nuclear weapons testing.

Other articles to read include: **Atom; Molecule.**

Linus Carl Pauling

A perfumer, sometimes known as a "nose," mixes scented oils to create a perfume blend.

Perfume

A perfume is a material that gives off a pleasant smell. Perfumes can be made from natural materials or from *synthetic (sihn THEHT ihk)* (artificially made) materials from coal and oil products. The finest natural perfumes come from oils taken from flower petals. Oils from such other parts of plants as bark, buds, leaves, roots, and wood can also be used to make perfumes. Animal parts are also used in certain perfumes.

Most perfume is used in soaps. People also spray liquid perfumes on their skin. Lipsticks, face and body lotions, and powders also contain perfume.

People have been wearing perfume for thousands of years. Perfumes and other scented products have also played an important role in religious ceremonies. The international perfume industry does many billions of U.S. dollars in business per year.

pH

A substance's pH is a number that describes how strongly *acidic* or *basic* the substance is. The pH scale starts at 0 and ends at 14. Substances that are acidic have a pH number less than 7. Substances that are basic have a pH number greater than 7. Substances that have a pH of 7 are considered *neutral* (neither acidic nor basic). Pure water has a pH of 7. Human blood has a pH of about 7.4.

Acids may taste sour and can be dangerous. They cause *chemical reactions* in metals. A chemical reaction takes place when one or more chemicals change into one or more different chemicals. Vinegar and citrus juices are acidic fluids. So is the liquid inside the stomach that helps the body *digest* (break down) food.

Basic substances may taste bitter and feel slippery. They can also burn the skin. Ammonia, which is sometimes used as a

Continued on the next page

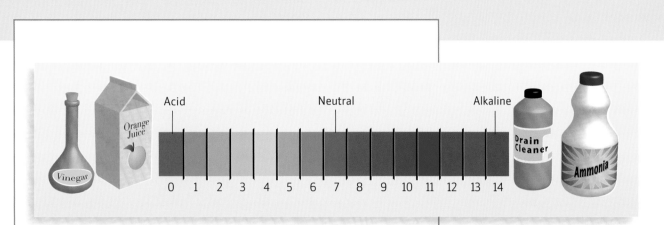

cleaning product, is an example of a basic substance. Basic liquids are also called *alkalis*.

Scientists often need to test the pH of such substances as soil or water. Soil that is too acidic or too basic is bad for growing certain crops. Some river and lake water has become too acidic because of *acid rain*. Acid rain is rain that carries chemicals from car exhaust and the gases released by power plants that burn coal. Fish and other creatures cannot live in water that is too acidic.

The abbreviation *pH* stands for *potential hydrogen*. A pH number tells chemists how many hydrogen *ions* (electrically charged atoms) are in a solution. The Danish biochemist Søren Sørensen invented the pH system in 1909.

Other articles to read include: **Acid; Base; Ion; Litmus; Neutralization.**

The pH scale ranges from 0 to 14. The pH number of an acidic liquid, such as vinegar or orange juice, is less than 7. The pH number of a basic (also called alkaline) liquid, such as ammonia or many drain cleaners, is greater than 7.

15	P	2 8 5
Phosphorus 30.973761		

Phosphorus
atomic symbol

Phosphorus

Phosphorus *(FOS fuhr uhs)* is a *chemical element* that all living things need to live and to grow. A chemical element is a material made up of only one kind of atom. Phosphorus is found in every living cell. It also has many industrial uses. In nature, phosphorus can be found only in a form called *phosphate*. This form is usually found in rocks.

Plants take in phosphorus from the soil. They use it to make energy. People and other animals need phosphorus for energy, too. They get it by eating plants or such foods as meat, milk, and eggs. Phosphorus is important for healthy teeth and bones.

One kind of phosphate is used to make such products as

Continued on the next page

Phosphorus *Continued from the previous page*

plastics, steel, detergent, and medications. Another kind is used in making safety matches. Pure phosphorus is used in some industrial processes. Most pure phosphorus is highly unstable. For example, one form of pure phosphorus will burst into flames if exposed to air.

Phosphates can threaten rivers, lakes, and wetlands. Phosphates in detergents can enter waterways through sewage systems. Large amounts of phosphates can promote the growth of simple organisms called *algae*. The algae use up the oxygen in the water. Fish and other things that live in the water then die off from a lack of oxygen.

Other articles to read include: **Element, Chemical.**

Phosphorus moves throughout the environment over long periods of time in a process called the phosphorus cycle. These movements happen at different rates in different places.

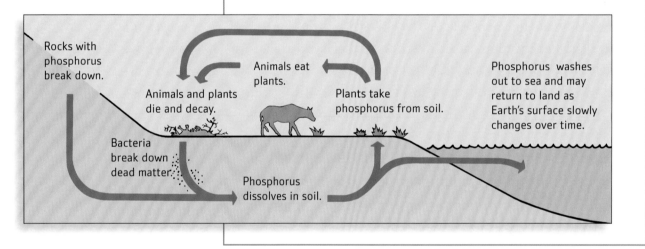

Rocks with phosphorus break down.

Animals and plants die and decay.

Animals eat plants.

Plants take phosphorus from soil.

Phosphorus washes out to sea and may return to land as Earth's surface slowly changes over time.

Bacteria break down dead matter.

Phosphorus dissolves in soil.

Photon

A photon *(FOH ton)* is a tiny bundle of pure energy. All forms of light are composed of photons. Photons come from such sources of natural light as the sun and stars. They can also come from sources that were made by people, including flashlights, campfires, and gas stoves.

Photons have no *mass* (amount of matter) and no electric charge. Photons make up all forms of light, or *electromagnetic energy*. Electromagnetic energy includes X rays, *infrared energy* (heat rays), and *visible light*. Visible light is the only form of

Continued on the next page

electromagnetic energy that humans can see with our eyes. The speed at which photons travel in a *vacuum* (space with almost no matter) is the speed of light.

Visible light often looks white to us. But it is actually made up of many colors. The color of a particular photon depends on how much energy that photon is carrying. For example, the *embers* (hot ashes) of a campfire look red or orange. This is because the photons from the fire are carrying less energy than the photons from the blue flames of a gas stove.

The German physicist Max Planck was the first to suggest the existence of light particles, in 1900. In 1905, the German-born physicist Albert Einstein proposed that light comes in tiny particles or bundles. These particles later became known as photons.

Other articles to read include: **Einstein, Albert; Electromagnetic spectrum; Light; Planck, Max Karl Ernst Ludwig.**

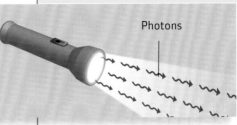

The photons that make up light and other forms of radiation act as both particles and waves. The speed at which photons travel through space—the speed of light—is the fastest that anything in the universe can move. It is 186,282 miles (299,792 kilometers) per second.

Physical change

A physical change is a change in the form or shape of *matter.* Matter is what makes up most of the objects around us. In a physical change, no new substances are created.

A physical change is often a change in the *state of matter.* The three common states of matter are gas, liquid, and solid. In a physical change, the matter's chemical structure stays the same. For example, ice melting into water is an example of a physical change. The state of the ice changes from solid to liquid. But ice's taste, smell, and other chemical properties do not change.

Turning a wooden log into sawdust is another example of a physical change. The wood's chemical qualities remain the same, even though the log has been cut into many tiny pieces.

A change in matter's chemical structure is called a *chemical change.* A chemical change can change matter's taste, smell, and ability to dissolve in liquid, among other things. Burning wood is an example of a chemical change. It creates new chemical substances—gases and ash.

Other articles to read include: **Chemical reaction; Gas; Liquid; Matter; Solid.**

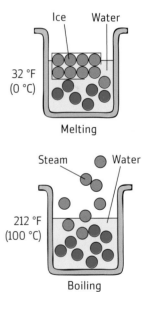

The melting of ice and the boiling of water are examples of physical change. When the temperature rises to 32 °F (0 °C), ice (solid water) changes into liquid water. When the temperature reaches 212 °F (100 °C), the liquid water changes into steam, a gas.

Physics

Physics *(FIHZ ihks)* is the study of *matter* and *energy.* All objects are made of matter. Scientists who study physics are called *physicists.*

Physicists try to understand what matter is and why it behaves the way it does. They want to know how it is put together and how it changes. They also try to learn how energy changes forms and how it goes from place to place. They try to learn ways to control energy. Physicists are also interested in how matter and energy work together.

The word *physics* comes from a Greek word meaning *natural things.* Information discovered by physicists is used in many other areas of science, including astronomy, chemistry, and geology. Physics also provides much useful information for new technological developments, including better designs of automobiles, airplanes, and computers and improved ways to treat diseases. Physics is even useful for explaining how such common items as vacuum cleaners and DVD players work.

Different physicists work in different ways. Some physicists perform experiments in laboratories. Other physicists think of new ideas and theories to explain how parts of the universe

Physicists once used a device called a bubble chamber to study subatomic particles (units of matter smaller than an atom). Tracks made by the particles as they passed through the chamber revealed information about the particles' mass (amount of matter), electric charge, and other characteristics.

Continued on the next page

A physicist uses smoke to study turbulence (the way air moves in response to heat, temperature, and other factors). This type of study, called aerodynamics, is useful in designing airplanes or understanding the weather.

Particle accelerators, such as the Large Hadron Collider in Europe, have replaced bubble chambers for studying subatomic particles.

work. Physicists must use a great deal of mathematics to explain their ideas. These explanations can be very complex.

Physics has many areas of study. These include electricity, heat, light, magnetism, mechanics, and sound. Some physicists study *atoms* and *molecules*. Atoms are tiny units of matter that combine to make molecules. Some physicists study the *subatomic particles* that atoms are made of, including *electrons, protons,* and *neutrons.* Still-smaller particles are often explored using huge machines called *particle accelerators.*

Through the centuries, physics has been closely linked to developments in technology and to advances in mathematics, astronomy, and other sciences. However, modern physics began in the late 1800's, when scientists began discovering subatomic particles. In the early 1900's, physicists began using *quantum (KWON tuhm) theory* and other new ideas to describe matter, energy, space, and time in ways that are very different from earlier descriptions.

Other articles to read include: **Atom; Biophysics; Energy; Matter; Molecule; Nuclear physics; Quantum mechanics.**

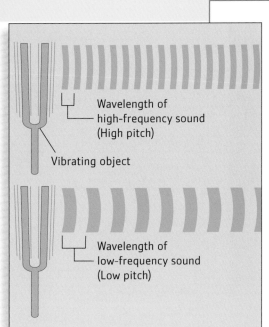

Wavelength of
high-frequency sound
(High pitch)

Vibrating object

Wavelength of
low-frequency sound
(Low pitch)

The pitch of a sound depends
on the frequency of the sound
waves made by the vibrating
object that produces the
sound. The higher the
frequency of the sound waves,
the higher the pitch of the
sound.

Max Karl Ernst Ludwig Planck

Pitch

Pitch is the highness or lowness of a sound. Pitch is determined by the *vibrations* of sound waves. Vibrations are quick, tiny movements back and forth or up and down. High-pitched sound waves vibrate faster than low-pitched sound waves. The speed at which a sound wave vibrates is called its *frequency.* Frequency is the number of complete vibrations per second. High-pitched sounds have higher frequencies than low-pitched sounds. When violin players *tune* (correct the pitch of) their instruments, they adjust each string so it will vibrate at the desired frequency.

Most sounds we hear are actually a blend of a number of pitches or frequencies. The sounds produced by a musical instrument, a whistle, or a siren, for example, have several frequencies at the same time.

Other articles to read include: **Frequency; Sound; Vibration; Waves.**

Planck, Max Karl Ernst Ludwig

Max Karl Ernst Ludwig Planck *(plahngk)* (1858-1947) was an important German scientist. He studied how objects *absorb* (take in) and release heat and other kinds of energy. In 1900, Planck developed an idea called *quantum (KWON tuhm) theory.* This theory totally changed the field of physics. Scientists had thought that energy flows continuously. Planck showed that energy actually flows in tiny units that he called *quanta.* One example of such a unit is called a *photon* (the smallest unit of light energy). All forms of light, including visible light and X rays, are composed of photons.

Planck was born in Kiel, Germany. He studied at the universities of Munich and Berlin. He taught physics at the universities of Munich, Kiel, and Berlin. In 1918, Planck was awarded the Nobel Prize in physics.

Other articles to read include: **Energy; Photon; Quantum mechanics.**

Plasma

Plasma *(PLAZ muh)* is sometimes called the fourth state of matter. The other three are *solids, liquids,* and *gases.* Plasmas consist of electrically charged particles. The sun and other stars and most other objects in space consist of plasma. Lightning bolts also consist of plasma, but few other plasmas occur naturally on Earth.

Artificially created plasmas have many practical uses. For example, electricity turns the gas in the tube of a neon sign into a plasma that gives off light. Ion rockets use plasma fuels for long trips through space.

Arc welding is an example of useful artificially created plasma. In this process, electricity is used to produce plasma at the high temperatures needed to join pieces of metal.

A plasma can be made by heating a gas to a very high temperature or by passing an electric current through it. Great heat or a flow of electricity causes the atoms in the gas to lose one or more electrons *(ih LEHK tronz).* Electrons are negatively charged particles that orbit the *nucleus* (core) of an atom. An atom that loses electrons has a positive charge and is called an *ion (EYE uhn or EYE on).*

The physical and electrical qualities of a gas change greatly when it becomes a plasma. They change because the ions and electrons in the plasma are separated. For example, most gases conduct electricity poorly and are not affected by magnetic fields. But a plasma conducts electricity well and is affected by magnetic fields. Gases consist of atoms that move around independently and in no definite manner. The electrons and ions in a plasma may move around in groups, usually in wavelike motions. Plasmas have qualities that are different from those of the three basic forms of matter.

Scientists hope someday to generate electricity by using plasmas to control the process of *nuclear fusion.* Nuclear fusion gives off tremendous amounts of energy when two lightweight atomic *nuclei* (plural of nucleus) unite to form a heavier nucleus.

Other articles to read include: **Electron; Gas; Fusion; Ion; Matter.**

Platinum

Platinum atomic symbol

Platinum *(PLAT uh nuhm)* is a silver-white metal that is more precious than gold. Platinum is also one of the heaviest *chemical elements.* A chemical element is a material made up of only one kind of atom. A piece of platinum weighs about 21 times as much as an equal volume of water.

Platinum is valuable for many reasons. It can be stretched into a fine wire or hammered into thin sheets. Platinum does not rust when exposed to air. It also resists strong acids. Platinum does not melt until the temperature reaches 3221.6 °F (1772 °C).

Platinum has many uses besides jewelry. Chemical laboratories often use containers made of platinum because heat and chemicals do not easily affect the metal. Platinum is an effective *catalyst (KAT uh lihst.)* A catalyst is a substance that helps start or speed up a chemical reaction. Automobile manufacturers use platinum in *catalytic converters.* These devices reduce harmful exhausts given off by car engines. The petroleum industry uses platinum as a catalyst in the conversion of oil into gasoline. Many tools used in surgery are made of platinum.

In the 1500's, *conquistadors* (Spanish conquerors) found silvery grains of an unknown metal mixed with gold deposits in Latin America. At the time, there were no known means for melting the grains to shape the metal. So miners threw the grains away. William Brownrigg, an English physician, recognized platinum as a new chemical element in 1750. By 1803, the English chemist William Wollaston had produced the first pure sample of platinum.

Other articles to read include: **Element, Chemical; Metal.**

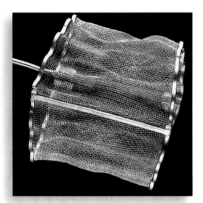

Platinum is used for many purposes, including making strong, heat-resistant wire meshes. Such meshes may be used by the oil industry in devices that break down oil. They may also be used in various areas of chemical research.

Polymer

A polymer *(POL ih muhr)* is a large, chainlike molecule *(MOL uh kyool).* Molecules are groups of atoms *bonded* (joined) together. Polymers are chemical compounds in which each molecule is made of two or more simpler molecules strung together. The simpler molecules are called *monomers.*

Continued on the next page

The monomers in a polymer are almost always identical. For example, starch is a polymer found in many plants. The monomer in starch is a simple sugar called glucose. A polymer may consist of thousands of monomers. Some polymers occur naturally. Others are *synthetic* (made by people).

Many common and useful substances are polymers. Starch and wool are natural polymers. Nylon and polyethylene, a tough plastic material, are synthetic polymers. Rubber, another polymer, can be natural or synthetic.

Polymers are often long and flexible. These characteristics give them many useful and unique properties. For example, rubber can be stretched to several times its normal length without breaking. In addition, many polymers do not dissolve easily because of the large size of their molecules.

Other articles to read include: **Ethylene; Molecule.**

PVC pipe (above) is made of polymers—long, chainlike molecules. The "links" are repeating patterns of groups of two carbon atoms, three hydrogen atoms, and one chlorine atom.

Porosity

Porosity *(paw ROS uh tee* or *poh ROS uh tee)* is a quality of many solid materials that indicates how many tiny holes or spaces they have. Materials that have many holes are said to be *porous (PAWR uhs* or *POHR uhs)*. Sandstone and limestone are examples of porous rock.

In some porous materials, the holes are connected to one another. Such materials include sponges and charcoal. Liquids and gases can easily pass through these holes and become *absorbed* (soaked up). The holes in other porous materials are not connected. Brick is an example of this kind of material. These materials usually cannot absorb liquids and gases very well.

Porosity is helpful in some materials. For example, charcoal can be used to filter the air. The holes allow air to pass through. But they trap unwanted substances. Porosity is not helpful in many other materials. For example, it reduces the strength of metals.

Other articles to read include: **Absorption and adsorption.**

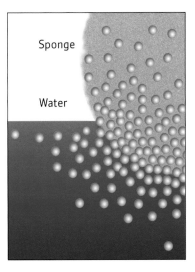

Sponges are very porous. Their holes are connected to one another, so they can quickly *absorb* (soak up) water and other liquids.

In nature, potassium is always found in combination with several other chemical elements. Potassium feldspar, a light-colored rock, also contains aluminum, silicon, and oxygen.

Potassium

19	K	2 8 8 1
Potassium 39.0983		

Potassium atomic symbol

Potassium *(puh TAS ee uhm)* is a silvery, metallic *chemical element*. A chemical element is a material that is made up of only one kind of atom. Potassium is the second softest metal, after lithium *(LIHTH ee uhm)*. Potassium is so soft it can be cut with a dull knife.

In nature, potassium is always found in combination with other chemical elements in compounds. Most potassium compounds occur in rock and clay grains. Potassium compounds also occur in soil. Plants need potassium to grow. Farmers use *fertilizers* (chemicals that help plants grow) containing potassium to keep crops healthy.

Potassium has a number of other uses. Potassium compounds are used to make glass, gunpowder, matches, soap, and a variety of medicines. The English chemist Sir Humphry Davy obtained the first pure samples of potassium in 1807.

Other articles to read include: **Element, Chemical; Metal.**

Potential energy

Potential *(puh TEHN shuhl)* energy can be thought of as "stored" energy. It is the result of something's position or other condition. Potential energy is different from *kinetic (kih NEHT ihk)* energy. Kinetic energy is the energy of motion.

Kinetic and potential energy can change from one form to the other. For example, a girl who swings backward on a swing set

A girl on a swing shows how *potential* (stored) energy can become *kinetic* (moving) energy. In the picture, the girl has kicked herself back from position A to position B. While hanging in position B—before she starts moving forward—she has a lot of potential energy but no kinetic energy.

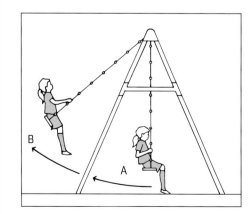

has potential energy at the top of her swing. This energy comes from her position in the swing. As she swings down, this potential energy is converted into the kinetic energy of her motion.

Continued on the next page

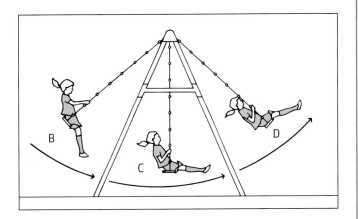

As the girl swings from position B to position D, she has a lot of kinetic energy but no potential energy.

There are different kinds of potential energy. Coal has potential energy in the form of chemical energy. That energy is stored in the arrangement of the *atoms* (tiny bits of matter) that make up the coal. A coal-burning power plant can convert this stored chemical energy to electric energy. Batteries store potential energy in the form of chemical energy that can be turned into electric energy.

Other articles to read include: **Energy; Kinetic energy; Motion.**

Pressure

Pressure is the action of a weight or force. If you place a heavy rock on a grape, the grape will be squashed by the pressure of the rock's weight. When you swim underwater, you feel the water pressing on your eardrums. When you blow up a balloon, the pressure of the air on the inside of the balloon makes it get larger. The greater the force applied, the greater the pressure will be. Pressure is measured in *pounds per square inch* in the inch-pound system and by the *pascal* in the metric system.

Atmospheric (at muh SFEHR ihk) pressure is created by the weight of the air in the atmosphere pressing on the air below it. The pressure at a mountaintop is less than the pressure at the base because less air is pressing from above.

Other articles to read include: **Force.**

The pressure made by air is related to the temperature of the air. Warm air weighs less than cool air. So air pressure is lower where the air is warmer. Air pressure is higher where the air is cooler. Warmer, lighter air rises, and cooler, heavier air sinks.

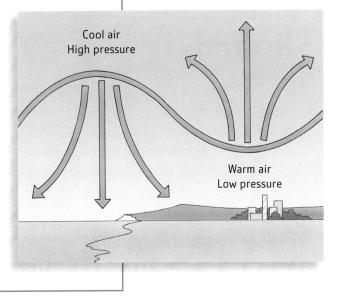

Cool air
High pressure

Warm air
Low pressure

Probability

Probability *(PROB uh BIHL uh tee)* is a branch of mathematics that deals with the chance that something will happen. If something is more *probable*, it is more likely to happen.

If you flip a coin, it will land either heads up or tails up. The coin is as likely to land heads up as it is to land tails up. So we say that the probability of it landing heads up is ½, or 50 percent. This probability holds true for each flip of the coin, no matter how many times the coin is flipped. The probability will not change, even if the coin has landed heads up three times in a row. On the fourth flip, the coin is equally likely to land either way.

Probability is the basis of a science called *statistics (stuh TIHS tihks)*. People who study statistics are called *statisticians (STAT uh STIHSH uhnz)* . Statisticians use probability to help predict many things. For example, they may try to predict the number of people who will vote for a political candidate or buy a particular soft drink.

Other articles to read include: **Mathematics; Statistics.**

When you flip a coin, the coin is as likely to land heads up as it is to land tails down, no matter how many times the coin is flipped.

Proton

A proton *(PROH ton)* is a particle with a positive electric charge found in the *nucleus (NOO klee uhs)* (core) of an atom. Protons are made up of three even tinier particles, called *quarks*. A proton has a diameter of approximately one-millionth of a *nanometer*. One nanometer equals one-millionth of a millimeter ($\frac{1}{25,400,000}$ inch).

The *nuclei* (plural of nucleus) of all but one kind of atom are made up of protons and another type of particle called a *neutron (NOO tron)*. Only the atoms of ordinary hydrogen have a nucleus without a neutron. The nuclei of these atoms have a single proton. All atoms of a *chemical element* have the same number of protons.

Continued on the next page

The number of protons in an atom is called the *atomic number* of that element.

A neutrally charged atom has an equal number of protons and *electrons (ih LEHK trons)*. Electrons orbit the nucleus. Each electron carries one unit of negative charge. This charge balances out the positive electric charge of each proton. As a result, the atom is electrically neutral.

Other articles to read include: **Atom; Electron; Element, Chemical; Neutron; Nucleus.**

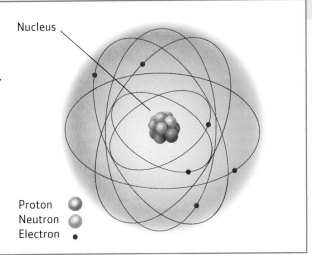

Nucleus

Proton
Neutron
Electron

Protons and neutrons make up the *nucleus* (core) of an atom. *Electrons* travel around the nucleus. An atom with no electric charge has equal numbers of positively charged protons and negatively charged electrons.

Pythagoras

Pythagoras *(pih THAG uhr uhs)* (580?-? B.C.) was a Greek mathematician and philosopher. He is best known for formulating the *Pythagorean theorem.* Pythagoras did not leave any writings. His ideas are known through the writings of his followers.

The Pythagorean theorem is a mathematical formula. It describes a special relationship between the lengths of the sides of a *right triangle.* A right triangle is a triangle with a *right angle* (a 90-degree angle). In a right triangle, the side opposite the right angle, called the *hypotenuse (hy POT uh noos),* is longer than the other two sides. Imagine a right triangle with sides of lengths A, B, and C, with C being the hypotenuse. The Pythagorean theorem states that the *squares* (values multiplied by themselves) of A and B, when added together, equal the square of C.

As a philosopher, Pythagoras taught that numbers were the essence of all things. He associated numbers with virtues, colors, and many other ideas. He also taught that the human soul is immortal and that after death it moves into another living body.

Little is known of Pythagoras's early life. Scholars believe that he was born on the Greek island of Samos. In about 529 B.C., he settled in Crotona, Italy. Pythagoras founded a *school* (brotherhood) among the high-ranking men of that city. But the people of Crotona killed most of the members in a political uprising. Historians do not know if Pythagoras escaped the violence or was among those killed.

Other articles to read include: **Angle; Geometry; Mathematics; Triangle.**

Pythagoras conducted experiments on the sounds made by vibrating strings of musical instruments. He identified mathematical patterns in the sounds.

Qq

Quantum mechanics

Quantum *(KWON tuhm)* mechanics is the study of the structure and behavior of *matter.* All objects and substances are made of matter. Quantum mechanics is especially useful for describing *subatomic particles.* Subatomic particles are smaller than *atoms,* one of the building blocks of matter. Quantum mechanics can be difficult to understand, and some of its claims seem strange. But quantum mechanics has been a great advance in *physics (FIHZ ihks).* Physics is the study of matter and energy.

Quantum mechanics has replaced *classical mechanics* as a description of the smallest known units of matter and their activity. Scientists still use the older theories for describing and predicting the behavior of objects that we ordinarily encounter in our daily lives.

In 1900, the German physicist Max Planck made the first discovery in quantum mechanics. Scientists had thought that hot objects give off energy in an unbroken stream. Planck showed that energy is actually given off in tiny bundles called *quanta. Quantum* is the singular of *quanta.*

The German-born physicist Albert Einstein built on Planck's ideas. Einstein showed that all light is given off in quanta. These "packets" were later called *photons.* The existence of quanta helps explain why light acts sometimes like a wave and sometimes like a particle. Physicists soon discovered that *electrons* and other subatomic particles also behave in a similar way. An electron is a negatively charged particle that orbits the *nucleus* (core) of an atom.

In 1913, the Danish physicist Niels Bohr discovered that the behavior of electrons in atoms is governed by quanta. An electron that absorbs a quantum of energy moves to a higher energy level. This move changes its orbit around the nucleus. When an electron gives off a quantum, the electron returns to the lower energy level. Electrons occupy only particular orbits. The orbits represent particular quanta of energy.

In 1927, the German physicist Werner Heisenberg found that it is impossible to precisely describe a particle's location and motion at the same time. If its location is precisely known, its motion cannot be precisely known, and vice versa. Physicists call this limitation the *uncertainty principle.*

Other articles to read include: **Bohr, Niels; Einstein, Albert; Matter; Mechanics; Physics; Planck, Max Karl Ernst Ludwig.**

Quark

The quark *(kwawrk)* is one of the most basic particles of *matter.* All objects and substances are made of matter. Quarks are *elementary particles.* This means that as far as scientists know, quarks are not made up of even smaller particles. There are six *flavors* (types) of quarks. They are: (1) *up,* (2) *down,* (3) *charm,* (4) *strange,* (5) *top,* and (6) *bottom.*

All quarks carry a fraction of an electric charge. This charge may be either positive or negative.

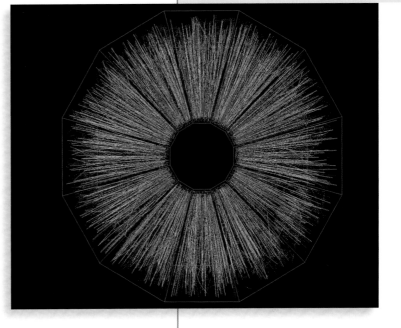

Hundreds of tracks made by quarks and other *subatomic particles* (particles smaller than an atom) radiate outward from the point of a collision between two beams of gold *ions* (charged atoms) in a computerized display.

Quarks make up one of the three families of particles that serve as "building blocks" of matter. The other two families are the *leptons* and the *fundamental,* or *gauge, bosons.*

Quarks have no measurable size. Physicists describe them as "pointlike." The top quark is the heaviest known elementary particle. It is almost as heavy as an entire atom of gold. The lightest quark, the up quark, has about 35,000 times less *mass* than the top. Mass is the amount of matter in an object.

A quark is always combined with one or two other quarks. For example, a *proton* consists of two up quarks and one down quark. A *neutron* is made up of two down quarks and one up quark. Protons and neutrons make up the *nuclei* (cores) of atoms, the basic building blocks of ordinary matter.

Strange, charm, bottom, and top quarks are much heavier than up and down quarks. These heavy quarks usually break down very quickly. For this reason, the heavy quarks do not exist in ordinary matter. Scientists have made them with special devices called *particle accelerators.*

The scientists Murray Gell-Mann, an American physicist, and George Zweig, a Soviet-born American physicist, each came up with the idea of quarks in 1964. Their original theories predicted three quarks. Scientists later thought that six quarks must exist. By 1995, they had found all six quarks.

Other articles to read include: **Boson; Mass; Neutron; Proton; Standard Model.**

Rr

Radiation

Radiation is energy given off as waves or small bits of matter. All life on Earth depends on radiation. Radiation comes in many forms. The most familiar is *visible light* (the light we see), such as the light from the sun or a flashlight. Other examples of radiation include the heat from a fireplace, signals that carry cell phone calls and wireless Internet access, and microwaves used to cook food.

Radiation occurs whenever energy moves from one place to another. Small bits of matter called *atoms* and *molecules* give off radiation to get rid of excess energy. When the radiation strikes a substance, it may transfer some or all of its energy to the substance. Often, the energy takes the form of heat, raising the temperature of the material. Except for visible light, most kinds of radiation are invisible to people.

There are two main types of radiation. One type is called *electromagnetic radiation*. It is made only of energy. All materials that have been heated give off electromagnetic radiation. Light, heat, and X rays are all examples of electromagnetic radiation.

The other type is called *particle radiation*. It consists of tiny bits of matter. Electrons and protons, two particles found in atoms, make up some particle radiation. Particle radiation often comes from *radioactive materials*. These materials release radiation because of changes in their atoms. Another type of particle radiation comes from certain nuclear reactions, such as those deep within the sun. The reactions in nuclear power plants also release particle radiation, along with the heat needed to produce electric power.

Radiation has many uses. Doctors use X rays to find broken bones and other problems in the body. The food industry uses low doses of radiation to kill bacteria in some foods.

Nuclear power plants get energy from *nuclear fission*. Nuclear fission is the splitting of an atom's *nucleus* (core). Fission releases large amounts of radiation. Some of the radiation is heat. This heat is used to turn water into steam. This steam then runs a machine called a *turbine* that produces electric power.

Continued on the next page

A technician checks samples of *ground water* (water found beneath Earth's surface) for evidence of radiation from buried nuclear wastes or natural sources.

Some forms of radiation can be dangerous. Light from the sun helps plants and other living things to grow, and it warms Earth. But it also causes sunburn and skin cancer. Nuclear power plants produce electric energy. But they also create radioactive waste that can harm living things.

Radiation can damage the body's cells. It can cause the cells to change in unusual ways or to die. The *doses* (amounts) of radiation received in daily life are too small to cause much immediate damage. But many small doses can lead to cancer or birth defects.

Scientists' understanding of radiation has changed over time. In 1864, the British scientist James Clerk Maxwell said that light is electromagnetic radiation. Scientists later found other forms of electromagnetic radiation. In the 1890's, natural radioactivity was discovered by the French scientists Antoine Henri Becquerel, Marie Curie, and Pierre Curie.

Other articles to read include: **Electromagnetic spectrum; Infrared light; Light; Microwaves; Nuclear energy; Radio wave; Ultraviolet waves; Waves; X rays.**

Radio wave

A radio wave is the longest kind of *electromagnetic wave.* Electromagnetic waves are moving patterns of electric and magnetic energy. Other kinds of electromagnetic waves include gamma rays, visible light, and X rays. Radio waves are invisible to people.

Like other types of electromagnetic waves, radio waves travel through empty space at the speed of light, 186,282 miles (299,792 kilometers) per second. Radio waves can pass through walls and other solid objects.

Radio waves are used in many communication devices. They are used to broadcast radio and television signals. Radio waves are also used by wireless devices, including cell phones, Global Positioning System (GPS) receivers, satellite

Continued on the next page

The two main kinds of radio waves are *AM (amplitude modulation)* and *FM (frequency modulation).* In AM broadcasts, the *amplitude* (strength) of the radio waves changes to match changes in the signals coming from the radio station. In FM broadcasts, the *frequency* (number of vibrations per second) of the waves changes to match the signals.

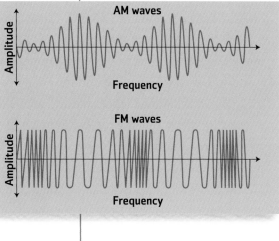

Radio wave *Continued from the previous page*

communication systems, police radios, and wireless Internet devices. Garage door openers and radio-controlled toys also use radio waves. Most radar systems detect such objects as airplanes, ships, cars, or clouds by bouncing radio waves off them. Microwaves are often considered to be a type of radio wave.

Radio waves enable astronomers to observe objects in space that cannot be seen with optical telescopes. Astronomers have detected radio waves from planets, *supernovae* (exploding stars) and galaxies with supermassive black holes at their centers.

Radio waves have different *frequencies (FREE kwuhn seez)* and *amplitudes (AM pluh toodz)*. The frequency is how rapidly the wave vibrates. The amplitude is how big the wave is.

Other articles to read include: **Electromagnetic spectrum; Waves.**

Scientists can use *radiocarbon dating* to figure out the age of an ancient object up to 50,000 years old. Burning a small part of the object creates carbon dioxide gas. Radiocarbon (carbon 14) atoms in the gas give off particles called *electrons* as they change into another kind of atom called *nitrogen 14.* Special machines can count the number of electrons, which gives scientists clues to the age of the object. ▼

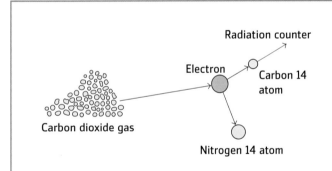

Radiation counter
Electron
Carbon 14 atom
Carbon dioxide gas
Nitrogen 14 atom

Radiocarbon

Radiocarbon *(RAY dee oh KAHR buhn)* is an *isotope (EYE suh tohp) (form)* of the *chemical element* carbon. A chemical element is a material made up of only one kind of atom. Radiocarbon is also called *carbon 14.* It is heavier than the regular form of carbon.

Radiocarbon is *radioactive.* That is, it gives off energy as its atoms *decay* (break down).

In nature, radiocarbon forms when high-energy atomic particles called *cosmic rays* smash into Earth's atmosphere. The rays cause nitrogen atoms to change into radiocarbon atoms.

Living things take in radiocarbon as long as they live. Plants take in radiocarbon from the carbon dioxide in the air. Human beings and other animals take in radiocarbon chiefly by eating plants.

Scientists can use radiocarbon to determine the age of fossils and other ancient objects. After a living thing dies, it no longer takes in radiocarbon. Researchers know the rate at which radiocarbon decays. By measuring the radiocarbon left in a material, they can determine how long ago it or the living materials from which it was made died. This process is called *radiocarbon dating.* It has helped scientists learn much about human beings, animals, and plants that lived up to about 50,000 to 60,000 years ago. Researchers also use radiocarbon to study biological actions in cells and tissues.

Other articles to read include: **Atom; Carbon; Isotope; Radiation.**

Radium

Radium atomic symbol

Radium *(RAY dee uhm)* is a *radioactive (ray dee oh AK tihv)* metallic *chemical element*. A chemical element is a material that is made up of only one kind of atom. Radioactive elements *emit* (give off) energy as their atoms *decay* (break down). Radium emits large amounts of radioactive energy. This radiation can be harmful to human health.

In the past, people used radium for many purposes. Physicians used radium for treating patients with cancer, because the radiation it emits can kill cancer cells. Today, there are many safer and cheaper ways to produce radiation for medical and other uses. The French scientists Pierre and Marie Curie *(KYOO ree)* and Gustave Bémont discovered radium in 1898.

Other articles to read include: **Curie, Marie Skłodowska; Curie, Pierre; Element, Chemical; Nuclear energy; Radiation.**

A speck of radium sends out rays of radiation made of particles called *alpha particles.* This image was made by placing a speck of radium on a special kind of photographic material.

Radius

A radius *(RAY dee uhs)* is a straight line from the center of a circle to any point on the circle's edge. A circle's edge is called its *circumference (suhr KUHM fuhr uhns).* A spoke in a bicycle wheel is an example of a radius. The wheel's tire is its circumference.

A circle can be described by the length of its radius. A circle's radius is one-half the length of the circle's *diameter (dy AM uh tuhr).* A diameter is a line that goes all the way across a circle, passing through its center.

A *sphere* also has a radius. A sphere is a solid figure shaped like a ball or a globe. A sphere's radius is a line from its center to a point on its surface.

Other articles to read include: **Circle; Diameter; Geometric shapes.**

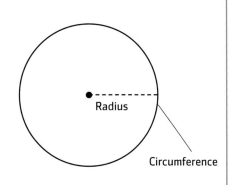

The radius of a circle is one-half the diameter of that circle. The radius can be used to determine the area of a circle. The area equals the radius multiplied first by itself and then by a ratio known as pi (3.14159).

Radon

Radon atomic
symbol

Radon *(RAY don)* is a heavy *radioactive chemical element*. Chemical elements are materials made up of only one kind of atom. Radioactive elements *emit* (give off) energy as their atoms *decay* (break down).

Radon occurs naturally as a gas. It forms when the chemical element radium *(RAY dee uhm)* decays. Radium is found in nearly all rocks and soil. Radon gas has no color or smell.

Radon gas can be very dangerous. In humans, high amounts of radon can cause cancer or other health problems. People may come into contact with radon in several ways. The gas can seep from soil and rocks into water and air. Radon can enter buildings through cracks in basements. Breathing air and drinking water containing radon can cause this chemical element to build up in the body.

People can test for high radon levels in their houses using kits available from stores and online sites. Contractors use a number of methods to lower radon levels in houses and other buildings.

Other articles to read include: **Element, Chemical; Radiation; Radium.**

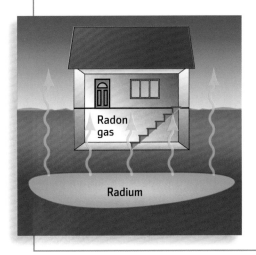

Radon gas can seep into a house's basement as radium in the rocks and soil below the house *decays* (breaks down).

Rainbow

A rainbow is a curved band of colored light that appears in the sky. A rainbow appears when the sun shines on raindrops. Sometimes both ends of the rainbow seem to touch the ground. A rainbow is not a physical object. Rather, it is a pattern of light.

No two people ever see the same rainbow. You are at the center of the rainbow you see. A person standing next to you would be at the center of a different rainbow. A different set of raindrops forms each rainbow.

Rainbows usually appear at the end of the day, after a storm has passed. To find a rainbow, turn away from the sun and face the shadow cast by your head. Now look up. If there is a rainbow, you will see it less than halfway between your shadow and a point straight above your head.

Usually, people see a *primary (PRY mehr ee)* (main) rainbow. It is red on the top of the curve and violet on the inside. Bands

Continued on the next page

of orange, yellow, green, and blue will appear between these colors, with orange at the top.

Sometimes a second, fainter rainbow appears higher up. This rainbow is violet on top and red on the inside. The colors between them are also reversed. Such a rainbow is called a *secondary rainbow*. In extremely rare cases, a *tertiary* (third) or *quaternary* (fourth) rainbow can appear on the same side of the observer as the sun. Because these rainbows are close to the sun, they are difficult to see. The colors of a tertiary rainbow are arranged in the same way as those in a primary rainbow. The colors of a quaternary rainbow are arranged in the same way as those of a secondary rainbow.

Rainbows appear because of the way light behaves. White light is made up of all the other colors of light. Each color has light waves of a different length. White light bends when it passes through a kind of glass called a *prism (PRIHZ uhm)*. Light waves of some colors bend more than others. This makes the white light separate into bands of colored light. Light passing through raindrops separates in the same way. The bands of colored light make up the rainbow that people see.

Other articles to read include: **Color; Light; Refraction; Waves; White light.**

Rainbows sometimes are seen as twins. This happens when the inside surfaces of raindrops reflect rays of sunlight more than once.

A rainbow forms when raindrops bend and reflect rays of sunlight. As the light bends while entering a raindrop, it breaks up into rays of different colors. These rays then reflect off the inside surface of the raindrop and bend again as they leave the raindrop. To find a rainbow after a storm, turn away from the sun and face the shadow cast by your head. Now look up. The rainbow will be about halfway between your shadow and a point above your head.

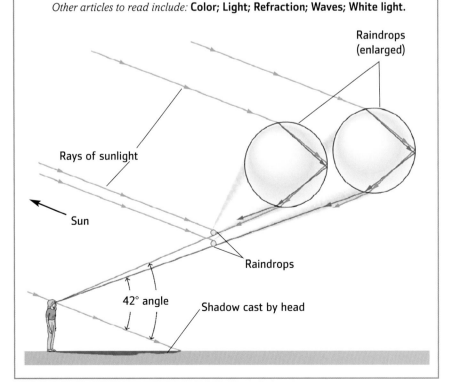

Raindrops (enlarged)

Rays of sunlight

Sun

Raindrops

42° angle

Shadow cast by head

Ray

A ray is a line or stream of energy. There are many types of rays. They include X rays, gamma rays, ultraviolet rays, *infrared rays* (heat rays) and *visible light rays*. All of these rays are forms of light. They are also known as *electromagnetic waves*. Electromagnetic waves are traveling patterns of electric and magnetic influence. Visible light rays are the only type of electromagnetic wave that human beings can see. Electromagnetic rays travel through space at 186,282 miles (299,792 kilometers) per second—the fastest speed that anything can move.

All rays can be changed in three ways. They can be reflected, *refracted* (bent), or *diffracted* (spread out). Rays are reflected when they bounce off certain materials. For example, rays of visible light are reflected from a mirror. Rays are refracted when they move from one material to another. For example, rays of light bend when they enter a *prism* (specially shaped piece of glass). Rays are diffracted when they pass close to an object or through a small hole. For example, light waves diffract as they pass around an object. This makes the edges of an object's shadow look fuzzy.

Other articles to read include: **Electromagnetic spectrum; Light; Radiation.**

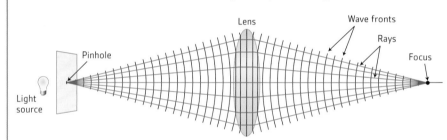

Light source · Pinhole · Lens · Wave fronts · Rays · Focus

Light rays *diffract* (spread out) after they pass through a pinhole. If the rays pass through a lens, they bend and then come together again at the focus.

Reflection

Reflection is the return of a wave of energy after it strikes a surface. The energy acts something like a ball bouncing off a wall. Reflection may happen to a wave of light, sound, or heat or to any other kind of energy.

One common source of reflection is a mirror. Most mirrors are made of glass with a metal back. Mirrors reflect most of the light that strikes them. A clear surface, such as window glass, reflects only a small amount of light. Most of the light passes through the glass.

An *echo* is another example of reflection. It happens when sound waves from a noise bounce off some object. When the reflected waves reach our ears, we hear an echo.

Continued on the next page

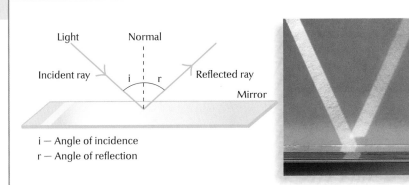

i — Angle of incidence
r — Angle of reflection

Radar systems detect the location of objects with the reflection of radio waves. For example, radio waves sent from a system may bounce off an airplane. The system can sense the reflected waves and determine the airplane's location, direction, distance, altitude, and speed.

Other articles to read include: **Echo; Light; Radio wave; Waves.**

A beam of light is reflected by a smooth surface, such as a mirror. After the beam is reflected, it travels away from the surface at an angle equal to the angle made by the original light beam. An imaginary line called the *normal* lies in the middle of the two angles.

Refraction

Refraction *(rih FRAK shuhn)* is the bending of light rays. Refraction occurs as light waves enter or leave a *transparent* (clear) material. For example, light may change direction as it passes from air into water or from water into air. Light travels at different speeds through different materials. A change in speed causes light to bend. Light must strike an object at an angle to refract. Refraction can change the way an object looks. The object may seem to have a different size, shape, or even location.

Light consists of waves of energy. Just like ocean waves, light waves have different *wavelengths*. We see these wavelengths as different colors. The shorter the wavelength, the more readily light can bend. Violet light has the shortest wavelength, so it bends the most. Red light has the longest wavelength, so it bends less than other colors.

Light can be refracted by a *prism (PRIHZ uhm)* (piece of glass). White light consists of many different wavelengths. A prism separates white light into a *spectrum* (rainbowlike band of colors). The different colors are bent at different angles. Similarly, rainbows occur because of the refraction of light passing through raindrops.

Other articles to read include: **Color; Light; Rainbow; White light; Wavelength.**

A pencil in a glass of water appears to be broken at the water's surface because the light from the pencil is *refracted* (bent) as it passes from water to air.

Can you bend a pencil?

Can you bend a pencil without breaking it? You can make a pencil look as if it has been bent by putting it in water.

What you need:

- a glass
- water
- a pencil

1. Fill the glass halfway with water. Put a pencil in the glass and lean it against the side.

2. Look at the water from above. The pencil will look bent.

3. Now take the pencil out of the water. Nothing has happened to the pencil after all!

What's going on:

Why did the pencil look bent when it was in the water? Light rays speed up as they leave the water and change direction before reaching your eyes. This makes the pencil look bent. The point of the pencil appears to be halfway up the glass!

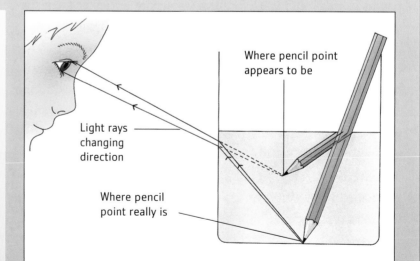

Where pencil point appears to be

Light rays changing direction

Where pencil point really is

http://bit.ly/128bQX3

Relativity

Relativity *(rehl uh TIHV uh tee)* is either of two theories of *physics* developed by the German-born American physicist Albert Einstein. Physics is the study of matter and energy. Einstein's theories explain the behavior of matter, energy, and even time and space. The first theory of relativity, called the *special theory of relativity*, was published in 1905. Einstein announced the second, the *general theory of relativity*, in 1915 and published it in 1916. These theories are two of the most *fundamental* (basic) ideas upon which modern physics is built.

Scientists before Einstein treated space and time as two different things. In his special theory of relativity, Einstein said that they were actually part of the same thing, which he called *space-time*. Space and time are *relative to* (dependent upon) the observer.

A famous example is often called *the twin paradox*. In this example, Einstein's theory explains how two people could experience time differently based on how fast they are moving. In the example, one brother stays on Earth for several decades, while his twin sets off in a spaceship, traveling close to the speed of light, for the same period. When the astronaut twin returns home, he finds his brother is an old man. But the astronaut is only a few months older. The two experienced time differently because one twin was traveling at a great speed relative to the other twin. Time passed more slowly for the traveler as his speed approached the speed of light. Scientists have since proven this theory using several different methods.

The general theory of relativity explains how gravity works. Einstein described gravitation as the ability of matter to *warp* (bend) space-time. The more massive an object is, the more it will warp space-time. For example, imagine two identical clocks placed at different distances from Earth's center. One is placed in orbit above Earth. The other is placed at the bottom of the ocean. A person observing both clocks would notice that the clock in the ocean was moving slower than the clock in orbit. That is because the force of Earth's gravity is different for each clock. The clock closer to Earth's gravitation experiences time at a slower pace.

Other articles to read include: **Einstein, Albert; Gravitation; Light, Speed of.**

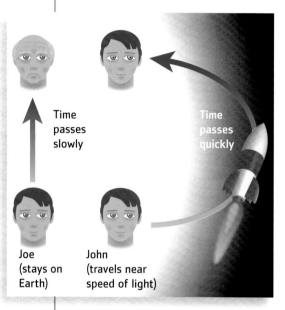

Time passes slowly

Time passes quickly

Joe (stays on Earth)

John (travels near speed of light)

The twin paradox is an example of the special theory of relativity. Joe and John are twins. Joe stays on Earth and ages in a normal way over many years. During this same time, John goes on a space trip, traveling at nearly the speed of light. Time passes more slowly. John ages as if only a few months have passed.

Rust

Rust is a red-brown coating that forms on iron or steel when the air around it is moist or wet. Rust forms when oxygen in the air combines with iron. Steel is iron mixed with other materials. The frame of a steel bicycle will rusts if it is left outside for a long time in damp, rainy weather. Rust makes the metal wear away and weaken. Rust is an example of *oxidation*.

Objects made of iron or steel should be kept dry or painted to prevent rust. They can also be coated with heavy grease or spray-on plastic to stop rust from forming. Iron can be mixed with other *chemical elements* to make metals that do not rust. These metals are called stainless steels. A chemical element is a material made of only one kind of atom.

Other articles to read include: **Corrosion; Metal; Oxidation.**

Rust eats away at the metal of a truck that was often left outside in the rain. Rust often forms when iron combines slowly with oxygen and water.

Rutherford, Ernest

Ernest Rutherford (1871-1937) was a British scientist. He developed a widely used model of the structure of *atoms*. Atoms are tiny building blocks of matter. Later, Rutherford became the first person to *split* (break up) the *nucleus* (core) of an atom. Because of his many contributions to science, he is often regarded as the father of nuclear science.

In 1911, Rutherford proposed that atoms are structured much like the solar system. A heavy nucleus forms the center of an atom, the way the sun forms the center of the solar system. Like the planets, particles of negative electric charge called *electrons* form the outer part of the system. But most of an atom is empty space. Later scientists determined that if an atom could be made 4 miles (6.4 kilometers) wide, the nucleus would only be about the size of a tennis ball.

Ernest Rutherford

Rutherford and the British chemist Frederick Soddy discovered that atoms of one chemical element can change into atoms of another element. Some atoms do so by giving off electrically charged particles, a type of *radiation*. Rutherford and Soddy published their finding in 1902. Rutherford won the 1908 Nobel Prize in chemistry for this work.

Rutherford was born in Nelson, New Zealand. He taught at McGill University in Montreal, Canada, and at the University of Manchester and Cambridge University in England.

Other articles to read include: **Atom; Nucleus; Radiation.**

Rusting

You can do some experiments to see what is needed to make rusting happen.

 Have a teacher or other adult help you with this experiment.

1. Put just enough room-temperature water in one jar to cover the bottom. Put a nail in the water. The top should stick up above the water's surface. Mark this jar "1" with the marker.

2. Put a nail in the second jar with no water. Mark this jar "2."

3. Ask a teacher or other adult to help you boil some water to remove any oxygen that may be mixed with the water. Put enough of this water in a third jar to cover the nail completely—almost to the top of the jar. Pour a little oil on top to keep air out of the water. Mark this jar "3."

4. Put just enough room-tempera-ture water in the fourth jar to cover the bottom. Before you put the nail in, stir plenty of salt into the water to make a strong salt solution. Mark this jar "4."

What you need:

- four glass jars
- a permanent marker
- water
- four **iron** nails
- a stove
- cooking oil
- salt

What's going on:

After a few days:

Jar 1: The nail will rust because there is air and water in the jar.

Jar 2: The nail will not rust very much because there is no water.

Jar 3: The nail will not rust very much even though it is in water, because the oil keeps out the air.

Jar 4: The nail will rust because there is water and air in the jar. The salt in the water speeds up the rusting, so the nail will rust more quickly.

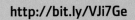
http://bit.ly/VJi7Ge

Ss

Schrödinger, Erwin

Erwin Schrödinger *(SHRAY dihng uhr)* (1887-1961) was an Austrian *physicist* (a scientist who studies matter and energy). Schrödinger developed a mathematical statement known as the "Schrödinger equation." It describes how *atoms* (tiny bits of matter) and other particles sometimes act like waves. Schrödinger based his equation on the ideas of Louis V. de Broglie, a French physicist. In 1924, de Broglie had proposed a theory that atoms and other particles show wavelike behavior. The Schrödinger equation became a basic part of a field of physics called *quantum mechanics*.

Schrödinger later worked to build on the theory of gravitation developed by the German-born physicist Albert Einstein. Schrödinger was also interested in the relationship between science and philosophy.

Schrödinger was born in Vienna. He worked as a professor of physics in several universities in Austria, Germany, and Switzerland. Schrödinger won the 1933 Nobel Prize in physics, along with the British scientist Paul Dirac, for their work on atomic theory.

Other articles to read include: **Atom; Gravitation; Quantum mechanics; Waves.**

Erwin Schrödinger

Scientific notation

Scientific notation is a way to write very large or very small numbers. Such numbers take up less space when written in scientific notation.

Scientific notation uses numbers called *powers of 10*. Powers of 10 can be written using positive or negative numerals.

The positive powers of 10 are used to write very large numbers. The positive powers of 10 always consist of a *1* followed by a number of zeros: 10, 100, 1,000, and so on. The particular power is equal to the number of zeros. For example, the number 10 is the first positive power of 10. It has one zero. The number 10,000 is the fourth power of 10 because it has four zeros.

Continued on the next page

Ten to the fourth power is written 10^4. The small numeral 4, which indicates the power, is called an *exponent*. The number 1,000,000 equals 10 to the sixth power. *Ten to the sixth power* is written 10^6. Through multiplication, these powers can be used to represent positive numbers. For example, the number 6,500,000 can be written in scientific notation as 6.5×10^6.

Negative powers of 10 are used for very small numbers. The first negative power of 10 (written 10^{-1}) is 0.1; 10^{-2} is 0.01, 10^{-3} is 0.001; and so on. The number 0.0002 is written as 2×10^{-4} in scientific notation.

Other articles to read include: **Multiplication; Number; Zero.**

Second

Second is the name of two separate units of measure. The first is used to measure time. The second is used to measure angles.

As a unit of time, a second is a *fraction* (portion) of a minute. There are 60 seconds in 1 minute, 60 minutes in 1 hour, and 24 hours in 1 day. Therefore, one second is $\frac{1}{86,400}$ of a day. This second is sometimes represented by the symbol *s*.

But days are not equal in length because Earth does not travel in a perfect circle around the sun. Therefore, measurements of time based on the day cannot be used for scientific work. Instead, scientists define a second by a particular vibration of an atom of the *chemical element* cesium *(SEE zee uhm)*. A chemical element is a material made up of only one kind of atom. The vibrations are measured by a device called an *atomic clock*. One second equals 9,192,631,770 such vibrations.

In *geometry (jee OM uh tree)*, a second is a fraction of an angle. Geometry is the study of shapes and angles. There are 60 seconds in each minute and 60 minutes in each *degree*. A circle has 360 degrees, so a second is $\frac{1}{1,296,000}$ of a circle.

Other articles to read include: **Angle; Circle; Degree; Time.**

In geometry, a second is a fraction of an angle. One-quarter of a circle is 90 degrees. One degree equals 60 minutes. One minute equals 60 seconds. So in a 90-degree angle, there are 5,400 minutes and 324,000 seconds.

90 degrees =
5,400 minutes =
324,000 seconds

Circle = 360 degrees

This silicon chip is smaller than a fingertip. Silicon is the main substance used to make computer chips.

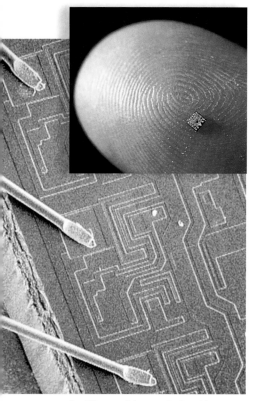

A silicon chip contains tiny metal circuits along which electric currents flow.

14	**Si**	2 8 4
	Silicon	
	28.0855	

Silicon atomic symbol

Silicon

Silicon *(SIHL uh kuhn)* is a hard, dark gray *chemical element.* A chemical element is a material made up of only one kind of atom.

Silicon is the main substance in computer chips and other electronic devices. It is also one of the most important building materials in the world.

Silicon is widely used for electronics because it is a *semiconductor.* A semiconductor can *conduct* (carry) electric currents more easily than glass and other *insulators* (materials that conduct almost no electricity). But silicon cannot conduct current as easily as copper and other conductors. Semiconductors work by controlling the tiny amounts of electricity that flow through them.

Silicon makes up about 28 percent of Earth's crust. Only oxygen is more plentiful. In nature, silicon occurs mainly as *silicon dioxide (dy OK syd),* also known as *silica.* Silicon is also found in compounds known as silicates *(SIHL uh kihts).* A silicate contains silicon, oxygen, and a metal.

Silicon dioxide is the main ingredient of sand and glass. It is used in ceramic products as well as electronic devices. Most rocks are mineral silicates. Silicates also make up cut stone, bricks, and concrete.

The Swedish chemist Jöns J. Berzelius (buhr ZEE lee uhs) discovered silicon in 1823. He developed the system of using letters of the alphabet as chemical symbols. Silicon's chemical symbol is *Si.*

Other articles to read include: **Element, Chemical; Electricity.**

47	**Ag**	2 8 18 18 1
	Silver	
	107.8682	

Silver atomic symbol

Silver

Silver is a soft, white metal. People have been using silver to make jewelry and coins for about 6,000 years. Silver is also a *chemical element* (a material that is made up of only one kind of atom).

Continued on the next page

Silver is a popular metal for making jewelry because it can be shaped more easily than any other metal except gold. Silver is also the shiniest of all metals. It reflects about 95 percent of the light that strikes it.

Silver conducts carries heat and electricity better than any other metal does. For this reason, it is used widely by the electrical and electronic equipment industries for wire and other items. Doctors use thin plates, wires, and drainage tubes made of silver during surgery, because silver helps kill bacteria.

Most countries have some silver, but it is expensive to mine. Peru leads the world in the production of silver, followed by Mexico and China.

Other articles to read include: **Element, Chemical; Electricity; Metal.**

Silver is a soft, whitish metal that can be shaped very easily. It is used to make many things, including tableware.

Sodium

11	Na	2 8 1
	Sodium	
	22.989770	

Sodium atomic symbol

Sodium *(SOH dee uhm)* is a silvery-white metal It is so soft that it can easily be molded or cut with a knife. Sodium is a common *chemical element* in Earth's crust. A chemical element is a material made up of only one kind of atom. In nature, sodium is never found in a pure state. It exists only in *compounds* (chemical combinations with other metals or minerals). One of the most common forms of sodium is sodium chloride, or table salt. It is found underground and in dry lake beds and in seawater.

Sodium compounds have many uses in industry. Sodium borate is used in making such products as soaps and water softeners. Sodium nitrate, also known as Chile saltpeter, is a valuable fertilizer. Sodium carbonate, called *baking soda,* is used for baking and as a gentle cleanser.

Pure sodium is used to produce some types of rubber and the metals titanium and zirconium. Sodium is also used in nuclear power plants to cool nuclear reactors, which produce extreme amounts of heat. However, pure sodium must be handled and stored with extreme care. When mixed with water, it can cause a violent reaction.

Other articles to read include: **Element, Chemical; Metal.**

Sodium is a silvery-white metallic element that has many important uses. It is so soft that it can easily be molded or cut with a knife.

Solid

Solid is one of the three basic *states* (forms) of matter. Nearly all the objects and materials that we see around us are made of matter. The other two basic states of matter are liquid and gas.

Solids have a particular size and shape. They also resist being *compressed* (squeezed) into a smaller space. Solids do not flow like a liquid or spread out like a gas. Their *molecules* (groups of atoms) cannot move around as freely as the molecules in liquids and gases. Most solids consist of small crystals packed together.

A solid can become a liquid if it is heated to its *melting point.* For example, ice—a solid—will change to water—a liquid—if heated to a temperature of 32 °F (0 °C). A solid may change directly to a gas or vapor, too. This process is called *sublimation.*

Other articles to read include: **Boiling point; Freezing point; Gas; Liquid; Matter; Melting point.**

The movement of atoms and molecules in a solid (right middle) is orderly. Solids form when liquids get cold enough for their atoms or molecules to line up in rigid arrangements. The atoms or molecules in a gas (far right) fly about in a disorderly way. Liquids (right) form when atoms or molecules in a gas lose a certain amount of energy. They stick together, and their motion becomes more orderly.

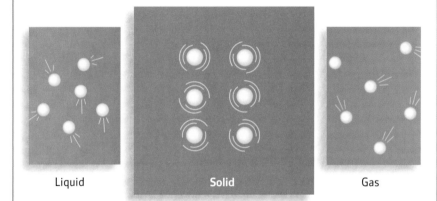

Liquid   **Solid**   Gas

A rock is a solid. It has a fixed size and shape, and it can be broken apart.

Water changes from a liquid to a solid when it freezes into ice.

Solution

A solution *(suh LOO shuhn)* is a mixture of two or more substances in which at least one of the substances *dissolves* (breaks up) into another. A solution can be a *liquid, solid,* or *gas.* A substance that causes another substance to dissolve is called a *solvent.* The substance that dissolves is called the *solute.*

The best-known solutions are liquid solutions. They form when a liquid, a solid, or a gas is dissolved in a liquid. For example, lemon juice, a liquid, can be mixed with water, another liquid, to make the solution called lemonade. Sugar, a solid, can be dissolved in the lemonade to make it tastier. The carbonated water used to make soft drinks is a solution made with water, a liquid, and carbon dioxide, a gas.

A solid solution usually forms when a liquid solution freezes. Lemonade poured into an ice cube tray and frozen to make ice pops becomes a solid solution. Sterling silver is another solid solution. It results when melted silver and copper are mixed and cooled. Solutions of metals are called *alloys.*

Air is an example of a gaseous solution. It is made up of nitrogen and oxygen, plus smaller amounts of argon, carbon dioxide, and other gases.

Other articles to read include: **Gas; Liquid; Solid; Solvent.**

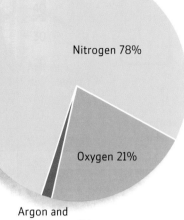

Nitrogen 78%

Oxygen 21%

Argon and other gases 1%

Air is an example of a gaseous solution. It is made up of different gases mixed together.

If you stir table salt into a glass of water, the salt will dissolve. The water is the solvent, and the salt is the solute. The resulting salty water is a solution. In a salt solution, the atoms of sodium and chlorine are surrounded by molecules of water.

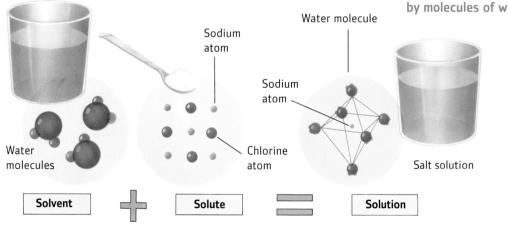

Water molecules

Sodium atom

Chlorine atom

Water molecule

Sodium atom

Salt solution

Solvent   +   **Solute**   =   **Solution**

Solvent

A solvent *(SOL vuhnt)* is a substance that causes another substance to *dissolve* (break up) to form a *solution (suh LOO shuhn)* (mixture). Water is the most common solvent. It dissolves an unusually wide variety of substances.

The term *solvent* is also used to refer to the substance in a solution that is present in the greater amount. The substance present in the lesser amount is called the *solute (SOL yoot)*.

Most solvents are liquids. If you stir table salt into a glass of water, the salt will dissolve. In this example, the water is the solvent and the salt is the solute. The resulting salt water is a solution. Substances such as ordinary salt and sugar are soluble *(SOL yuh buhl)* in water. That is, they will dissolve in water. Substances that will not dissolve in a substance are called *insoluble (ihn SOL yuh buhl)* in that substance. However, many substances that are insoluble in one substance may be soluble in another. For example, oil is insoluble in water but soluble in gasoline.

Solvents have many uses. They are used to produce cleaning fluids, ink, paint, and such artificial fibers as nylon.

Other articles to read include: **Liquid; Solution.**

A sonic boom occurs when an object, such as an airplane, traveling faster than the speed of sound creates a shock wave. People on the ground hear the boom when the wave reaches them. ▼

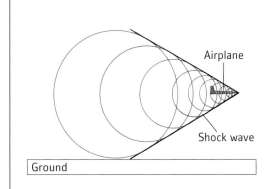

Airplane

Shock wave

Ground

Sonic boom

A sonic boom is a loud noise caused by an object that is moving faster than the speed of sound. At sea level and a temperature of 59 °F (15 °C), sound travels in air at a speed of 1,116 feet (340 meters) per second. Thunder is a sonic boom created by lightning. Part of the sound of a gunshot is a sonic boom created by the speeding bullet.

The fastest airplanes can also create sonic booms. To a person on the ground, the sonic boom created by a plane may sound like a clap of thunder. The noise comes from a *shock wave* produced by the object. A shock wave is a change in air pressure that builds up around the edges of an object that is moving faster than the speed of sound.

Sonic booms cannot seriously hurt people, though they can damage hearing if they are loud enough. Sonic booms sometimes break windows or crack walls.

Other articles to read include: **Sound; Sound, Speed of.**

A trombone produces a sound when the player causes the air inside the instrument to vibrate.

Sound

Sound is something we hear. Every sound we hear is made when an object *vibrates (VY braytz),* making quick, tiny movements back and forth or up and down. When an object vibrates, the air around it vibrates, too. These vibrations *(vy BRAY shuhnz)* in the air travel outward in all directions from the object. When the vibrations enter our ears, the brain interprets them as sounds.

The word *sound* also refers to the traveling waves made by vibrations. In that sense, something can make a sound even if no one is near enough to hear it.

Sound waves are something like the waves on water. If you drop a small stone into a still pond, you will see circles of waves traveling outward from the place where the stone hit the water. But sound waves are different from water waves in an important way. Water waves travel only along the surface of the water. That is, these waves spread only in two dimensions. Sound waves travel in three dimensions. You can think of them as *spheres* (round bodies) expanding in all directions from the source of the vibration.

Sound can move through many materials besides air. Sound waves can travel through water, solid earth, wood, glass, brick, or metal.

Continued on the next page

All sounds are caused by vibrations. A frog croaks by forcing air over its vocal chords, making them vibrate.

But there is no sound in outer space, because there is no air or other material for sound waves to travel through.

Scientists describe sound waves in a number of ways. These ways include *frequency (FREE Kwuhn see), pitch, wavelength, intensity, and loudness.* When an object vibrates quickly, it produces many sound waves that travel close together. Frequency is the number of vibrations made by an object in a given time. A pattern of waves traveling slowly and far apart is a low-frequency wave. A pattern of waves traveling quickly and close together is a high-frequency wave. Scientists use a unit called *hertz* to measure frequency. One hertz equals one *cycle* (vibration) per second.

Most people can hear sounds with frequencies from about 20 to 20,000 hertz. For example, a person's voice can produce frequencies from 85 to 1,100 hertz. Bats, cats, dogs, dolphins, and many other animals can hear sounds with frequencies far above 20,000 hertz.

Pitch is the highness or lowness of a sound. High-pitched sound waves vibrate faster than low-pitched sound waves do. Wavelength is the distance from the *crest* (peak) of one wave to

Continued on the next page

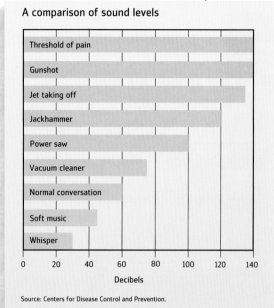

A comparison of sound levels

The intensity of sounds is measured in units called *decibels.* Every increase of 10 decibels represents a tenfold increase in the power of a sound wave.

A tuning fork makes the sound of a particular musical note, depending on how it vibrates.

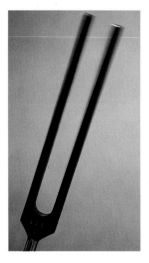

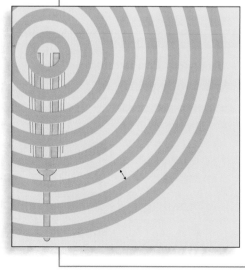

Sound waves form when a vibrating object causes the material around it to vibrate. The substance in which sound waves travel is called a *sound medium.* If no sound medium is present, there can be no sound. Sound waves commonly travel through air and water, but they can also travel through iron and many other materials.

the crest of the next wave. Shorter waves have more energy than longer waves. Intensity is a measure of the power of sound waves. Intensity differs from loudness. Loudness refers to how strong a sound seems to be when we hear it.

Other articles to read include: **Decibel; Echo; Frequency; Radio wave; Sonic boom; Vibration; Wavelength; Waves.**

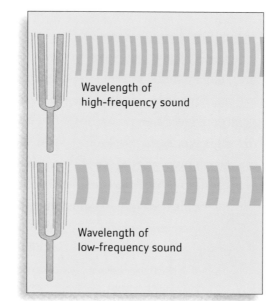

Wavelength of high-frequency sound

Wavelength of low-frequency sound

Frequency is the number of vibrations made by an object in a given time. As the frequency increases, the *wavelength* decreases. The frequency of a sound determines its *pitch.* High-pitched sounds have higher frequencies than low-pitched sounds.

Sound, Speed of

The speed of sound is how fast sound waves travel. The speed of sound can change, depending on the material the waves are passing through. Sound travels faster through liquids and solids than it does through gas. Temperature can also affect the speed of sound. Sound almost always travels faster through warmer materials than it does through cooler materials.

The Bell X-1, an experimental U.S. rocket plane, in 1947 became the first plane to fly faster than the speed of sound.

At sea level and a temperature of 59 °F (15 °C), sound travels through air at 763 miles (1,228 kilometers) per hour. But at 212 °F (100 °C), sound travels through air at a speed of 864 miles (1,391 kilometers) per hour. At 77 °F (25 °C), sound travels through seawater at 3,425 miles (5,512 kilometers) per hour. In contrast, sound travels through steel at 11,659 miles (18,763 kilometers) per hour.

Light travels faster than sound. For this reason, people see a flash of lightning before they hear the sound of thunder.

Other articles to read include: **Light, Speed of; Sonic boom; Sound.**

A square is a flat figure that has four equal straight sides and four right angles. This square is 2 inches (5 centimeters) high and 2 inches (5 centimeters) wide.

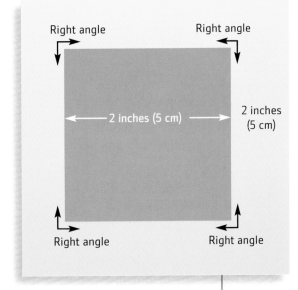

Right angle   Right angle

←———— 2 inches (5 cm) ————→

2 inches
(5 cm)

Right angle   Right angle

Square

A square is a flat shape with four straight sides of equal length. A square has four *right angles*. A right angle is a 90° angle. It is shaped like the capital letter "L."

One way to describe the size of a square is to measure its *area*. Area is the amount of space inside a shape. To find the area of a square, multiply the length of any side by itself. For example, consider a square with sides 5 units in length. The area of the square is 25 square units— that is, 5 x 5.

Perimeter *(puh RIHM uh tuhr)* is another measure of a square. Perimeter is the distance around a shape. To find the perimeter of the same square, add the lengths of all the sides: $5 + 5 + 5 + 5 = 20$. Because the sides of a square are equal, you can also find the perimeter by multiplying any side by 4 (4 sides × 5 units each).

Some math problems call for the *square* of a number. This is the number multiplied by itself. For example, 25 is the square of 5, because $5 × 5 = 25$.

Other articles to read include: **Angle; Geometric shapes.**

The square root of a group of 25 apples—which is 5 apples—can be seen by spacing the apples out in 5 equal rows and 5 equal columns.

Square root

The square root of a given number is a number that results in that given number when it is multiplied by itself. For example, 5 is a square root of 25, because $5 × 5 = 25$. The symbol for a square root, √, is called a *radical sign*. It enables us to write the previous example as $\sqrt{25} = 5$. The negative number −5 is also a square root of 25. The result of multiplying two negative numbers together is a positive number. Therefore, $−5 × −5 = 25$.

The easiest way to find a number's square root is to use an electronic calculator. In the late 1600's, the English mathematician Isaac Newton described a complex method of finding square roots using basic arithmetic.

Other articles to read include: **Multiplication; Newton, Sir Isaac; Number.**

Standard Model

The Standard Model is an important set of ideas in *physics*. Physics is the study of matter and energy. The Standard Model describes the tiny particles that make up matter. It also explains how those particles act on one another. All the objects and materials in the world around us are made of matter. Scientists have made many correct predictions about the basic physical parts and rules of the universe based on the Standard Model.

According to the Standard Model, ordinary objects are made up of *atoms*. An atom is made up of three main types of particles: *protons (PROH tonz)*, *neutrons (NOO tronz)*, and *electrons (ih LEHK tronz.)* Protons and neutrons make up the *nucleus (NOO klee uhs)* (core) of an atom. The electrons orbit the nucleus. Neutrons and protons are made up of even smaller particles called *quarks*.

Particles act on one another through *forces*. The *electromagnetic force* attracts electrons to the nucleus. The *strong force* holds quarks together in protons and neutrons. The *weak force* is involved in the breakdown of certain kinds of particles. A fourth force, called *gravitation*, causes objects to be pulled toward one another. Gravitation is not part of the Standard Model at this time. Many scientists are working to create a theory of the forces of nature that includes gravitation.

Other articles to read include: **Atom; Electron; Force; Gravitation; Neutron; Proton.**

Static electricity makes this girl's hair stand on end.

Static electricity

Static electricity is the build-up of an electric charge. An object may build up either a positive or a negative charge.

All objects are made of tiny particles called *atoms*. An atom has a center called a *nucleus*. The nucleus has a positive charge. Around the nucleus are negatively charged particles called *electrons*.

Some atoms can gain or lose electrons easily. The electrons can rub off from one object to another. The object that loses electrons becomes positively charged. The object that gains electrons becomes negatively charged.

Continued on the next page

Static electricity *Continued from the previous page*

Consider a person walking across a rug. Electrons from the rug can jump onto the person's body. The person becomes negatively charged. The person may get a shock on touching something metal, such as a doorknob. The shock comes from the extra electrons jumping onto the metal.

Static electricity can also occur when you rub a balloon on your shirt. The rubbing causes electrons to transfer from your shirt to the balloon. The shirt then has an overall positive charge because it has lost electrons. The balloon takes on a negative charge because it has picked up electrons. Opposite charges attract each other. As a result, the balloon will stick to your shirt.

Static electricity has many uses in homes, businesses, and industries. For example, the copying machines found in most offices are electrostatic copiers. They make copies of printed or written material by attracting negatively charged particles of *toner* (powdered ink) to positively charged paper. Static electricity is also used in air cleaners to pull dust, smoke, bacteria, or pollen out of the air.

Other articles to read include: **Electricity; Electron.**

Statistics can be presented in different ways. The table below shows the annual yearly catch of certain kinds of fish.

▼

Worldwide fish and shellfish catch		
Chief kinds	**Annual catch**	
	In tons	**In metric tons**
Carp, barbel, cyprinid	23,649,000	21,454,000
Herring, sardine, anchovy	22,173,000	20,115,000
Cod, hake, haddock	8,495,000	7,707,000
Shrimp, prawn	7,187,000	6,520,000
Tuna, bonito, billfish	6,960,000	6,314,000
Clam, cockles, arkshell	5,701,000	5,172,000
Squid, cuttlefish, octopus	4,755,000	4,314,000
Oyster	4,731,000	4,291,000
Tilapia, cichlid	3,917,000	3,553,000
Salmon, trout, smelt	3,448,000	3,128,000
Scallop	2,397,000	2,174,000
Mussel	1,886,000	1,711,000
Crab	1,720,000	1,561,000
Flounder, halibut, sole	1,205,000	1,094,000
Shark, ray, chimaera	812,000	736,000
Shad	651,000	590,000
Abalone, winkle, conch	542,000	492,000
Eel	303,000	275,000
Lobster	275,000	250,000
Krill, plankton	173,000	157,000

Statistics

Statistics *(stuh TIHS tihks)* is a set of methods that are used to collect and figure out information. Statistical methods help people identify, study, and solve many problems. These methods help people make good decisions about uncertain situations.

People use statistical methods in a wide variety of jobs. Physicians use such methods to find out if certain drugs help in the treatment of people with particular medical problems. Weather forecasters use statistics to help them improve their weather predictions. Engineers use statistics to help make products safer. Statistical ideas help scientists design experiments and determine if the experiments

Continued on the next page

provided accurate information. *Economists (ih KON uh mihsts)* use statistics to predict future economic conditions. Economists study how goods and services get produced and how they are given out to the public.

Other articles to read include: **Mathematics; Probability.**

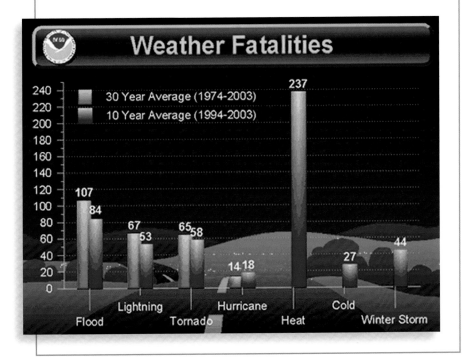

A graph shows statistics on the average number of people killed per year by dangerous weather conditions during two different periods.

In steam heating, water is changed to steam in a *boiler.* The steam passes through pipes to *convectors,* where the steam releases its heat to the room. As the steam cools, it becomes liquid again. The water then flows back to the boiler. ▼

Steam

Steam is water that has been changed into gas. It is at least as hot as 212 °F (100 °C), the boiling point of water. Steam has no color, and you can see through it. The white cloud that you can see over the spout of a kettle is not steam. It is a cloud of tiny drops of water. The white cloud forms as steam cools. Steam at a temperature much higher than the boiling point is called *superheated steam.*

Boiling water makes steam. Water stays at 212 °F until it all turns to steam. A volume of water must take in a lot of heat to

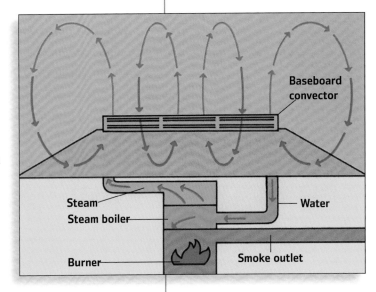

Continued on the next page

Steam is a gaseous, colorless state of water. Stand well back and watch a boiling kettle. (Have an adult with you as you observe.) As the steam from the spout moves away from the kettle, it quickly *condenses* (becomes cooler and turns back into tiny drops of water). Condensation makes the white cloud you can see. These are clouds of water drops, not steam.

Steam   *Continued from the previous page*

change into steam. This heat is released when the steam cools and changes back to liquid water.

Steam is used to move energy from one item, such as coal, wood, or natural gas, to a place where this energy is needed. For example, coal can be used to heat water to make steam. The steam is used to turn devices called *turbines*. The turbines, in turn, power machines called *generators* that produce electric power. Steam is also used in heating homes, in working with chemicals, and in making food pure.

Other articles to read include: **Boiling point; Condensation; Evaporation; Vapor.**

Streamlining

Streamlining means shaping an object so that it moves easily through a *fluid* (liquid or gas). Streamlining reduces *resistance*— that is, a force that opposes the object's motion. For example, a speedboat meets resistance as it travels through water. As the boat moves forward, the water pushes it in the opposite direction. A jet also meets resistance from the air as it flies. Resistance is also called *drag*.

The path that a fluid follows around an object in a steady flow is called a *streamline*. If an object is streamlined, the fluid divides smoothly at the front. The fluid then passes easily around the object and meets at the object's tail. But if the object is not streamlined, the fluid may swirl and twist violently as it passes around the object. These motions are called *eddy flows* or *eddies*. They increase the drag on the object.

Continued on the next page

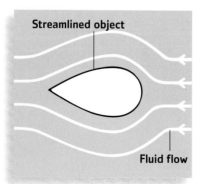

Streamlined object

Fluid flow

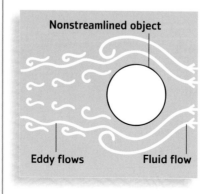

Nonstreamlined object

Eddy flows   Fluid flow

A streamlined object (far left) meets little resistance from a fluid flowing past it. A round object (left) causes *eddies* that increase its resistance to a flowing fluid.

The best streamlined shape for an object depends on whether that object is to travel slower or faster than sound. That is because speed affects the pressure of the fluid and how air turbulence behaves around the object. For travel slower than sound, an object should be somewhat rounded in front and come to a point at the tail. Submarines and fish have this shape. For travel faster than sound, an object should have a pointed front. Engineers design some airplanes and rockets to have this shape. The pointed shape helps reduce the effects of shock waves caused by moving faster than sound.

Other articles to read include: **Aerodynamics; Fluid; Gas.**

String theory

String theory is an idea about the nature of *matter* and the forces that affect matter. All the objects and materials in the world around us are made of matter. A *theory* is an explanation for something based on known facts. String theory is used in the study of *physics* (the study of matter and energy).

Matter is made of *elementary particles.* Such particles are smaller than an atom and have no known smaller parts. Common theories of physics, together called the Standard Model, treat elementary particles as points. But in string theory, these particles are tiny strings that can *vibrate* (shake) in different ways. Different patterns of shaking would look to us like different particles.

Some scientists hope that string theory might provide a single combined explanation of all four of the known basic forces of nature. These forces are: (1) the electromagnetic force, (2) the strong nuclear force, (3) the weak nuclear force, and (4) gravitation. Scientists currently explain the first three forces using an idea called *quantum theories.* They describe gravitation using a theory called *general relativity,* which is not a quantum theory. Since the mid-1980's, physicists have developed many forms of string theory, including a group of superstring theories. However, the theory is still incomplete and providing evidence for it has proved difficult.

Other articles to read include: **Force; Gravitation; Quantum mechanics; Relativity.**

Sublimation

Dry ice, the solid form of carbon dioxide, *sublimes* (changes from a solid to a gas) at normal temperatures.

Sublimation *(SUHB luh MAY shuhn)* is the process in which a solid changes directly into gas or vapor. Often, a solid substance will melt to liquid when it is heated. Further heating will turn the liquid to gas. In sublimation, the substance never becomes liquid. It simply turns from a solid to a gas.

A few common materials, including iodine *(EYE uh dyn)* and dry ice (solid carbon dioxide), undergo sublimation under normal conditions. These substances are said to *sublime (suh BLYM)*. Many substances, including water ice, will sublime under unusual conditions.

Sublimation can be used to separate or purify certain materials. A process called *freeze drying* removes water in the form of ice and other materials by sublimation. Freeze drying is used in food preservation.

Other articles to read include: **Freezing point; Gas; Melting point; Solid; Vapor.**

16 ◄—— Minuend
–5 ◄—— Subtrahend
11 ◄—— Remainder or difference

A subtraction equation has three kinds of numbers—a *minuend,* a *subtrahend,* and a *remainder* (also called the *difference*).

Subtraction

Subtraction *(suhb TRAK shuhn)* is the taking away of a number of things from a larger number. You take them away to find how many things are left. Only things that are alike can be subtracted. For example, you cannot subtract a number of apples from a larger number of books. Subtraction is one of the four basic steps of arithmetic. The other steps are *addition, division,* and *multiplication.*

Each part of a subtraction problem has a name. The answer is the *remainder,* also known as the *difference.* The number being subtracted is the *subtrahend (SUHB truh hehnd).* The number from which the subtrahend is taken is called the *minuend (MIHN yu ehnd).* For example, in the equation $5 - 3 = 2$, the 5 is the minuend, the 3 is the subtrahend, and the 2 is the remainder.

Other articles to read include: **Addition; Mathematics.**

Only "like things" can be subtracted. You cannot subtract apples from oranges. You can only subtract oranges from oranges.

Suppose you have a set of 8 oranges.

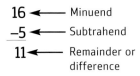

Suppose you want to take away a set of 5 oranges.

You will have 3 oranges left.

Sulfur

Sulfur atomic symbol

Sulfur is a yellow material that is found in many parts of the world. It is a *chemical element,* a material that is made up of only one kind of atom. Sulfur has no taste or odor.

Sulfur has been used for many purposes for hundreds of years. The ancient Greeks and Romans used it as a cleaner, bleach, and medicine. Later, sulfur was important as one of the main ingredients in gunpowder. Today, sulfur is used in a variety of products, including paint, paper, shampoo, and medicines.

Deposits of pure sulfur can be found in nature. Sulfur is also found in coal, crude oil, natural gas, oil shales, and many minerals. Before 1900, material erupted from volcanoes was a common source of sulfur. Today, most sulfur comes from sulfur compounds found in oil and natural gas.

All plants and animals need small amounts of sulfur to live. Many foods, including cabbage and onions, are rich in sulfur.

Other articles to read include: **Element, Chemical.**

Sulfur

Superfluid

A superfluid is an unusual kind of liquid. It flows absolutely freely. An ordinary liquid flows with *resistance.* Resistance is a force that opposes the motion of a body. In an ordinary fluid, this resistance is called *viscosity (vihs KOS uh tee).* Molasses, for example, has high viscosity. It does not flow easily. Water has low viscosity. It flows much more easily than molasses. But a superfluid has no viscosity at all. For this reason, superfluids can climb in and out of open containers.

Scientists have found only two substances that can become superfluids. Both of them are forms of the *chemical element* helium. A chemical element is a material that is made up of only one kind of atom. Both forms of helium must be chilled to very low temperatures to become a superfluid.

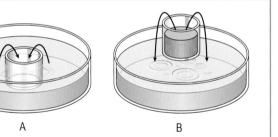

A   B

The superfluid form of helium can "crawl" up the side of a beaker. In experiment A, an empty beaker placed in a bowl of the superfluid gradually fills up. In experiment B, the helium flows out of a beaker suspended over a bowl of superfluid.

Continued on the next page

Superfluid *Continued from the previous page*

Superfluids have many unusual qualities not found in regular fluids. For example, spinning a container of superfluid creates tiny whirlpools called *vortexes (VAWR tehks ehz)* in the fluid. A vortex will continue to spin as long as the liquid remains a superfluid. In addition, a superfluid can flow through a finely packed powder. It can also *conduct* heat—that is, allow heat to pass through itself—at a tremendous rate.

Other articles to read include: **Fluid; Helium; Liquid.**

The water strider is an insect that relies on surface tension to allow it to move across the surfaces of ponds and lakes.

Surface tension

Surface tension *(TEHN shuhn)* causes a liquid to act as if it had thin, elastic skin. Surface tension enables the surface of water to support some objects that would normally sink. For example, needles, razor blades, and certain insects will not sink if placed carefully on water. Different liquids have different amounts of surface tension. Compared with water, the liquid metal mercury has a very high surface tension. Many types of alcohol have a low surface tension. Surface tension also causes a liquid to rise in a thin tube when the tube is dipped in the liquid. This effect is called *capillary (KAP uh lehr ee) action.*

Liquids are made up of tiny bits of matter called *molecules.* Molecules at the boundary of a liquid act differently from molecules in the middle. In the middle, each molecule is attracted to the other molecules around it. These attractions are usually equal in all directions. But molecules near the edge also interact with molecules outside the liquid, in neighboring materials. The attraction of the molecules outside the liquid may be different than the attraction of the other liquid molecules. This lack of balance produces surface tension.

At the surface of a pool of water, for example, air molecules weakly attract water molecules. However, the molecules inside the pool attract the surface molecules more strongly. This difference results in an overall inward force. The force causes the surface to act like a thin, elastic skin.

Other articles to read include: **Capillary action; Liquid.**

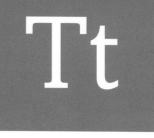

Temperature

Temperature is a measure of how hot or cold something is. Temperature is not the same as *heat*. In science, temperature is the amount of *thermal energy* a substance or object contains. The level of an object's thermal energy depends on the movement of its *atoms* and *molecules* (small bits of matter) in relation to one another. Hot objects have higher energy levels than cold objects do. Heat is the movement of thermal energy from one object to another.

Tools that measure temperature are called *thermometers*. Thermometers measure temperature in different *scales*. A scale marked on a thermometer shows degrees, usually numbered from coldest to hottest. The two most common temperature scales for thermometers show *degrees Fahrenheit* (°F) and *degrees Celsius* (°C). Celsius degrees are used in the metric system of measurement. Digital thermometers display the temperature in numerals.

Scientists believe there is a lower limit to temperature. If all the thermal energy in a substance were removed, the motion of its molecules and atoms would virtually stop. The lowest possible temperature in the universe is −459.67 °F (−273.15 °C). This temperature is called *absolute zero*. However, there does not seem to be an upper limit to temperature. For example, the temperatures inside stars can be many millions of degrees.

Other articles to read include: **Absolute zero; Degree; Celsius scale; Fahrenheit scale; Freezing point; Heat; Melting point.**

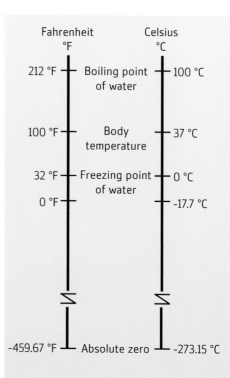

The two most common temperature scales are the Fahrenheit *(FAR uhn hyt)* and Celsius *(SEHL see uhs)* scales.

Time

Time is one of the world's deepest mysteries. We often think of time as flowing or moving forward. We also think of time as a way to put events in a certain order. You remember that on your vacation, you visited a science museum *after* you spent a day at a waterpark. But these ideas only describe the way we experience time. They do not explain what time really is. Throughout history, people have struggled to better understand time.

Continued on the next page

Time *Continued from the previous page*

Time and change go together. As you read this sentence—right now—you are experiencing the present. Now, the event of reading the last sentence is already fading into the past. New events are becoming part of the present. The simple act of reading the previous paragraph reveals three important features of our experience of time. First, the present moment seems more real than the past or the future. Second, we tend to think of time as moving or flowing. Third, time often appears to flow at different rates. An hour of a dull class may seem much longer than an hour of playing an exciting video game.

These seemingly simple characteristics lead to difficult questions about time. Do moments of time actually "flow" by? If they do, how does this happen? Why does time seem to flow in only one direction? Is it possible to move backward in time? Are the past, present, and future really different?

Devices that were used to keep track of time before the invention of mechanical clocks include the hourglass (top) and the sundial (above).

Scientists today know that time can be slowed down or sped up in two different ways. First, the faster you travel, the slower time passes. A classic example uses a set of identical twins. One twin lives on Earth. The second twin boards a space ship. The ship can travel close to the speed of light. After a few hours of traveling very fast in the space ship, the second twin returns to Earth. After the trip, the twin on the space ship has barely aged. However, the twin who remained on Earth is much older.

Second, gravity can change the rate at which time passes. For example, time passes more slowly for a person standing on Earth than for a person floating in space. Earth's gravity slows time for the person standing on the planet.

Early people probably kept time by watching changes in nature that took place again and again. They noticed the movements of objects in the sky. The rising and setting of the sun became a day. Early people also saw that the moon seems to change a little bit each day—from a curved shape to a round shape and then a curved shape again. This *cycle* (change) takes place over a 29 ½-day period. That period became a month.

Continued on the next page

The changing of the seasons gave people another way to keep time. They saw that the sun seemed to move slowly eastward among the stars. The sun made a full circle around the sky over four seasons—winter, spring, summer, and fall. This cycle of seasons took about 365 ¼ days. That period became a year.

The sundial was one of the earliest tools used to measure time. A sundial has a part that casts a shadow when the sun shines on it. As the sun moves across the sky from east to west during the day, the shadow moves and points to numbers that tell the hours.

An hourglass or sandglass tells time by using sand that trickles through a narrow tube. A water clock tells time by allowing water to drip slowly from one container into another.

By the 1700's, people had invented clocks and watches. These early machines were able to tell time to the minute. Electric clocks appeared in the mid-1800's. These clocks replaced the power of a spring with electric current to drive the clock mechanism. Through the 1900's, several new ways to keep accurate time were invented. For example, many modern clocks rely on the vibration of a quartz crystal to keep time. The crystal vibrates a certain number of times per second. The most accurate time is kept by *atomic clocks*. These clocks use the properties of a single atom to keep time. Atomic clocks are accurate to one second over many millions of years.

Other articles to read include: **Gravitation; Relativity.**

The world is divided into 24 time zones. As a result, people from the United States must set their watches forward when traveling eastward from one zone to another.

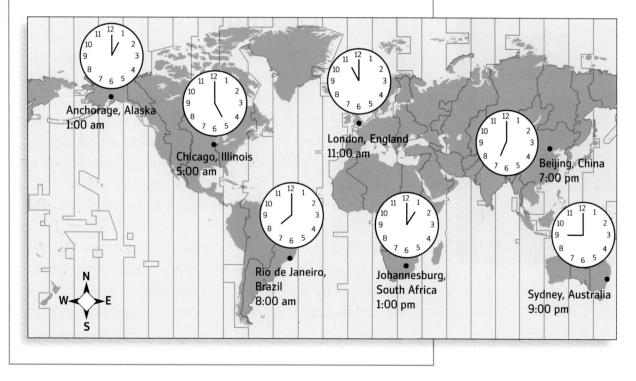

Anchorage, Alaska
1:00 am

Chicago, Illinois
5:00 am

London, England
11:00 am

Beijing, China
7:00 pm

Rio de Janeiro, Brazil
8:00 am

Johannesburg, South Africa
1:00 pm

Sydney, Australia
9:00 pm

Tin

50 Sn	2 8 18 18 4
Tin	
118.710	

Tin
atomic symbol

Tin is a silvery metal that people have used for more than 5,000 years. Tin is a *chemical element* (a substance that contains only one kind of atom).

Tin is very useful because it can be formed into many different shapes. Ancient people combined tin with copper to make an *alloy* (mixture) called *bronze*. They used bronze for such articles as weapons and tools. Today, tin is used mostly in the production of *tin plate*. Tin plate is made by coating steel with a very thin layer of tin. Most tin plate is made into tin cans.

Tin is also used in many other kinds of products. Most paper clips, safety pins, straight pins, and staples are made of steel or brass coated with tin. In addition, tin is used for making *solders (SOD uhrz)*. Solders are alloys used to join or mend metal surfaces, such as those of pipes.

Tin is a silvery metal that is found mostly in Earth's southern hemisphere. It is used to make many products, including tin cans.

Other articles to read include: **Element, Chemical; Metal.**

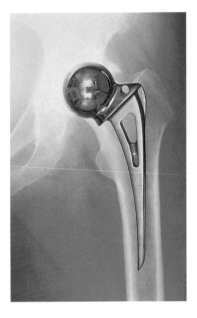

An artificial hip joint made of titanium is shown in position in a patient's hip and upper leg.

Titanium

22 Ti	2 8 10 2
Titanium	
47.867	

Titanium
atomic symbol

Titanium *(ty TAY nee uhm)* is a strong, light-weight, silver-gray metal. Titanium is a relatively common *chemical element* in Earth's crust. A chemical element is a material that is made up of only one kind of atom. Objects made of titanium are stronger than steel objects of the same weight. Titanium resists *corrosion (kuh ROH zhuhn)* caused by the salt in seawater and sea air. Corrosion is the destruction of a material caused by the chemical action of a gas or liquid.

Titanium is an important element in *alloys (AL oyz)*. Alloys are combinations of two or more metals. Ship and submarine parts made of titanium alloys can work in saltwater for long periods without corroding. Alloys of titanium are also used to make many

Continued on the next page

other objects, including rocket engines, artificial knee and hip joints, bicycles, and golf clubs.

Although titanium is useful, it is expensive to produce. It never appears naturally in metallic form because it *bonds with* (is attracted to) oxygen easily and strongly. Before it can be used, it must be separated from the *ores* in which it is found. An ore is a mineral or rock containing a valuable element.

Other articles to read include: **Alloy; Element, Chemical; Metal.**

Triangle

A triangle *(TRY ANG guhl)* is a flat shape with three straight sides. The sides meet at three points called *vertices (VUR tuh seez)*. Each *vertex* (the singular of vertices) forms an angle with two of the sides. The sum of the three angles is always 180 *degrees,* often written 180°. A degree is a small unit of measurement.

There are different types of triangles. A *scalene (skay LEEN) triangle* has three sides of different lengths. An *isosceles (eye SOS uh leez) triangle* has at least two equal sides. An *equilateral (EE kwuh LAT uhr uhl) triangle* has three sides of equal length.

Triangles can also be sorted by their angles. A triangle with every angle smaller than 90° is an *acute (uh KYOOT) triangle.* An *obtuse (uhb TOOS) triangle* has one angle larger than 90°. A *right triangle* has one *right angle,* which is 90°.

Other articles to read include: **Angle; Degree; Geometric shapes.**

Different kinds of triangles are classified according to the lengths of their sides and the angles of their corners. In these diagrams, the blue lines mark equal sides of a triangle. The red symbols mark equal angles. The green square marks a *right angle,* an angle of 90°.

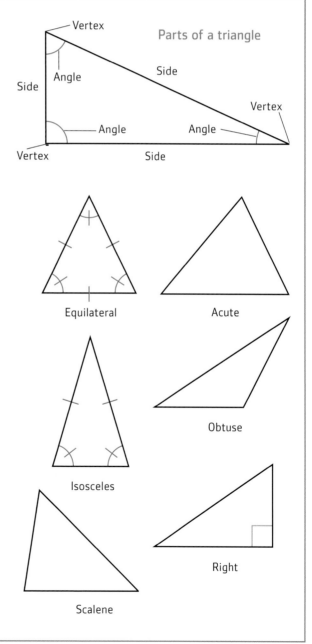

Parts of a triangle

Vertex

Side

Angle

Side

Angle

Angle

Vertex

Vertex

Side

Side

Equilateral

Acute

Isosceles

Obtuse

Scalene

Right

Trigonometry is used by a boater to navigate his course across the sea.

In nature, tungsten is found in the mineral wolframite.

Trigonometry

Trigonometry *(TRIHG uh NOM uh tree)* is a *branch* (form) of mathematics that deals with triangles. In particular, it deals with the relationship between the angles and sides of triangles. Trigonometry is used in such sciences as astronomy and *physics* (the study of matter and energy). Trigonometry is also used in *navigation* and *surveying*. People use navigation to figure out the position and path of a ship or other vehicle. Surveying involves measuring and mapping the land.

Triangles have three sides and three angles. Trigonometry shows how these six parts of a triangle are related. A person can use trigonometry to "fill in the blanks" for unknown parts of a triangle. For example, you might only know the measurements of one side of a triangle and two of its angles. But you can use trigonometry to find the measurements of the triangle's other two sides and the remaining angle.

Plane trigonometry involves triangles on a flat surface, such as a sheet of paper. *Spherical trigonometry* involves triangles on a spherical surface, such as Earth's surface.

Other articles to read include: **Angle; Mathematics; Triangle.**

74	**W**	2 8 18 32 12 2
	Tungsten 183.84	

Tungsten atomic symbol

Tungsten

Tungsten *(TUHNG stuhn)* is a hard, silver-white metal. Tungsten is a *chemical element*. A chemical element is a material that is made up of only one kind of atom. In nature, tungsten is found in a mineral called *wolframite (WUL fruh myt)*. Tungsten is also called *wolfram (WUL fruhm)*.

Tungsten is a very useful material. It has the highest melting temperature of any metal. For this reason, it is used in equipment that must work properly in extreme heat. Tungsten is also used to make steel harder and stronger. Tungsten steel tools last longer than ordinary steel tools. There are tungsten parts in electric lights and in televisions and other electronic equipment. There are also tungsten parts in the *ignition (ihg NIHSH uhn) systems* of automobiles. Ignition systems help start vehicles.

Other articles to read include: **Element, Chemical; Metal.**

Uu

Ultraviolet rays

Ultraviolet rays are a form of light. The sun is the chief source of natural ultraviolet rays that strike Earth. Ultraviolet light can also be produced in some kinds of lamps. The sun produces ultraviolet light in many *wavelengths*. Wavelength is the distance between the *crests* (peaks) and *troughs* (lows) in a series of waves. Ultraviolet light is invisible to people. But experiments have shown that bees, butterflies, and other insects can see ultraviolet light. The reflection of ultraviolet rays off certain insect wings, for example, reveals patterns that help insects identify mates.

Ultraviolet rays can be harmful. People can get a painful sunburn if their skin is exposed to too many ultraviolet rays over a short period. An extremely bad sunburn or overexposure to the rays over many years may lead to skin cancer. Sunscreen lotion helps protect skin from ultraviolet rays. Good sunglasses help protect the eyes.

Ultraviolet rays can also help people. Some types of ultraviolet rays can kill germs that cause disease. Some ultraviolet rays produce vitamin D in the body. Lamps that send out ultraviolet rays are used to treat acne and other skin disorders. Scientists study ultraviolet rays from distant stars to learn more about the universe.

Other articles to read include: **Electromagnetic spectrum; Light.**

Ultraviolet markings cannot be seen on flowers in visible light (top). But when these flowers are photographed in ultraviolet light (above), we can see markings that tell bees where to find *nectar* (a sweet liquid produced in flowers).

Uranium

92	U	2 8 18 32 21 9 2
Uranium		
238.02891		

Uranium
atomic symbol

Uranium is a *radioactive (RAY dee oh AK tihv)* silvery-white metal. Radioactive elements *emit* (give off) energy as their atoms *decay* (break down). Uranium is the second-heaviest *chemical element* found in nature. A chemical element is a material that is made up of only one kind of atom.

All large nuclear power plants use uranium to produce electric energy. A softball-sized piece of uranium can produce more

Continued on the next page

This "button" of uranium, used as fuel in a nuclear power plant, can produce more energy than a trainload of coal.

Uranium *Continued from the previous page*

energy than a trainload of coal weighing three times as much. Uranium also produces the huge explosions of some nuclear weapons.

Uranium is found mostly in rocks, in very small amounts. Uranium can be found in even smaller amounts in rivers, lakes, and oceans. Canada produces more uranium than any other country. In the United States, Arizona, Colorado, New Mexico, Texas, Utah, and Wyoming have deposits of uranium.

The German chemist Martin H. Klaproth discovered uranium in 1789 in pitchblende, a dark, bluish-black mineral. In 1896, French physicist Antoine Henri Becquerel discovered that uranium is radioactive.

Other articles to read include: **Element, Chemical; Fission; Nuclear energy; Radiation.**

Vacuum

A vacuum *(VAK yoom)* is a space with almost no *matter* in it. All the objects and materials around us are made of matter. Scientists have discovered that no space can ever truly be empty. Even the space between the stars, called *interstellar space,* has a tiny bit of matter. On Earth, scientists have been able to remove most of the air from certain areas by creating specially sealed containers. So when scientists talk about a vacuum on Earth, they are talking about an area in a container with most of the air taken out.

We use vacuums in many ways. A vacuum cleaner uses a vacuum to suck up dust and dirt. Vacuum bottles have a vacuum between their double walls to help keep drinks hot or cold. This vacuum has few air molecules to carry heat between the outer air and the drink. Food manufacturers use vacuums to make such instant foods as soup and powdered milk. That is because foods dry out quickly in a vacuum. Some foods, including frozen meat or canned vegetables, are packed in a vacuum to keep them from spoiling.

Other articles to read include: **Matter.**

Technicians lower a space probe into a vacuum chamber for testing before its launch to Mars. Such chambers can be used to *simulate* (re-create) the airless conditions encountered in space.

Vapor

Vapor *(VAY puhr)* is a gas. Solids and liquids can become vapor when heated. Steam is a vapor. It is a vapor of water. Water vapor is always present in the air. Water vapor that has changed to liquid forms clouds, dew, rain, and snow.

The change from liquid into vapor is called *vaporization (VAY puhr uh ZAY shuhn). Evaporation (ih VAP uh RAY shuhn)* and *boiling* are types of vaporization. In evaporation, the change to a vapor takes place slowly. In boiling, the change happens very quickly. The vaporization of a solid without first becoming a liquid is called *sublimation (SUHB luh MAY shuhn).*

Other articles to read include: **Boiling point; Evaporation; Gas; Liquid; Solid; Steam.**

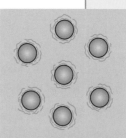

Slow-moving molecules at lower temperature

Fast-moving molecules at higher temperature

Evaporation occurs when the molecules of a sustance have enough *thermal energy* (heat) to break the bonds that hold them together. They can then escape from the substance's surface as vapor. Heat is a kind of *kinetic energy* (energy of motion).

Velocity

Velocity *(vuh LOS uh tee)* is the rate at which an object moves through space in a given direction. Velocity is expressed in units of speed and time, such as inches per second or kilometers per hour.

Velocity is not the same as *speed.* Speed describes the rate of motion. But it does not describe the direction of the motion. Velocity always describes both the rate of motion and direction of motion.

Velocity can be *uniform* or *variable.* An object with uniform velocity would keep traveling in the same direction and at the same rate. An object with variable velocity would change either its speed or its direction while traveling. A change in a moving object's velocity is called *acceleration.* Acceleration is how much the velocity changes over a certain time.

Other articles to read include: **Acceleration; Motion.**

Velocity is not the same as speed. Speed describes the rate at which a bicyclist or other object is moving. Velocity also describes the direction of that motion.

Vibration

A vibration *(vy BRAY shuhn)* is a fast back-and-forth motion. Almost everything vibrates. But the vibrations may be too weak, too fast, or too slow for us to notice. The rate of a vibration from side to side is called *frequency*. The size of a vibration—that is, how far the vibration moves from side to side—is called the *amplitude*.

Very large vibrations happen during earthquakes. Ocean waves also produce vibrations. Smaller vibrations happen in everyday objects. For example, a car vibrates because of small explosions inside the engine. Our ears enable us to hear sounds by detecting sound waves—a type of vibration—in the air. Many sounds are produced by vibrating objects.

Vibrations can be useful. For example, tapping a salt shaker causes vibration. This vibration makes the salt flow. In medicine, vibrating devices are used to treat sore muscles.

Vibrations can also cause problems for people and machines. Frequent, strong vibrations in a car or other vehicle can make people feel uncomfortable. In machines, vibrations can cause noise, wear, and breakage.

Other articles to read include: **Frequency; String theory; Waves.**

The sounds produced by the vibrations of the strings on an electric guitar are translated to electrical impulses by a type of microphone on the guitar called a pickup. The impulses are then transmitted to an *amplifier,* which strengthens the impulses. Loudspeakers change the impulses back into sound.

Viscosity

Viscosity *(vihs KOS uh tee)* is a measure of how difficult it is for a *fluid* (liquid or gas) to flow. For example, molasses flows slowly. It has a high viscosity. Water flows much more easily. It has a low viscosity.

Fluids are made up of tiny groups of atoms called *molecules*. To flow, the molecules must move past one another. But several factors oppose a fluid's ability to flow. The molecules collide or rub against one another. The molecules are also attracted to one another by electric forces. The collisions, *friction* (rubbing), and attractions create viscosity. In many instances, the size of the molecules in a liquid can determine the viscosity. Large

Continued on the next page

molecules, such as those in motor oil, do not move around each other as easily as do smaller molecules, such as those in water. The larger molecules create more collisions and friction. Such substances have a higher viscosity.

Viscosity changes with temperature. In liquids, molecules are close together. As a result, they have a strong attraction to one another. But when a liquid is heated, its molecules move apart, limiting the number of collisions and the amount of friction. The attraction between molecules grows weaker. Therefore, raising the temperature of a liquid lowers its viscosity.

In gases, the molecules are far apart. A gas's viscosity comes mainly from collisions between molecules. Heating a gas makes its molecules move faster and collide more often. For this reason, hot gases have a higher viscosity than cold ones.

Other articles to read include: **Fluid; Gas; Liquid; Superfluid.**

Volume

Volume *(VAHL yuhm)* is the amount of space something takes up. Both solids and liquids have a definite volume. Gases do not have a definite volume because they fill any container that holds them.

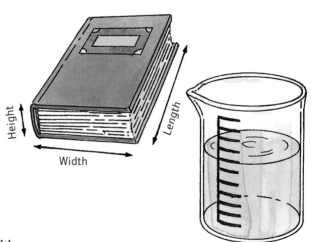

The unit of measurement for volume is the *cube*. It has edges of equal length. The volume of a solid, such as a book, is found by multiplying the length of the book by its width and height. Solids may be measured in cubic feet or cubic meters.

The volume of a liquid, such as water, is often measured in special containers that have marks showing different volumes. Many people in the United States measure liquid volume in gallons, quarts, pints, and fluid ounces. A gallon equals 4 quarts, a quart equals 2 pints, and 1 pint equals 16 fluid ounces. In the metric system, liquids are measured in milliliters and liters. One liter equals 1,000 milliliters.

Other articles to read include: **Density; Liquid; Metric system; Solid.**

Volume is the amount of space taken up by something. Both solids and liquids have a specific volume. The volume of a rectangle-shaped solid, such as a book, can be found by multiplying its length by its width by its height. The volume of a liquid, such as water, is often measured in special containers that have marks showing different volumes.

Ww

The wattage (W) of a light bulb is usually marked on the top of the bulb as a number followed by a capital W. This bulb has a wattage of 60.

Electromagnetic waves not affected by gravitation travel in a straight line. Their electric and magnetic fields move back and forth at right angles to each other and at a right angle to the energy flow. Scientists can determine the distance between two points where the electric and magnetic fields repeat. This distance is called the *wavelength* of the electromagnetic radiation. ▼

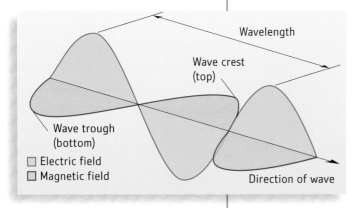

Watt

The watt *(wot)* is a widely used unit of electric power. Although the watt is a unit of the metric system of measurement, it is used in countries that have not adopted this system. The symbol for the watt is *W.* The watt was named for James Watt, a Scottish engineer and inventor. In the 1700's, his improved engine design first made steam power useful.

The number on a light bulb shows its *wattage* (use of power measured in watts). For example, a light bulb operating at 100 *volts* and using 2 *amperes (AM peers)* consumes 200 watts (100 volts × 2 amperes). The volt is a unit for measuring the force of electric energy. The ampere is a unit used to measure electric current.

The watt also is used to measure mechanical power. A machine uses a power of 1 watt if it uses 1 *joule (jowl or jool)* of energy in 1 second. A joule is a unit for measuring the amount of work a machine or person does.

Other articles to read include: **Ampere; Electricity.**

Wavelength

Wavelength is the distance from the *crest* (peak) of one wave to the crest of the next. Wavelength is one way to measure waves.

The number of waves that passes a given point in a given time is called the *frequency* of the series of waves. As the frequency increases, the wavelength tends to decrease. The shorter the wavelength, the more energy the wave has, if the waves being compared have the same *amplitude* (height).

Different forms of light have different wavelengths. Gamma rays have the shortest wavelength. Radio waves have the longest wavelength. Some long radio waves measure more than 6,000 miles (10,000 kilometers) in length. Thus, gamma rays carry more energy than radio waves do. Waves of sound, air, and water can also be measured in wavelengths.

Other articles to read include: **Electromagnetic spectrum; Frequency; Light; Radio wave; Wave.**

Waves

Waves are movements that carry energy from place to place. Waves can move through water, air, and other materials. The up-and-down movements of water in the ocean are waves. Sound and light also travel in waves.

Waves have three basic characteristics. *Wavelength* is the distance from the *crest* (peak) of one wave to the next. *Amplitude* is the height of a wave. *Frequency* is the number of waves that passes a single point in a certain amount of time.

It is easy to start a wave. If you throw a stone into a large, still pond, ripples will travel outward from the point where the stone entered the water. The ripples are actually a number of ring-shape-waves. Each wave is wider, but all have the same center—the stone's entry point. Energy produces the waves, and the waves carry energy.

Waves can also carry information. They can move through *fields* (areas) where an electric or magnetic force can be felt. Radio and television broadcasts and cellular telephone messages travel through the air on radio waves.

Another simple wave experiment involves two people and a rope. Each person holds one end of the rope. When one person moves an end of the rope up and down sharply, energy moves from that person's hand and travels through the rope. As the energy passes through the rope, the rope moves up and down but not forward.

Continued on the next page

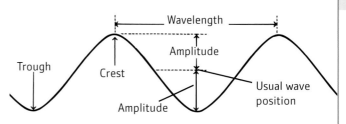

Most waves look like hills and valleys. The hills are called *crests,* and the valleys are called *troughs.* The *amplitude* is a measure of how much the wave rises or falls from its usual position. *Wavelength* is the distance between the crest of one wave and the crest of the next.

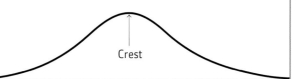

A solitary wave has a single crest with no trough. Solitary waves often form in shallow water channels.

A transverse wave travels in a direction *perpendicular* to that in which the material—in this case a rope—moves. That is, the crest of the wave moves from left to right. As the wave passes through the rope, the rope moves up and down.

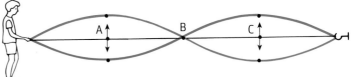

A longitudinal wave travels in the same direction as the material it is traveling through. Points A and C move up and down, but point B does not.

Waves *Continued from the previous page*

There are two main kinds of waves. Some waves travel in the same direction as the material they are traveling through. These waves are called *longitudinal (LON juh TOO duh nuhl) waves*. Sound waves are longitudinal waves. The second kind of wave moves in a different direction than the material it is traveling through. These waves are called *transverse (trans VURS) waves*. A rope wave is a tranverse wave because it moves up and down while the wave moves from one end of the rope to the other.

Other articles to read include: **Electromagnetic spectrum; Frequency; Light; Radio wave; Relativity; Wavelength.**

This table shows units of measurement in the inch-pound system and their equivalents in the metric system. People who use the inch-pound system usually measure temperature in degrees Fahrenheit. Temperature in the metric system is measured in degrees Celsius.

Weights and measures

Weights and measures are standards we use to describe the physical properties of things. These properties include size, weight, temperature, and time.

Weights and measures are essential for science and technology. They are also needed for trade and manufacturing. All countries enforce the uniform use of measurement standards within their borders.

Continued on the next page

Units of measurement

To measure length or distance

1 foot	=	12 inches	=	about 30 ½ centimeters
1 yard	=	3 feet	=	almost 1 meter
1 mile	=	5,280 feet	=	about 1 ⅗ kilometers

To measure area

1 square foot	=	144 square inches	=	929 square centimeters
1 square yard	=	9 square feet	=	over ⅘ square meter
1 acre	=	4,840 square yards	=	about ⅖ hectare
1 square mile	=	640 acres	=	259 hectares

To measure volume

1 tablespoon	=	3 teaspoons	=	almost 15 milliliters
1 cup	=	16 tablespoons	=	237 milliliters or almost ¼ liter
1 pint	=	2 cups	=	473 milliliters or almost ½ liter
1 quart	=	2 pints	=	946 milliliters or almost l liter
1 gallon	=	4 quarts	=	about 3 ¾ liters

To measure weight

1 pound	=	16 ounces	=	454 grams or almost ½ kilogram
1 ton	=	2,000 pounds	=	907 kilograms or almost 1 metric ton

To measure temperature

°F	=	$\frac{9}{5}(°C) + 32$
°C	=	$(°F - 32)\frac{5}{9}$

The most widely used measurement system is the *modern metric system,* which is known as the International System of Units. People commonly refer to this system by the initials *SI,* which stand for its name in French: *Système International d'Unités.* The metric system includes such units as grams and kilograms for measuring *mass*—a measure related to weight— and meters and kilometers for measuring length and distance. Temperature in the metric system is measured in degrees Celsius.

The United States is the only large country in which people still use the *inch-pound system* of measurement. The inch-pound system includes feet, yards, and miles for measuring length or distance. It also includes ounces for measuring small weights and tons for measuring large weights. People who use the inch-pound system measure temperature in degrees Fahrenheit. The inch-pound system is sometimes called the *customary system* or the *English system,* though it is no longer used in England.

Other articles to read include: **Ampere; Celsius scale; Decibel; Degree; Fahrenheit scale; Horsepower; Metric system; Ounce; Volume; Yard.**

A tape measure shows measurements for both the inch-pound system and the metric system.

White light is made up of many different colors. When white light passes through a prism, a rainbow is seen on the other side. ▼

White light

White light is the mixture of all the types of light that people can see. For this reason, white light is also called *visible light.* Passing white light through a *prism (PRIHZ uhm)* produces a rainbow of colors. A prism is a specially shaped piece of glass. The rainbow shows all the colors that make up white light. These colors are red, orange, yellow, green, blue, and violet. Indigo, which is closely related to blue, is sometimes included in this list. The basic colors of light we can see make up the *visible spectrum.*

Many other colors, such as shades of brown, are a combination of different colors from the spectrum. White light is white because it is a combination of all the colors of the spectrum. There are many kinds of light people cannot see, including *ultraviolet light* and *infrared light.*

Other articles to read include: **Color; Electromagnetic spectrum; Light.**

Work

Work is what happens when a force moves an object over a distance against *resistance*. Resistance is a force that opposes the motion of an object. An example of resistance is *friction*. Friction is what makes two objects *resist* (act against each other) when one is pushed or pulled across the other. *Gravity,* which pulls objects near Earth's surface toward its center, also creates resistance. Work can be done by a person, a machine, or some other thing that produces a force that causes movement. In the metric system, work is measured using a unit called the *joule.*

Two things determine how much work is done. One factor is the amount of force used. The other is how far the object moves. In the science of physics *(FIHZ ihks),* work happens only when a force is strong enough to move an object. People do work when they lift, push, or pull an object from one place to another. People also do work when they rotate an object, such as a jar lid. Work is not the same as effort. People do not do work when they hold an object without moving it—even though they may become tired.

Other articles to read include: **Force; Friction; Gravitation; Motion.**

Work is done when a *force* moves an object. Pushes and pulls that change an object's motion are types of forces. When you push a wheelbarrow, you are doing work.

People also do work when they lift an object, such as a piece of furniture.

X rays

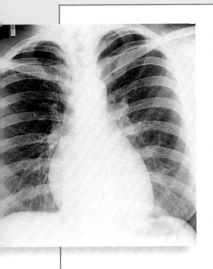

X rays are one of the most useful forms of energy. They are widely used in medicine. Doctors use X rays to make pictures of the bones and organs inside the body. These pictures are called radiographs *(RAY dee oh grafs)*, or simply *X* rays. Radiographs let doctors see broken bones, lung disease, or other problems without having to cut into the body. Dentists take radiographs to find tiny *cavities* (holes in teeth).

X rays produce pictures by passing through a patient's body onto a sheet of photographic film or special plastic. Shadows of the patient's bones or organs are made on the film or plastic, because the bones and organs block some of the X rays. Doctors "read" these shadows to learn about the condition of the body.

X rays can produce changes in the substances they enter. For this reason, they can be dangerous. But doctors also use X rays to kill cancer cells.

X rays have many other uses in science. Astronomers study X rays that come from stars and other hot objects in the universe to learn about the objects' temperature and makeup. Other scientists use X rays to determine how *atoms* (tiny bits of matter) are arranged in crystals.

In industry, inspectors use X rays to examine products for cracks and other defects. Workers also use X rays to check the quality of such mass-produced products as computer chips and other small electronic devices. Scanners at airports use X rays to check baggage for weapons or bombs.

X rays were discovered in 1895 by the German scientist Wilhelm Roentgen *(VILL helm REHNT guhn)*. He called them *X* rays because at first he did not understand what they were. *X* is often used as a symbol for the unknown.

X rays are a form of *electromagnetic energy,* or light. Another form of electromagnetic radiation is *visible light*. But human beings cannot see X rays.

Other articles to read include: **Electromagnetic spectrum; Energy; Light; Radiation.**

A chest X ray (left) shows the shadows of the heart, the lungs, and the ribs. Such images can help physicians "see" into patients' bodies to detect lung disease, broken bones, and other problems.

A medical technician prepares to make *radiographs* (X-ray pictures) of a patient.

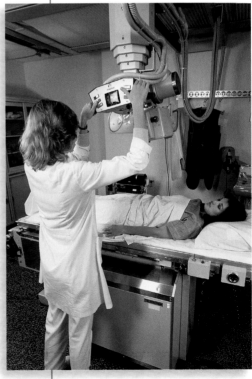

Yard

A yard is a unit of length in the *inch-pound system* of measurement. This system is commonly used in the United States. One yard is equal to 3 feet or 36 inches. One yard equals 0.9144 meter in the *modern metric system* of measurement.

Yards can also be used to measure *area*. Area is the amount of surface contained within a certain boundary. A *square yard* is a figure with two dimensions—length and width—that measures one yard on each side. To find the area of a figure with two dimensions, multiply the lengths of two sides that meet at a corner.

A *cubic (KYOO bihk) yard* is a figure with three dimensions—length, width, and height—that measures one yard on each edge. It measures *volume* (the amount of space something occupies). To find the volume of a solid, three-dimensional figure, multiply the length by the width by the height.

Other articles to read include: **Meter; Metric system; Volume.**

Yards, marked with white lines, are used to divide football fields.

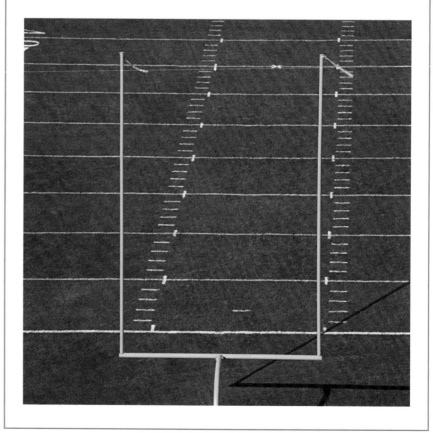

Zero

Zero is the name of the *digit 0*. It is sometimes called *naught (nawt)*. It is used to show the absence of an amount.

Digits are the numerals from 0 to 9. A digit's position in a number tells its value. In the number 246, for example, the digit *2* stands for two hundreds (or 200). The digit *4* stands for four tens (or 40). The digit *6* stands for six ones (or 6). To write the number 206, we must show that there are no tens. The digit 0 serves this purpose.

Adding zero to a number gives the original number. Subtracting zero also gives the original number. Any number multiplied by zero is zero. Division by zero is impossible. Zero is an even number.

There is evidence that the Maya of Central America were using symbols for zero by about A.D. 250. The Hindus in what is now India had developed such a symbol by the late 800's. The Hindu symbol spread from India and was adopted in Europe during the late 1400's. The word *zero* probably came from the word *ziphirum,* a Latin form of the Arabic word *sifr.* Sifr comes from the Hindu word *sunya,* which means *void* or *empty.*

Other articles to read include: **Decimal system; Digit; Number.**

Zero is used to indicate the absence of anything. In the number 206, the zero (shown in red) indicates that there are no tens in this number.

206

Zinc is a bluish-white metallic element.

30	Zn	2 8 18 2
Zinc		
65.39		

Zinc atomic symbol

Zinc

Zinc is a shiny, bluish-white metal. It is a useful metal that can be bent or molded into a variety of shapes. Such metals as iron and steel are often coated with zinc to keep them from rusting. Zinc-coated metals are used to make roof gutters and other products. Zinc is also used in electric batteries. Since 1982, United States pennies have been made from a zinc *alloy* (mixture) coated with a thin layer of copper. Although zinc is a hard metal, it breaks easily at room temperature.

Zinc is a *chemical element.* A chemical element is a material that is made up of only one kind of a atom. Plants and animals need zinc for normal growth.

Zinc is never found in a pure state in nature. It is always found with other chemical elements. Zinc can be combined with other metals to form many important *alloys.* Brass is an alloy of copper and zinc. Bronze is an alloy of copper, tin, and zinc.

Other articles to read include: **Element, Chemical; Metal.**

The index is an alphabetical list of important topics covered in this book. It will help you find information given in both words and pictures. The page number or numbers after a heading tell you where to look for information about a topic. For example, there are references to **Liter** on pages 142 through 143 and also on page 166.

When there is an article on a topic in *The Discovery Science Encyclopedia*, the page number or numbers appear in **boldface**. For example, the boldface pages for the article on **Acid** appear along with references to that topic in other encyclopedia articles. When there are many references to a topic, they are sometimes organized under subtopics, as they are under **Atom**.

Sometimes, an index heading refers you to information in other headings in the index. For example, **Air** has a "See also" reference to additional information on this topic under **Atmosphere**. The "See" reference for **Air pressure** tells you that all the information on this topic will be found under **Atmospheric pressure**.

When an entry can mean more than one thing, there are words in parentheses to help you distinguish between these different meanings—for example, **Earth** (element) and **Earth** (planet).

A page number in *italics* refers to an illustration only. For example, a picture for **Afterimage** appears on 49, but there is no other reference to this topic in the text on this page or the facing page.

The publisher gratefully acknowledges the following sources for photographs. All maps and illustrations unless otherwise noted are the exclusive property of World Book, Inc.

8-9 © Thomas Zimmerman, Getty Images; © iStockphoto

10-11 WORLD BOOK photo; AP Images; © Dreamstime

12-13 © Mary Kate Denny, PhotoEdit; U.S. Mint

14-15 Boeing; © Roger Ressmeyer, Corbis

16-17 Granger; © Dennis MacDonald, PhotoEdit

18-19 Granger; © Dreamstime; © Charles D. Winters, Photo Researchers; © Tony Freeman, PhotoEdit

20-21 © Bettman/Corbis

22-23 © Corbis; © David R. Frazier

24-25 Granger

26-27 © Brian Bell, Photo Researchers; © David Parker, Photo Researchers

28-29 © iStockphoto; © Sueddeutsche Zeitung Photo/Alamy Images

30-31 © Image Asset Management/SuperStock

32-33 Nobel Foundation

36-37 © PhotoDisc/Getty Images; Granger; WORLD BOOK photo

38-39 © PhotoDisc/Getty Images; © Maximilien Brice, CERN; © Shutterstock

40-41 AP Images; © Shutterstock; © Dreamstime

42-43 © Shutterstock; © Shutterstock

44-45 © Geri Lavrov, SuperStock; © PhotoAlto/SuperStock

46-47 © Shutterstock; © Nick Hawkes; Ecoscene/Corbis; © Swerve/Alamy Images; © Shutterstock

48-49 © Russ Lappa, Photo Researchers; WORLD BOOK photo

50-51 © Crispin Hughes, Alamy Images

52-53 WORLD BOOK photo; © Roger Ressmeyer, Corbis

56-57 © Hulton Archive/Getty Images

58-59 WORLD BOOK photo; Mary Evans Picture Library

60-61 © Kevpix/Alamy Images; Art Archive

62-63 © Bill Aron, PhotoEdit

64-65 © Charles D. Winters, Photo Researchers

66-67 © Bettmann/Corbis; © Earl & Nazima Kowall, Corbis

70-71 WORLD BOOK photos

72-73 PhotoDisc; WORLD BOOK photo

74-75 Granger

76-77 © Shutterstock; © Crown Copyright/Health & Safety Lab/Photo Researchers

78-79 WORLD BOOK photo; © Corbis

80-81 © Hulton Archive/Getty Images; © Bettmann/Corbis

82-83 © Shutterstock; © Shutterstock; © Owen Franken, Corbis

84-85 WORLD BOOK photo; © Shutterstock

86-87 © Shutterstock

88-89 © Mehau Kulyk, Photo Researchers

90-91 NASA/SOHO/ESA; AP Images

94-95 © Shutterstock

98-99 © Sunstar/Photo Researchers; © Sion Touhig, Getty Images

100-101 © Floris Leeuwenberg, Corbis; © Shutterstock

102-103 Granger; CERN; © Hulton-Deutsch Collection/Corbis

104-105 © SPL/Photo Researchers

106-107 © Bettmann/Corbis

108-109 © Shutterstock

110-111 WORLD BOOK photos

112-113 © Martin Dohrn, Photo Researchers; © Alfred Pasieka, Photo Researchers; © Tom Prettyman, Photo Edit; © Pat Behnke, Alamy Images

114-115 © Charles D. Winters, Photo Researchers; © Image Bank/Getty Images

116-117 © Getty Images; Granger

118-119 WORLD BOOK photo

120-121 © Bill Bachmann, Alamy Images; © Geoff Tompkinson, Photo Researchers; © Douglas C. Jones, Edison National Historic Site; North Wind Pictures

122-123 WORLD BOOK photo; © Dave Parker, Photo Researchers

124-125 © Robert Karpa, Masterfile; © PCL/Alamy Images

126-127 © Agripicture/Alamy Images; © Comstock/Alamy Images

128-129 © Richard Hutchings, Photo Researchers; © Andrew Lambert, SPL/Photo Researchers

130-131 © PhotoDisc/Getty Images; © Peter Ryan, Photo Researchers

132-133 AP Images; NASA/NSSDC; © Airforce, Army, Navy News/Alamy Images

134-135 © Shutterstock; © Keren Su, Corbis; © Jessica Rinaldi, Corbis; © Corbis; © David H. Wells, Corbis

136-137 © AIP Emilio Segre Visual Archives

138-139 © James King-Holmes, FTSS/Photo Researchers; © Shutterstock; WORLD BOOK Photo

140-141 © Bill Pugliano, Getty Images; © Charles O'Rear, Corbis; © Roger Ball, Corbis

142-143 © Sally Morgan, Ecoscene/Corbis; © Baldwin H. Ward, Corbis

146-147 © Gary S. Settles, Photo Researchers

148-149 © Time/Life Pictures from Getty Images; WORLD BOOK Photo

150-151 CNRI, Photo Researchers

152-153 © S. Terry, Photo Researchers; © Phillipe Psaila, Photo Researchers; © Carl Frank, Photo Researchers

154-155 Granger Collection; © Charles E. Steinheimer, Getty Images

156-157 © AFP/Getty Images

158-159 © David R. Frazier, Photo Researchers; LBNL/Photo Researchers

162-163 Granger Collection; © Everett Collection/Alamy Images

164-165 © Rosenfeld Images Ltd./Photo Researchers; © Shutterstock; © Pascal Alix, Photo Researchers

166-167 © Shutterstock

168-169 © Ilya naymushin, Reuters/Corbis; © PRISMO ARCHIVO/Alamy Images; © Mary Evans Picture Library/Alamy Images; Granger Collection

170-171 © Hemis/Alamy Images

174-175 © Yoav Levy, Phototake from Alamy Images; © Yoav Levy, Phototake from Alamy Images; © CERN

176-177 © Pictorial Press Ltd/Alamy Images; © Andre Jenny, Alamy Images

178-179 © David A. Barnes, Corbis; © Shutterstock

180-181 WORLD BOOK Photo

182-183 © Shutterstock; Granger Collection

184-185 © Photo Researchers

186-187 © H. Mark Heidman Photography/Alamy Images

188-189 © C. Powell, P. Fowler & D. Perkins, SPL/Photo Researchers

190-191 © Geogphotos from Alamy Images

192-193 WORLD BOOK Photo

196-197 Alice Dole; © World History Archive/Alamy Images

198-199 © Mary Evans Picture Library/Alamy Images

200-201 © Steven Dalton, Photo Researchers; © Andrew Syred, SPL/Photo Researchers; © Eastfoto; © A.B. Joyce, Photo Researchers

202-203 Christopher L. Coughenour, Drexel University; Aerofilms

204-205 © Dennis Hallinan, Getty images; © Jerry Herman, Getty Images

206-207 WORLD BOOK Photo

208-209 © David R. Frazier

212-213 © Aaron Haupt, Frazier Photolibrary

214-215 © Alexis Rosenfeld, Photo Researchers; WORLD BOOK Photo

216-217 © Terry Wild

218-219 © Brand X Pictures from Alamy Images; © picturedimensions from Alamy Images

220-221 © Charles D. Winters, Photo Researchers; © Anthony-Masterson, Corbis; Zefa

222-223 © Sinclair Stammers, Photo Researchers; © Kevin Fleming, Corbis; © Edward Kinsman, Photo Researchers

224-225 © U.S. Department of Energy/Photo Researchers; NASA/JPL/UA/ Lockheed Martin; © Dominic Burke, Alamy Images

226-227 © Shutterstock

228-229 WORLD BOOK Photo

230-231 © Superstock; © David Parker, Photo Researchers

232-233 © Robert Harding Picture Library from Alamy Images; © Dennis Macdonald, Alamy Images; Saint Mary of Nazareth Hospital Center; © Larry Mulvehill, Photo Researchers

234-235 © Mark Douel, Getty Images; © Astrid & Hanns-Frieder Michler, Photo Researchers